How Insurgency Begins

How and why do rebel groups initially form? Prevailing scholarship has attributed the emergence of armed rebellion to the explosion of pre-mobilized political or ethnic hostilities. However, this book finds both uncertainty and secrecy shrouding the start of insurgency in weak states. Examining why only some incipient armed rebellions succeed in becoming viable challengers to governments, *How Insurgency Begins* shows that rumors circulating in places where rebel groups form can influence civilians' perceptions of both rebels and the state. By revealing the connections between villagers' trusted network structures and local ethnic demography, Janet I. Lewis shows how ethnic networks facilitate the spread of pro-rebel rumors. This in-depth analysis of conflicts in Uganda and neighboring states speaks to scholars and policymakers seeking to understand the motives and actions of those initiating armed rebellion, those witnessing the process in their community, and those trying to stop it.

Janet I. Lewis is Assistant Professor of Political Science at George Washington University. Her research and teaching focus is on political violence, ethnic conflict, and state formation, especially in Africa. Her work has received several honors, including awards for Best Article published in 2017 in *Comparative Political Studies*, Best Article published in 2017 in the *American Journal of Political Science*, and Best Article or Chapter using qualitative methods published in 2018 from the Qualitative and Multi-Methods Section of the American Political Science Association.

CAMBRIDGE STUDIES IN COMPARATIVE POLITICS

OTHER BOOKS IN THE SERIES

Continued after the index

How Insurgency Begins

Rebel Group Formation in Uganda and Beyond

JANET I. LEWIS

CAMBRIDGE
UNIVERSITY PRESS

CAMBRIDGE
UNIVERSITY PRESS

University Printing House, Cambridge CB2 8BS, United Kingdom

One Liberty Plaza, 20th Floor, New York, NY 10006, USA

477 Williamstown Road, Port Melbourne, VIC 3207, Australia

314–321, 3rd Floor, Plot 3, Splendor Forum, Jasola District Centre,
New Delhi – 110025, India

79 Anson Road, #06–04/06, Singapore 079906

Cambridge University Press is part of the University of Cambridge.

It furthers the University's mission by disseminating knowledge in the pursuit of
education, learning, and research at the highest international levels of excellence.

www.cambridge.org
Information on this title: www.cambridge.org/9781108479660
DOI: 10.1017/9781108855969

First published 2020

A catalogue record for this publication is available from the British Library.

ISBN 978-1-108-47966-0 Hardback
ISBN 978-1-108-79047-5 Paperback

Contents

Figures

Tables

Acknowledgments

This project benefitted from the generosity of numerous people and institutions. I gratefully acknowledge this assistance and my great fortune to receive it.

First and foremost, I thank the hundreds of Ugandans – villagers, military officers, journalists, civil servants, and others – who generously shared their time with me. Ugandans have a well-deserved reputation for their warmth, and I am honored that so many trusted me to use their recollections and insights in a manner that would advance knowledge. I owe special thanks to Gerald Tushabe, Mo Adiga, and Richard Karemire for their guidance and friendship. I am also grateful to those who lent their expertise in identifying contacts and linguistic and/or political expertise in interpreting what I was hearing throughout Uganda, in particular Julius Okwana in Acholi; Hippo Rashid in West Nile; Abraham Odeke in Tororo; Albert Wabudia in Busia; James Tweny in Lango; and Richard Otim and Francis Akoiro in Teso. Innovations for Poverty Action's Uganda office – especially Vianney Mbonigaba and Charity Komujurizi – provided excellent advice on the field experiment and helped me identify my fantastic enumeration team in Teso, which was led by Juliet Ajilong, Edmund Emulu, and Moses Olich. I benefitted from research affiliations with Uganda's Center for Basic Research and the Makerere Institute for Social Research and thank the Uganda Bureau of Statistics for sharing their data with me. Thanks also to Randy Harris, "Duke" Ellington, and Jeremy Lebowitz, who lent their deep experience in Uganda to help guide my fieldwork.

The seeds of my interest in identity-based conflict were planted during my undergraduate experience at Stanford. For their teaching and important advice as I started down the path of studying political science, I thank Byron Bland, Susan Okin, and Judy Goldstein. For helping me begin to understand the craft of fieldwork, research, and academic writing, I thank Steve Stedman. During these formative years, my host family – the Coetzees – in Belhar, South Africa, and the community at Seeds of Peace taught me up close about the painful realities of violent, identity-based conflict and the potential for reconciliation. I'm glad that many friends from Seeds of Peace have stayed close, sustaining me personally and professionally. Finally, I am so grateful to Emile Bruneau, who entered my life during these years first as my rugby coach, then as a dear friend and fellow scholar of conflict and peace. Our conversations have made deep imprints in me about the potential for science and human connection to make the world a more peaceful place, and about how to live courageously. I hope that my contributions will emulate, in a small way, Emile's extraordinary legacy of bringing light and knowledge where they had not previously shone.

This book grew out of my dissertation work in Harvard's Government Department. I owe my deepest intellectual debt to my dissertation committee: Robert Bates, Nahomi Ichino, Steve Levitsky, and Monica Toft. Their formidable talents and wide-ranging perspectives taught me to strive to ask important questions and answer them in a deeply informed, rigorous way. I greatly appreciate Nahomi and Steve's broader professional mentorship as well. During graduate school, an excellent group of graduate students supported me personally and professionally: Nichole Argo, Jen Bachner, Brett Carter, Amy Catalinac, Andrew Coe, Sheena Greitens, Andy Harris, Cat Kelly, Elena Llaudet, Kristen Looney, Brenna Powell, Chris Rhodes, Claire Schwartz, Sarah Shehabuddin, Omar Wasow, and Sarah Zukerman-Daly. The structure of this book's empirical chapters is owed to thoughtful feedback from Brett.

During graduate school, I was also fortunate to develop collaborations and friendships with Guy Grossman and Jennifer Larson. Our conversations made me a much better scholar and led to several insights about politics that inform this book. Jenn's incisive contributions to our joint work strengthened several of this book's components. For example, she built a formal model, which is also presented in our 2018 coauthored article in *International Organization,* that undergirds a key piece of the theory in Chapter 2. We also collaborated intensively on the field experiment discussed briefly in Chapter 5; we present the design and findings from that experiment more fully in our 2017 coauthored article in the *American Journal of Political Science.*

My year at Yale's Program on Order, Conflict, and Violence allowed me to develop this project and to join an inspiring community of scholars dedicated to the study of conflict. I thank Stathis Kalyvas for building that program, for making that year possible, and for his advice and intellectual inspiration then and since. I am also grateful to Elisabeth Wood and Keith Darden for helpful conversations and to Ana Arjona, Gina Bateson, Ellie Powell, Pia Raffler, and Jessica Trisko Darden for their feedback and friendship that year at Yale. Finally, a hearty thanks to Evgeny Finkel and Sarah Parkinson for their great insights and laughter then in New Haven and now in Washington, DC.

Numerous people have provided excellent feedback on pieces of this manuscript. At a manuscript workshop hosted by Harvard in 2013, Fotini Christia, David Cunningham, Mai Hassan, Rich Nielsen, Roger Petersen, Kara Ross Camarena, and Scott Straus generously read the full manuscript and provided crucial, constructive comments. Participants at Uppsala University's Peace and Conflict Research Department Speaker Series, the Olympia Summer Academy, George Washington University's Comparative Politics Workshop, Temple University's Comparative Politics Colloquium, and Duke University's Security, Peace, and Conflict Seminar Series also provided helpful feedback on pieces of the project. I owe thanks to Sean Yom for the connection between my theory and a line from T. S. Eliot's "Hollow Men" at the start of Chapter 4. At these and other venues, several scholars provided helpful comments: David Art, Laia Balcells, Leore Ben-Chorin, Mark Berlin, Nathaniel Cogley, Jangai Jap, Peter Krause, Michael Gilligan, Reyko Huang, Nelson Kasfir, Peter Kingstone, Matthew Lange, Theo McLauchlin, Stephen Rangazas, Nicholas Sambanis, Hillel Soifer, Paul Staniland, Livia Schubiger, Prerna Singh, Chris Sullivan, Jessica Stanton, and Peter Von Doepp.

The Department of Political Science at the United States Naval Academy (USNA) provided an inspiring environment as I developed this manuscript, as teaching midshipmen reminded me daily to consider the broader implications of my research. My colleagues at USNA – especially Mike Kellermann, Brendan Doherty, Matt Testerman, Stephen Wrage, Evelyn Lunasin, Susan Margulies, Joan Shifflett, and Elizabeth Yates – provided friendship and support that made the completion of this manuscript possible. During those years, while not directly affiliated with USNA, Jenny Hamilton and Andy Marshall provided excellent research assistance on the dataset on rebel group formation in eastern and central Africa. My thanks also go to Robert Lee, Bliss Leonard, Abi Mariam, and Sean Reilly for their helpful research assistance. In my final months of revising this manuscript, I moved to an excellent intellectual home for doing so: the Department of Political Science at George Washington University. Thank you to my colleagues there for believing in the promise of this project.

My sincere thanks also go to several institutions that provided grants to make this work possible. I received funding to conduct early fieldwork from Harvard's Committee on African Studies and Weatherhead Center for International Affairs. The Weatherhead Center also served as an excellent intellectual community during graduate school and funded my book workshop. My fieldwork in Uganda was supported by grants from the Smith Richardson Foundation, the National Science Foundation, and the US Institute for Peace. Analysis and writing for this project were supported by a Hartley R. Rodgers Merit fellowship at Harvard, a grant from the Harry Frank Guggenheim Foundation, and a residential fellowship at Yale's Program on Order, Conflict, and Violence (OCV). USNA provided summer funding for revising this manuscript and related articles, and the Minerva Research for Defense Education Faculty program funded building the dataset on rebel group formation in eastern and central Africa.

My deepest gratitude goes to my family, whose support made this project possible at every stage: my mother, Doris; my father, Fred; my sister, Joanna; and especially my husband, Simon. He deserves a medal for the steady stream of patience, support, and fresh bread he provided, and for helping me find fulfillment and joy along the way – especially after the birth of our daughters, Aliza and Ariel, as I completed this book.

PART I

RETHINKING HOW ARMED CONFLICTS BEGIN

I

Introduction

In 2009, *The New York Times* declared that Uganda was "one of the safest, more stable nations in this patch of Africa."[1] Uganda had reached a turning point just four years prior when the last of several rebel groups that had operated there fled beyond its borders. This relative stability persists today. But for older Ugandans, memories of decades of political violence remain.

The last rebel group operating extensively on Ugandan soil was the notoriously violent Lord's Resistance Army (LRA). From the late 1980s until the mid-2000s, armed conflict between the LRA and the Government of Uganda led to the displacement of an estimated 1.8 million people in northern Uganda. Roughly 25,000 children were abducted by rebels into servitude as fighters, "wives," and porters, sometimes forced to harm or kill their family members.[2] The United Nations Under-Secretary-General for Humanitarian Affairs and Emergency Relief called this situation in northern Uganda in 2003 the world's "largest forgotten emergency."

The LRA's ability to survive for over two decades and its disturbing willingness to use frequent, gruesome violence against civilians have led observers to classify it with the world's most reviled insurgent groups, like the Khmer Rouge in Cambodia, the Revolutionary United Front (RUF) in

---

[1] Jeffrey Gettleman, "Rafting in Uganda – Wild on the Nile." *The New York Times.* May 20, 2009.

[2] Civil Society Organizations for Peace in Northern Uganda, "Counting the Cost: Twenty Years of War in Northern Uganda." February 2006. Estimates of abducted youth vary widely, with one estimate reaching more than 66,000. See J. Annan, C. Blattman, and R. Horton. 2006. The State of Youth and Youth Protection in Northern Uganda: Findings from the Survey of War-Affected Youth. Kampala: UNICEF Uganda.

Sierra Leone, and the Shining Path (Sendero Luminoso) in Peru. Although diminished in recent years – the LRA has not attacked within Uganda's borders since 2005 – its remnants have occasionally resurfaced in remote jungles of the northeastern Democratic Republic of Congo (DRC), south and western Sudan, and the Central African Republic. At its height in Uganda, and more recently beyond Uganda, brazen acts of mass murder, sexual violence, and abduction marked the LRA's path.

How do groups like the LRA come about? Why are they sometimes not stopped before they become so violent and difficult to contain? Why on the other hand – in the wording of several former Ugandan insurgents and counterinsurgents I interviewed – are some rebel groups "nipped in the bud" by the states they confront, before becoming much of a threat?

These questions motivate this book, which aims to answer them with a straightforward approach: It scrutinizes how rebel groups start. It seeks to describe and explain what people who initiate rebellion do when they first come together with the aim of violently challenging a state and how nearby citizens and the state respond.

This approach is revealing – about how insurgencies begin and about the challenges of learning about violent conflict's emergence. When the LRA first started, it did not look much like the large, cruel organization it later became. Instead it was a small group with few weapons that sought to persuade local citizens – often through song and friendly interaction, not through coercion – to withhold information about their activities from the government. In fact, in its earliest days, the LRA looked similar to the other fifteen rebel groups that have formed in Uganda since 1986, the period that concerns this book and that followed the current president's seizing power.

To analysts of violent conflict, it may be surprising that so many rebel groups in addition to the LRA have formed in Uganda in recent decades. Little is known about many of these rebel groups because they began as small, clandestine groups, making just a faint imprint, if any, on the historical record. As a result, several that failed early are also missing from the standard databases on civil conflict and are thus not considered in the large swath of recent scholarly analyses that rely on these datasets. For example, the LRA is the sole Ugandan rebel group that appears after 1986 in the widely used Correlates of War dataset.[3] Only seven appear in the more fine-grained Uppsala Conflict Data Program and the Peace Research Institute of Oslo's (UCDP/ PRIO) Armed Conflict Database.[4]

---

[3] Sarkees and Wayman 2010.   [4] Gleditsch et al. 2002.

The absence of several groups reflects their rapid demise; most were defeated before gaining a capacity for mass violence. Only four groups – the LRA, the Holy Spirit Movement (HSM), the Uganda People's Army (UPA), and Allied Democratic Forces (ADF) – managed to become viable threats to the Ugandan government. The remaining twelve failed to hold a base on Ugandan territory for more than one or two months; they were either destroyed or forced to retreat across an international border. The early failure of these groups is also what makes them informative to study and poses the central puzzle that this book aims to address: If these groups formed under similar initial conditions, why did only some, like the LRA, become a viable threat to Uganda's stability?

This book is focused primarily on Uganda, but it speaks to a broader set of rebellions and fundamental questions about them. How does insurgency begin? Why and how do people start rebel groups?[5] Why do "weak states" often fail to expediently defeat new armed groups that challenge their authority, and how do weak states become strong?

In a sense, these questions are well-trodden. As Figure 1.1 shows, the majority of political violence in recent decades occurred within states, not between them. By one estimate, one-third of countries have experienced internal armed conflict since the 1950s.[6] Recognition of this pattern and interest in its causes have generated an expansive body of research on this topic since the early 1990s.

However, little if any of this work aims to examine *the initial stages of rebel group formation*. This is the case largely because doing so requires evidence that is quite hard to come by; rebel group formation often occurs in remote areas with minimal media presence or internet access. As noted previously, fewer than half of Uganda's rebel groups since 1986 are captured in fine-grained conflict datasets like that of UCDP/PRIO; over three-quarters of prominent recent studies of conflict onset rely on this dataset or less detailed ones.[7] For reasons I detail next and for which

---

[5] I limit my discussion in this book to armed conflict between a state and a non-state actor originating from within that state, and I use the phrases "rebellion," "civil conflict," and "internal armed conflict" interchangeably.

[6] Esteban, Mayoral, and Raj 2012.

[7] Arriving at this figure entailed identifying and reviewing all articles from January 2003 to December 2019 in ten prominent, peer-reviewed political science journals in order to identify those that undertook quantitative empirical analysis of the onset, incidence, or recurrence of civil war, internal armed conflict, rebellion, or state-based ethnic conflict (not intraethnic conflict or riots). The analysis identified 189 articles that met these criteria, 147 of which (77.8 percent) relied on the Correlates of War (COW) dataset, the UCDP/PRIO Armed Conflict Dataset (Gleditsch et al. 2002), Fearon and Laitin's (2003) dataset,

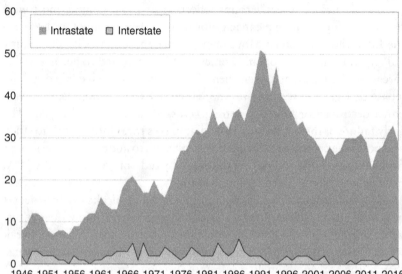

FIGURE I.I Incidence of internal armed conflict far exceeds interstate war since 1946

This is a stacked graph; the width of each shaded portion indicates the number of ongoing, state-based conflicts in each category and the upper threshold of the dark band indicates the total sum of ongoing intra- and interstate conflicts. Data are from the Uppsala Conflict Data Program/Peace Research Institute Oslo's (UCDP/PRIO) Armed Conflict Dataset. Intrastate conflicts occur between a state and a non-state actor. Interstate conflicts shown here are those between two or more states that resulted in at least twenty-five recorded battle-related deaths in a calendar year. Neither category includes "internationalized intrastate conflicts" (proxy wars).

I provide evidence in the chapters that follow, there is good reason to believe that, especially in weak states, such omissions exist far beyond data on Uganda.

A full understanding of the origins of insurgent violence must include rebel group behavior *before* groups hone their capacity for large-scale violence. From a theoretical standpoint, there is little reason to believe that the initial stages of rebellion are governed by the same forces as later

or Sambanis's (2006) dataset to measure the primary DV. The ten journals were *American Journal of Political Science, American Political Science Review, Conflict Management and Peace Science, Comparative Political Studies, International Organization, International Security, Journal of Conflict Resolution, Journal of Peace Research, Journal of Politics,* and *World Politics.*

stages. From a policy standpoint, there may be an opportunity for intervention in the period after a rebel group's formation but before its violence
is broadly covered by news media, and thus on our analytic radar. For
example, as Russell Hardin observed about Northern Ireland, "If the first
few [Irish Republican Army (IRA)] cells had been stopped, there might not
have been twenty-five years of such violence."[8] While the commonly used
Correlates of War dataset dates the "onset" of the LRA conflict to 1993, the
LRA initially formed in 1988. A focus into the earliest stages of insurgency
promises to offer insight into how internal armed conflict ends *before* large-
scale violence and its attendant humanitarian costs accrue.

In sum, the difficulty of observing the full range of rebel group starts in
a given time and place and poses a fundamental obstacle for the study of
conflict's emergence. The best chance for furthering knowledge on this
topic is to obtain systematic evidence on rebel group formation in the rare
contexts where it is possible to do so. This book does precisely that with
a detailed study of all rebel groups that formed in Uganda since 1986 –
including those that failed too early to be included in most retrospective
accounts and datasets. In doing so, I aim to advance our understanding of
how and why armed groups emerge in contexts like Uganda and why only
some, like the LRA, become viable.

1.1 THE ARGUMENT

The argument at the core of this book is that *information* – especially what
nascent rebels, the civilians that surround them, and states that they
challenge do and do not learn and believe about one another – strongly
influences the behavior of these parties during the initial stages of insurgency, and therefore whether or not aspiring rebels become viable threats.
As described in the section on scope conditions, this argument applies
primarily to rural areas of weak states, where insurgent groups are most
likely to form.

When a small group in such contexts initially comes together and
makes plans to violently challenge a state, few "facts on the ground"
have been established. Local villagers, the state, and even the aspiring
rebels themselves do not know how formidable the rebels will eventually
become – and thus *rumors* about their strength and righteousness relative
to the government, and thus their potential to succeed, are potent and

---

[8] Hardin 1995, 146.

unverifiable. In Chapter 3, I show that nascent rebel groups often do not yet even have a name. In such highly uncertain environments, rumors rule.

Insurgencies typically begin as small, clandestine groups – not as the well-known, army-like forces that they may later become. Because they are typically small and poorly resourced, nascent groups can be easily destroyed, even by relatively weak states. Therefore, the main threat to such vulnerable, incipient groups is whether or not they prevent the government from learning of their identity and location.

Many other studies of insurgency also put civilian support of the insurgents at the center of insurgents' ability to survive. However, their understanding of "support" usually emphasizes material support, such as joining the fighting ranks or providing food, money, weapons, or shelter. This book instead posits that incipient rebels need a very specific type of support from civilians: secrecy. Civilians who live where rebel groups form often learn basic information about where they were last seen and who they are. If just a few civilians provide this information to the government, this can lead to the nascent rebels' demise. This understanding of local noncombatants' role in nascent insurgency also differs from common views of violent conflict's emergence as a public, protest-like movement – a form of collective action that boils over into violence. This distinction yields several related insights at the core of the book.

First, understanding the dire threat that civilian informants pose to fragile, nascent rebels helps elucidate nascent *rebels' behavior*, especially regarding where they form and how they use violence (Chapter 4). Aspiring rebels, I argue, typically choose to form their groups in areas where they have an informational advantage – near their home area or where they have other strong connections to the local population – maximizing their chances of successfully controlling the information environment. Furthermore, due to a lack of monitoring capability and thus credible punishment mechanisms, nascent rebels rarely coerce civilians. Instead, during the initial phases, rebels often seek to score small, easy victories against government forces that minimize their military costs and serve as useful fodder for rumors. Such victories create opportunities to seed boastful rumors about the rebels' competence and good intent (and the government's lack thereof), which can help generate local pro-rebel narratives and influence nearby villagers to keep rebels' identity and whereabouts a secret. Even rebels that later become terribly violent, like the Khmer Rouge in Cambodia, RENAMO in Mozambique, and even the LRA in Uganda, were more pacific toward local civilians when they initially emerged.

The theory presented here helps us understand why this is the case: in this early phase, incipient rebels' would-be capabilities and "true" intent are inherently ambiguous, and thus rebels attempt to signal positive traits to civilians through their use of violence (and lack thereof). These dynamics change, making rebel coercion of civilians and more daring attacks against the government more likely, after rebels have developed information networks in the communities where they operate as well as coercive capacity.

Second, because of the vulnerability of nascent rebels, the most important influence on whether nascent rebels will survive to become viable groups is the *behavior of local civilians* (Chapter 5). These civilians observe rebels forming in their midst and can choose to provide information (or not) about nascent rebels' identity and location to the government. Civilians make this decision based on their expectations about the rebels' capabilities and the justness of their cause, about which they learn from people they trust – their kin. Thus, the structure of kinship networks among civilians where rebels form importantly influences incipient rebels' chances for becoming viable; kinship networks shape what people hear and believe about nascent rebels. Specifically, I argue that the types of kinship network structures that tend to underlie ethnically homogeneous areas are more likely to spread rebels' rumors effectively, leading few civilians to leak information about rebels to the government. By contrast, because of unhelpful network structures among civilians in heterogeneous areas, pro-rebel rumors are less likely to spread there, and therefore more civilians decide to inform the government what they know about the rebels. In short, while rebel groups initially form in both ethnically homogeneous and heterogeneous areas, because the different kinship structures in each shape how information flows, only those that form in homogeneous areas are likely to survive long enough to become a viable threat.

Finally, this argument indicates the importance of *the state's ability to access civilian information networks*, thereby ending nascent rebel groups and deterring new ones from forming (Chapter 6). Attempts at rebellion will be much more rare in areas where state's informational capacity is stronger since the likelihood of being detected there is higher. Knowing this, most potential rebel initiators will be deterred from attempting organized violence in the first place. This argument about the diminished likelihood of rebellion onset in areas of state strength is uncontroversial – in fact, many scholars, building on Max Weber's classic work, define strong states as those that do not have rebels operating on their territory. The primary contribution here, elaborated below, is to illuminate *why*

strong states see few rebel groups forming on their territory. While existing accounts emphasize the importance of states' military strength, infrastructure, or service delivery, I argue that the *informational penetration of
the state,* especially in rural areas, is crucial to deterring rebel formation
and limiting the likelihood of rebel viability.

1.2 CONTRIBUTION

1.2.1 Learning from Incipient Rebel Violence and Early-Failed Rebellions

While there is an expansive body of research that examines the "outbreak," "origins," and "onset" of internal armed conflict, due to the
inherent difficulty of studying clandestine activities that occur in remote
regions, few people explicitly study how insurgencies *begin*. Most classic
theories about internal conflict only briefly reference, if at all, how groups
of individuals with political goals initially come together and build organizations with the intent to commit violence against the state. Many center
on rebellion-building activities like rebel recruitment or finance but take
for granted the existence of an organization to absorb these resources.[9]

A lack of data about the start of internal armed conflict exacerbates this
lack of theory. As noted earlier, almost 80 percent of recent quantitative
articles on conflict onset use one of what Samuel Bazzi and Chris Blattman
call "the four major datasets"[10] on internal armed conflict. None of these
datasets aim to capture the initial phases of conflict, opting instead to
include only conflicts (and thus rebel groups) when at least twenty-five
battle-related deaths have been recorded in news media in a calendar year.
In a data collection effort I describe at the end of this chapter and in
Appendix D, I attempted to collect more comprehensive data about rebel
groups that formed in eastern and central Africa since 1997. The most

---

[9] For example, for Gates 2002, 1, "a rebel group is assumed to have already formed and is
engaged in armed military combat with governmental forces." Similarly, Weinstein (2007)
primarily focuses on how initial endowments of rebel groups shape dynamics of recruitment and violence that occur after violence is well underway. Both works thus illuminate
a set of issues very distinct from the initial dynamics of rebel group formation. Yet as
Nathan Leites 1970, 51, notes in his classic work on insurgency and counterinsurgency,
"(T)he distinction between tactical nuclear war and conventional war is hardly greater than
the distinction between an embryonic and a matured insurgency: between one in
a formative stage, where ... challenge to the established order is beginning; and one in
the advanced stage, where the insurgent civil and military organization is already strong."
[10] Blattman and Bazzi 2014, 8.

detailed of these datasets – the PRIO/UCDP Armed Conflict Dataset[11] – captures only 32 percent of the groups in this new dataset.

These problems may be particularly severe because, as I argue in Chapter 2, incipient rebels often commit only sporadic, small-scale violence for months or longer when they initially form and often do not take public credit for initial attacks due to concerns about detection. Because states may not detect incipient rebels, or may want to discredit them, states also have incentives to keep these attacks out of national news media – or to characterize them as attacks of mere criminals or bandits. In other words, recent quantitative research on conflict onset suffers from a selection problem.[12]

Of course, evidence about the initial phases of conflict is not necessary for studying most questions about medium- and large-scale conflicts, especially those about processes like patterns of violence that occur after viable rebel groups have already formed. Why should we also study the very initial stages of insurgency, prior to a group becoming viable – arguably a narrow slice of an enduring rebel group's lifespan?

First, as emphasized earlier, without examining these phases, we cannot fully understand how insurgencies begin – and, thus, how they may be detected, prevented, or ended before they become quite violent. Second and crucially, a sole focus on already-viable rebellions means that most existing studies cannot distinguish the correlates of the *initial* start of violence from that of conflict's *escalation*.[13] I highlight next why this matters when studying the controversial relationship between ethnicity and the start of civil conflict.

Furthermore, our absence of knowledge on conflict's initial stages means there is little awareness of the widespread phenomenon of incipient rebel groups failing before becoming much of a threat. Yet, as Daniel Byman argues, "for every group that becomes an insurgency, dozens – or perhaps hundreds – fail."[14] In recent news articles and nongovernment and international organizations' reporting from conflict regions, it is common to find mention of "small" rebel groups that go unnamed

---

[11] Gleditsch et al. 2002.
[12] I more fully describe this problem and demonstrate the inferential problems it causes, especially for understanding ethnicity's role in rebel group formation, in Lewis 2017. For additional discussion of the omissions resulting from uses of battle-death thresholds as a key inclusion criterion, see also Zukerman-Daly 2012; Finkel 2015; Blaxland 2018.
[13] For work examining later stages of conflict escalation – the distinct causes of low-intensity conflict, defined as minimum twenty-five battle-related deaths, and high-intensity conflict, defined as minimum 1,000 battle-related deaths – see especially Eck 2009; Webster 2019.
[14] Byman 2007, 1.

because they end before gaining much notoriety, especially in exceptionally weak states like the Democratic Republic of the Congo and the Central African Republic. While reporting on the Iraqi insurgency tended to focus on the major groups, Dexter Filkins wrote in 2005 that "Iraqi and American officials in Iraq say the single most important fact about the insurgency is that it consists not of a few groups but of dozens . . . Each is believed to have its own leader and is free to act on its own."[15]

This problem of limited reporting on the initial phases of rebellion, especially for early-failed rebel groups, is also evident in the historical record, in which typically only the most enduring groups are documented in any depth. In Sri Lanka, for example, while one usually associates recent conflict with the Tamil Tigers (LTTE), several other rebel groups operated during the period that the LTTE formed. Jeyarathnam Wilson states that there were thirty-seven Tamil militant groups, but "only five were of significance."[16] The Tamil Tigers survived the longest and caused the most casualties; scholars have painstakingly retraced their trajectory, while most other Sri Lankan groups remain obscure. Similarly, analysts tend to associate insurgency in Ethiopia with the Tigray People's Liberation Front (TPLF), which succeeded in toppling the government in 1991. Yet when the TPLF began in the 1970s, numerous other rebel groups operated in Ethiopia.[17] Today, little is known about the other groups, which never grew to the strength of the TPLF.

A natural response to the difficulty of obtaining information about early-failed groups has been to focus solely on the rebellions about which we do have substantial information. For example, in his seminal work on Latin American guerilla movements, Timothy Wickham-Crowley concedes the prevalence of failed incipient rebellions but explains he does not study them due to data collection challenges: "(G)uerilla movements appeared throughout Latin America in the 1960s, but most died an early death . . . failures left but few traces on the historical record, too few for the close analysis required here."[18] Indeed, in other prominent, qualitative comparative studies of rebellion, scholars caveat that they are only able to study the "major" groups, acknowledging that several other, less prominent groups existed.[19]

---

[15] Dexter Filkins, "Profusion of Rebel Groups Helps them Survive in Iraq." *The New York Times*, December 2, 2005.
[16] Wilson 2000, 126.   [17] Berhe 2004.   [18] Wickham-Crowley 1993, 16.
[19] E.g. Goodwin 2001; Staniland 2012a.

In sum, limited documentation of the initial stages of insurgency – and particularly the omission of early-failed rebel groups – has limited both quantitative and qualitative work on conflict onset. I argue in Chapter 2 that it has also contributed to the persistence of a long-standing scholarly debate about whether the *motives* of would-be rebelling populations, versus factors that make rebellion more *feasible,* are more important in causing the start of organized armed conflict. This book provides a window into incipient rebellion and offers a systematic approach to analyzing unusually comprehensive evidence about aspiring rebels.

1.2.2 Understanding the Importance of Rumors in Rebellions' Start

Rumors are a ubiquitous feature of politics and warfare, yet they are largely absent from dominant theories of the start of organized armed conflict within states.[20] Rumors are likely to be especially important in the uncertain *initial* stages of insurgency, before each side's capabilities are fully demonstrated. As the opening words of Jeremy Weinstein's *Inside Rebellion* read, "Word of the rebels came first in the form of rumors." Similarly, in Evgeny Finkel's *Ordinary Jews,* the chapter about Jewish armed resistance against Nazis opens with "Initially, there were rumors [about the new armed group]."

By directly examining the initial stages of insurgency in the chapters that follow, the importance of local networks in influencing rebel group formation becomes clear: They can transmit rumors about nascent rebels. And when the rumors travel through networks of trust – kinship networks in many rural contexts – they are often widely adopted among members of the network.

This book's emphasis on rumors diverges from most recent scholarship on conflict onset, which instead emphasizes structural factors that make people want to rebel, such as discrimination or exclusion of their group, or material factors that make rebellion feasible like access to financing for recruits and weapons. The theory of nascent rebellion presented here instead builds on the literature on counterinsurgency, which has long emphasized the importance of information. In David Kilcullen's words,

---

[20] Rumor's importance has been demonstrated in conflict zones, in Greenhill and Oppenheim 2017, and rumors play a central role in theories and evidence on how interethnic riots start in urban contexts (e.g. Varshney 2003; Bhavnani, Findley, and Kuklinski 2009.) However, prior social science work has not specified their relevance to initial armed group formation. The sole exception I know of is Larson and Lewis 2018.

"In this battlefield [of insurgency and counterinsurgency], popular perceptions and rumor are more influential than the facts and more powerful than a hundred tanks."[21]

While foundational research has shown the fundamental importance of information to the extent and character of violence during civil war[22] – especially the irregular warfare that is the subject of this book[23] – and recent, pathbreaking work has shown the importance of social networks to sustaining rebellion[24] and shaping perceptions of threat that fuel mobilization during civil war[25] – this book's contribution is to bring related insights to how rumors spread and influence rebellions' *start*.

1.2.3 Ethnicity and Kinship Networks

Scholars have long noted the relevance of ethnic identity to armed rebellion,[26] but *how* and *why* ethnicity matters remain areas of considerable continuing debate. While an initial wave of literature using country-level data failed to find a relationship between a country's ethnic diversity and conflict onset,[27] studies using subnational data have found a substantively and statistically significant relationship between concentrations of ethnic groups within a country and conflict onset.[28] Understanding the mechanisms that underlie this relationship remains the central challenge to understanding how ethnicity influences the start and escalation of conflict. The theory and evidence presented in this book offer a micro-level look inside the "black box" of this process.

This book proposes a previously overlooked reason why shared ethnicity can propel communities to rebellion. Ethnic groups in sub-Saharan Africa and much of Asia are comprised of an underlying web of kinship ties;[29] these ties serve as conduits of trusted, word-of-mouth information. In the chapters that follow, I argue that certain *kinship network structures* among civilians in the villages where rebels form can make those civilians vulnerable to rumors that nascent rebels seed in the communities where they launch. These rumors are about difficult-to-verify aspects of the incipient rebels' expected competence and

---

[21] Kilcullen 2010, 38.   [22] Kalyvas 2006.
[23] Berman and Matanock 2013; Berman et al. 2018.
[24] Parkinson 2013; Staniland 2014.   [25] Shesterinina 2016.
[26] Walter and Denny 2014.   [27] Fearon and Laitin 2003; Collier and Hoeffler 2004.
[28] Toft 2002; Toft 2003; Weidmann 2009.   [29] Horowitz 2000, 57.

righteousness, or of interpretations of government actions. If such rumors spread widely, through trusted channels of shared kinship, they can generate beliefs among civilians that those living near them broadly support the rebels – which, in turn, dissuades civilians from informing the government about a new rebel group forming in their midst. This buys the rebels crucial time to build their own intelligence networks and a small army that can pose a viable threat. Using a variety of historical and anthropological sources, as well as fieldwork in Uganda, the book argues that the types of *kinship network structures that can help rebels by spreading their rumors often underlie areas that are ethnically homogeneous.* Ethnic demography reflects kinship groups' patterns of migration and settlement, and thus certain ethnic demographic patterns reflect certain underlying kinship network structures.

Empirical evidence from Uganda presented in Chapters 3 and 5 suggests that ethnicity had little to do with the initiation of insurgency, but rather the network structures underlying ethnic demographic patterns influenced already-formed rebel groups' prospects for survival beyond their infancy. I show that some ethnic grievances that are thought to have caused Ugandan rebellions in fact emerged *out of* the initial phases of insurgency; kinship networks likely shaped the emergence and solidification of grievance narratives in ethnically homogeneous areas and stymied their formation in ethnically heterogeneous areas. In other words, the narratives were not preconditions to the start of rebellion but instead appear to have resulted from it.

Such findings support recent theories and evidence suggesting that ethnic narratives are highly responsive to the dynamics of violent conflict.[30] A key implication is that while previously held ethnic grievances may be helpful to aspiring rebels, their existence is not a necessary condition for nascent rebels to become viable – and to later be known as an "ethnic rebellion." Yet this suggests that it may be easy for observers to retrospectively attribute a conflict's "root causes" or "origins" to grievances or hate, when in fact grievances were ignited *by the early phases of violence.* These distinctions are not trivial, especially since these microfoundations of ethnicity's role in conflict should inform our thinking about pathways for preventing the start and escalation of violent conflict.

---

[30] Valentino 2004; King 2007; Kalyvas 2008a; Christia 2012.

1.2.4 Information and State Capacity

Most scholarly works conceptualize strong states as those that competently provide collective goods to its citizens. For example, prominent accounts stress that state strength entails providing protection from external threats,[31] protection of property rights,[32] provision of rule of law,[33] a strong sense of national identity,[34] or a capacity to carry out its policies – particularly formation of a professionalized bureaucracy that allows states to administer and fund the production of these goods.[35]

This study, instead, highlights the importance of domestic intelligence institutions, which channel information about potential threats from localities back to the central government. Specifically, this book emphasizes a state's *informational penetration* of its territory, arguing that it not only allows states to end incipient rebellions before they escalate but helps to deter individuals from launching rebellion in the first place. In doing so, this book joins with those who emphasize the population's "legibility" to the state[36] and applies related, foundational ideas about states' monitoring capacity[37] to the start of rebel group formation.

While theories of conflict onset have long highlighted the relevance of a state's capacity to cope with rebels operating on its territory, they tend to focus on the military strength or infrastructural reach of the state. With the exception of historical literature on colonial states' maintenance of order, intelligence institutions are rarely emphasized in works on how relatively weak states bring about order. Further, scholars who do argue that a state's coercive weakness makes it ripe for internal conflict[38] rarely *observe* how certain conditions of fragile states influence the initial decisions of would-be rebel leaders.

In Chapter 6, I describe how Uganda's ruling party extended the state's civil intelligence institutions until they penetrated every region, and indeed every village of Uganda. While intelligence institutions in developing countries are sometimes associated with coercion or repression, interviews throughout rural Uganda indicate that the creation of these systems in Uganda was more subtle, usually relying on a mix of persuasion, political ideology, prestige, and financial incentives to induce civilians to serve as informers – both those with formal and public informant roles, and those with public or clandestine informant roles. To my knowledge,

---

[31] Tilly 2005.   [32] Bates, Grief, and Singh 2002.   [33] O'Donnell 1993.
[34] Herbst 2000; Darden and Mylonas 2012.   [35] Geddes 1996; Soifer 2016.
[36] Scott 2008; Lee and Zhang 2017.   [37] Fearon and Laitin 2003.
[38] Bates, Grief, and Singh 2002; Fearon and Laitin 2003; Bates 2008.

the intelligence functions of these institutions and their role in preventing rebel formation in Uganda have not yet been well-documented. Interview evidence from government intelligence forces and former rebels provides a clear picture of these dynamics and indicates the importance of these institutions to deterring rebel group formation in Uganda today.

Why are domestic intelligence institutions not a central focus of the conflict onset literature? First, from a pragmatic standpoint, intelligence collection is difficult to observe since it often happens in secret, leaving scant traces for observers to analyze. It is simply much easier to measure a state's terrain, military, and roads. Second, the omissions from historical accounts and conflict datasets that motivate this book – those of the initial phases of insurgency and of early-failed rebel groups – also likely play a role in the lack of appreciation for intelligence in the state-building process. The fact that many attempted rebel groups fail early clarifies that states often detect and therefore can end nascent rebellions before those rebels develop substantial military capacity. As I argue further in Chapter 6, these dynamics present a critical role for the state's informational reach.

1.3 SCOPE CONDITIONS

This book's arguments pertain to the emergence of a particular, common form of intrastate armed conflict: insurgency against a weak state. I follow Kalyvas and Balcells (2010) in conceptualizing *insurgency* as a technology of warfare used during irregular fighting; it is used by non-state actors against stronger state actors and is characterized by "unconventional," hit-and-run tactics rather than "conventional" open warfare. By "weak states," I mean those that have limited institutional presence and limited ability to administer territory much beyond the capital city; tax collection and other state-provided services are minimal in rural areas.[39] Police stations may be nominally present but generally lack the resources and the capacity to operate effectively over a large territory, and are easily avoided since they are clustered near trading centers. Furthermore, as I argue in this book, weak states often have limited access to information in their peripheral territories, which makes it difficult for them to detect and thus to deter emergent internal, violent challengers.

---

[39] Using this conceptualization of weak states, I am following Herbst 2000 and Fearon and Laitin 2003, among others.

By limiting its focus to armed groups that challenge the authority of states – either by taking over a state or by controlling some of its territory – this book does not consider violence that occurs *among* non-state actors, such as when neighboring groups raid one another's villages. It also does not examine the dynamics of new rebel groups forming when two or more small, previously formed rebel groups merge into a new group, nor when groups form via splintering off of a prior, larger group. Instead, it examines the steps people take when starting to build a new armed group where one did not previously exist. This nascent group may, if it becomes viable, later go on to merge with other groups or fragment into several new groups.

Insurgency is the most common form of organized, armed challenge to a state, typically occurring in rural areas and accounting for about two-thirds of large-scale civil wars between 1944 and 2004,[40] and likely a much larger share of small- and medium-scale civil wars.[41] Re-analyzing Balcells and Kalyvas's (2010) data indicates that since the end of the Cold War, non-state actors in civil wars are most likely to use tactics of insurgency in weaker states (proxied by GDP per capita); they more often used conventional warfare in stronger (higher income) states.[42] Figure 1.2 shows these patterns.

Because of this book's focus on rural, weak state contexts, several of its core arguments do not easily travel to urban or stronger state contexts, like

[40] I use Kalyvas and Balcells's 2010 data to arrive at this number, collapsing their "irregular" and "SNC" categories into one category of "insurgency." Kalyvas and Balcells (2010) put forth a threefold typology based on the combined tactics of the rebels and the state; if the rebels use guerilla tactics while the state has a conventional army, they call this *irregular* warfare, if both the rebels and the government use sophisticated military tactics, they call this *conventional* warfare, and if the rebels use guerilla tactics while the government also uses unsophisticated tactics, often because of extreme state weakness or implosion, they call this *symmetric non-conventional (SNC)* warfare. Because I am just focusing on the rebel side, and because I posit that both a militarily sophisticated and an unsophisticated government would be relatively stronger than a rebel group in its infancy, I consider both of what Kalyvas and Balcells call *irregular* and *SNC* conflicts to count as insurgency.

[41] Non-state actors can employ conventional warfare if they start with substantial coercive capacity, which is most commonly the case when challengers emerge from within a national army, pitting at least one faction of the national army against that which retains allegiance to the incumbent government. McLauchlin 2015 calculates that about 22 percent of new rebel groups from 1946 to 2011 emerged from a national army.

[42] More broadly, civil conflict is most common in poorer states; one of the few, robust empirical regularities of the sizeable body of work on the country-level risk factors for small-scale and large-scale internal conflict is the negative association between GDP per capita and both types of conflict onset. See especially Hegre and Sambanis 2006.

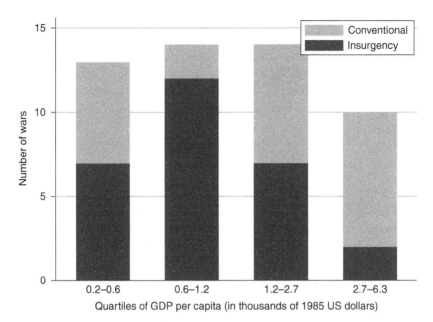

FIGURE I.2 Technologies of civil war, 1989–2004
Civil war list and technology of warfare data are from Kalyvas and Balcells (2010).
Per capita GDP data are from Fearon and Laitin (2003) using World Bank data.
Quartiles are not of equal size due to missing data.

the outbreak of "the Troubles" in Northern Ireland or the Syrian civil war,
where aspiring rebels face different types of challenges. However, this focus
is also arguably one of the book's strengths, since we know the least about
rebel group formation in weak state contexts. Most recent major, in-depth
scholarly works on the *start* of rebellion focus on settings of relatively strong
states or foreign occupiers.[43] Yet especially in Africa, armed groups are most
likely to emerge from rural areas, whereas antigovernment mobilization is
more likely to take the form of protests, riots, or terrorism in urban areas.[44]

In sum, this book limits its scope to understanding the start of insurgency in the weak state contexts in which insurgent groups are most likely

[43] E.g. Petersen 2001; Lawrence 2010; Zukerman-Daly 2012; Della Porta 2013; Staniland
2014; Finkel 2015; Sullivan 2015. Recent exceptions focused on Africa include Weinstein
2007; Reno 2011; Roessler 2016; I address how this work builds on and diverges from
these and other works in Chapter 2.
[44] Leventoğlu and Metternich 2018.

to form, and for which the least light has been shed to date. In the final chapter of this book, I consider how rebel group formation differs in stronger state contexts. In such contexts, I argue, barriers to entry for new armed groups are higher and thus groups start less frequently – but when they do, they more often draw on stronger organizational foundations and can be more immediately, explosively violent.[45]

1.4 EVIDENCE

1.4.1 Why Uganda?

This book studies these questions with a focus on rich micro- and meso-level data from Uganda between 1986 and 2006. Closely studying one country allows for more detailed and precise data collection than cross-national studies. This approach also allows for the collection of critical evidence that prior studies lack: information about all rebel groups that formed in a given period of one country – even groups that did not survive long.

Uganda is an excellent environment to do so for several reasons. Since sixteen groups operated in Uganda during this period, my approach allows for systematic comparison of groups within a single national political context; the current president has been in power since January 1986. Also, because violence in Uganda stemming from these conflicts had ended by 2007, when I began fieldwork for this project, I avoided several complex ethical and logistical challenges of collecting data in an ongoing conflict zone. Yet, because the conflicts I was studying had occurred relatively recently and due to a blanket amnesty law there, key actors were still alive and could discuss their experiences with relative candor. According to data from Uganda's Amnesty Commission, over 22,000 former Ugandan rebels have received amnesty under these provisions, receiving a "soft-landing" package from the government, which includes a blanket and about $200 each.[46]

Uganda is also a substantively important case. Internal armed conflict has affected sub-Saharan Africa more than any other part of the world

---

[45] I also touch on this argument in the penultimate section of Chapter 2, which addresses alternative explanations.

[46] Prior to Uganda's Amnesty Act, a presidential pardon was in place for former rebels who disavowed violence. See Caroline Lamwaka, "President Pardons All Rebels." *The New Vision*, April 12, 1988.

since the early 1990s.[47] While large-scale civil wars are becoming less common in contemporary Africa,[48] the most common form of rebellion there is similar in kind to those at the center of this book: rebels that are weak, operate in states' peripheries, and produce low-intensity violence.[49] Instability and rebel group formation continue to threaten the livelihoods of Africans in several states; about 80 percent of military and police personnel serving worldwide in UN stability operations are stationed in Africa.[50] Further, Uganda – a country of over 40 million people – is positioned at the center of a region has suffered from a great deal of political violence. It borders eastern DRC, South Sudan, Rwanda, Kenya, and Tanzania. Uganda's recent relative stability has positioned it to be a major player in regional security; since 2007, Ugandan military officers have led the African Union peacekeeping force in Somalia (AMISOM), and Uganda has been the largest troop-contributing country to the force.

1.4.2 Evidence from Uganda

The primary data collection challenge of this project – and the most difficult one – was to determine how many rebel groups had operated in Uganda since 1986 and to ascertain basic facts about how those groups formed. To do so, I used data from Uganda's Amnesty Commission, in combination with triangulating among information from current and former intelligence officials in the capital and outlying areas, former rebels, local journalists, and a set of Ugandan newspaper articles on armed conflict from that period. Specifically, I started with a list of twenty-nine rebel groups, which came from an Amnesty Commission database of all individuals who, as of July 2008, had received amnesty from the Ugandan government for their participation in a rebel group. The database listed each individual's rebel group affiliation. I eliminated thirteen of these listed groups either because I determined that they ended prior to 1986 or because I could not find any evidence that these groups committed a single act of violence on

---

[47] I measure "affected by internal armed conflict" by the number of ongoing conflicts per year and quantity of battle-related deaths per year. Regional patterns of internal armed conflict incidence are displayed and summarized in the Human Security Report (2010, chapter 10). See also Goldstone et al. 2010.

[48] Williams 2011, 4. [49] Straus 2012.

[50] Author's calculation based on data at "UN Missions Summary of Military and Police," www.un.org/Depts/dpko/dpko/contributors/, accessed December 28, 2015.

Ugandan territory. "Briefcase" rebel groups – those that exist in public proclamations only, likely because an individual seeks to capture the attention of the media or government while never building an actual group or committing violence – are a well-known phenomenon in Uganda. To make determinations about which purported rebellions had existed as groups that aimed to violently challenge the state, I gathered and reviewed a set of Ugandan, English-language[51] newspaper articles that reference armed conflict from 1986 to 2002, conducted interviews in the areas where the groups reportedly formed, and consulted with Uganda's intelligence services, including the head of Uganda's Chieftancy of Military Intelligence.[52] For more discussion of how I arrived at this list of sixteen rebel groups, including close calls, please see Appendix A.

To examine patterns of rebel violence, including correlates of where these rebel groups formed and became viable, I use quantitative data from Uganda's census, geographic and household survey data from Uganda, and the Ugandan newspaper articles described previously. Where information about the location of rebel group formation and early violence was incomplete or I was concerned about accuracy, I supplemented this evidence with information from over 250 interviews. Of these interviews, 170 were with former rebel commanders, intelligence officers and foot soldiers, local government officials that operated where rebels launched, Members of Parliament, military leaders, intelligence officers, and conflict experts such as Ugandan academics and NGO leaders. The remainder was with civilians, described next. As much as possible, I verified information about the timing and location of events described in this book with multiple sources from multiple regions and with distinct roles in the conflict (e.g. rebel, civilian, or state-affiliated actor).

To learn about civilians' experiences and beliefs, in addition to the information gleaned from the interviews described previously,

---

[51] In practice, this likely constitutes the strong majority of Ugandan newspaper articles on armed conflict, since most non-English-language newspapers in Uganda are translations of the English-language version. I collected these articles from archives at the Makerere University Business School and the Centre for Basic Research in Kampala, Uganda, as well as at the Library of Congress in Washington, DC. Newspapers reviewed included: *The Citizen, The Monitor, The New Vision, The Star, The Weekly Focus,* and *The Weekly Topic.*

[52] The two Ugandan institutions responsible for internal intelligence are the Chieftancy of Military Intelligence, a military agency, and the Internal Security Organization, a civilian agency. I also consulted several Internal Security Organization officials as I determined this list of rebel groups.

I conducted interviews with civilians in rural areas of Uganda where rebels groups had formed. This effort included sixty-eight semi-structured individual interviews and fourteen focus groups with civilians in four areas that were affected by the early stages of conflict for four different rebel groups: the Acholi, Bukedi, Teso, and West Nile regions.[53] In doing so, I sought to balance breadth of contexts examined – each of these four regions had distinct rebellions, political histories, and local ethno-linguistic groups – while ensuring reasonable depth of knowledge gained for each region. I discuss the paired comparison research design that drove selection of the case studies in Chapter 5. For a list and more discussion of the interviews and focus groups, see Appendix B. I conducted research for this study in over fourteen months of fieldwork throughout several regions of Uganda (in twenty districts[54] and twenty-nine counties, shown in Figure 1.3) between August 2007 and February 2011.

To more closely probe a key proposed casual mechanism about news traveling more widely in ethnically homogeneous than heterogeneous areas (among other research questions not addressed in this book), in collaboration with Jennifer M. Larson, I conducted a field experiment in two villages of Soroti district. I trained and supervised the enumeration team for the duration of the experiment, which took place in May and June 2013.[55]

This body of evidence cannot offer a comprehensive or decisive history of these rebellions. Instead, it allows for insight into key actors' interpretations of certain key events during the formation of these rebel groups that cannot otherwise be captured. Gathering detailed information about beliefs and recollections on sensitive, complex topics often requires extended back-and-forth exchanges and relationships of trust between interviewer and informant that are difficult to attain through other methods for eliciting opinions and experiences. Furthermore, while it can be quite difficult to obtain reliable information about events related to violent conflicts, the technique of triangulating among multiple interviews,

---

[53] In Teso, I conducted focus groups in Soroti and Kumi. In Bukedi, I conducted focus groups in Tororo and Busia. In West Nile, I conducted focus groups in Nyadri, Koboko, and Yumbe. In Acholi, I conducted focus groups in Gulu, Pader, and Kitgum. The focus groups ranged from 6 to 23 participants; the total number of focus group participants was 169. Details are in Appendix B.

[54] The districts in which I conducted interviews, based on 2009 district boundaries, are Amuria, Arua, Busia, Gulu, Kitgum, Koboko, Kabarole, Kampala, Kasese, Kumi, Lira, Luwero, Masindi, Mbale, Mukono, Nyadri, Pader, Soroti, Tororo, and Yumbe.

[55] Details about this experiment can be found in Larson and Lewis 2017.

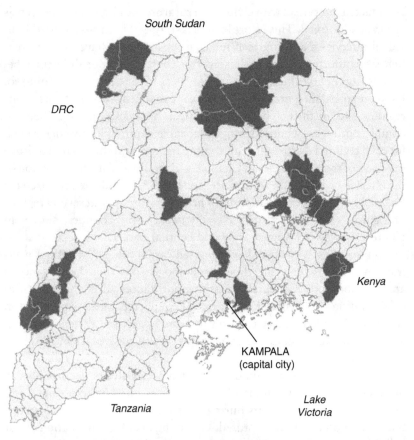

FIGURE 1.3 Location (county) of interviews conducted in Uganda

along with local newspaper articles, can make it possible to capture
sequences and description of basic patterns of behavior.[56] Where evidence
from different individuals – especially if those individuals represent distinct types of actors in a conflict (e.g. insurgent and counterinsurgent) –
converged on a similar description of a single event, perception of local
attitudes, or pattern of behavior, I judged that this constituted considerable evidence in favor of its accuracy.

[56] Local Ugandan newspapers were often less useful than interviews because articles overlooked or provided highly ambiguous information about violent events, particularly
during the initial phases of rebellions.

1.4.3 Beyond Uganda: Dataset of Rebel Group Formation in Eastern and Central Africa

While the empirical core of this book draws on scrutiny of events in Uganda since 1986, it is useful to probe whether the patterns uncovered there are relevant elsewhere. In a concluding section of each empirical chapter that follows (Chapters 3 through 6), I consider the extent to which findings from Uganda may apply in other states. To do so, I rely on qualitative studies from other scholars focused on weak states around the world, and when possible, on descriptive statistics from a new dataset on rebel groups in eastern and central African states.

This dataset aims to capture all non-state armed groups that formed in central and eastern Africa from January 1, 1997,[57] until the end of 2015 that had political goals and made concrete plans to violently challenge the authority of the state. The coding protocol was designed to include even those groups that failed soon after launching their group, committing only minimal violence. I defined central and eastern Africa inclusively, attempting to collect data about rebel group formation in twelve countries: Burundi, the Central African Republic, the Democratic Republic of the Congo, Ethiopia, Kenya, Malawi, Mozambique, Rwanda, Sudan, South Sudan, Tanzania, and Zambia.[58]

To identify potential groups, the research team started with actors listed in the Armed Conflict Location and Event Dataset (ACLED).[59] Because we were aiming to capture new, anti-state armed groups, we did not include groups that had fragmented from prior armed groups.[60] We determined whether actors from that dataset should be counted using the same criteria used to identify groups in Uganda; I discuss in detail how we operationalized and applied these criteria, among other details about the dataset, in Appendix D. This effort resulted in a dataset of eighty-three armed groups. Since the aim was to probe the external validity of findings

---

[57] We chose this date as our start date because of the need to rely on the ACLED dataset as a crucial source; its data for Africa starts on this date.

[58] For additional analyses shown in Chapter 6, we identified rebel groups and coded a subset of variables for eight additional countries in southern Africa: Angola, Botswana, Lesotho, Madagascar, Namibia, South Africa, Swaziland, and Zimbabwe. Including these countries resulted in the addition of six additional rebel groups to the dataset, bringing the total to eighty-nine groups.

[59] Raleigh et al. 2010.

[60] On the importance and dynamics of rebel fragmentation in Africa, see especially Woldemariam 2018.

from Uganda, these eighty-three groups do not include Ugandan rebel groups.[61]

Because the evidence used to identify rebel groups relied primarily on articles from newspapers, the resulting dataset surely undercounts the true number of new rebel groups that formed in these countries. In the analyses that follow, I discuss potential biases resulting from likely omissions. Still, by explicitly trying to capture all groups, and by scrutinizing the very initial phases of group formation and violence, this dataset captures rebel group formation at a level of detail unmatched by prior armed group-level datasets. The eighty-three groups we capture in central and eastern Africa are over three times as many groups as prior datasets include for these countries; only 32 percent of the rebel groups our research team identified are included in the UCDP/PRIO non-state actor list,[62] and only 35 percent are in the National Consortium for the Study of Terrorism and Responses to Terrorism's (START) Global Terrorism Database (GTD).[63]

Beyond identifying rebel groups, this data collection effort entailed coding a series of variables on the organizational basis of each group (or lack thereof), groups' patterns of initial violence, and others. Because the available information on these groups is often highly lacking in detail, there is considerable missingness in this data; I report findings in the pages that follow with attention to transparency on this matter (see especially Table 3.2 and the surrounding discussion).

---

[61] Because of uneven quality of information about the existence of new rebel groups, we coded a variable about the certainty of the existence of these groups. Of the eighty-three groups we included, coders assessed that there was "high" certainty that fifty-nine of these groups existed as an organized armed group that sought to challenge the authority of the state; there was "medium" certainty about the existence of sixteen groups, and "low" certainty about eight groups. High certainty means that researchers identified more than two credible sources (including local media) that verify the existence of an armed group meeting our criteria. Medium certainty means no more than two credible sources suggested existence of a group, or that there are few (not more than three) conflicting reports that are difficult to explain. Low certainty means that researchers could only identify one credible report of a rebel group, and/or there is good reason – e.g. political context – to believe that this may not have been a real group, or there are more than three conflicting reports that were difficult to explain. For several countries, coders judged that new rebel groups had likely formed that coders were unable to capture due to poor information. Coders agreed that there were likely more than eighty-three new rebel groups that formed in these countries between 1997 and 2015.

[62] Gleditsch et al. 2002.

[63] National Consortium for the Study of Terrorism and Responses to Terrorism (START) 2012.

1.5 OVERVIEW OF THE BOOK

This book aims to build knowledge about insurgent group formation by examining the strategic context faced, respectively, by nascent insurgents, the communities they operate near, and the states they confront. Chapter 2 presents the book's theoretical arguments. It describes and defends the key assumptions on which the arguments presented in the book rely, and shows how these assumptions lead to expected empirical patterns about the initial stages of insurgency.

The book then turns to the evidence. Chapter 3 provides background about rebel group formation in Uganda since 1986 and shows that several features of rebel group formation in Uganda are common in other central and eastern African countries. This discussion provides context and support for key assumptions underpinning the book's theory – especially that rebels often start as small, poorly resourced, clandestine groups, and not as large, public protest movements.

Chapters 4, 5, and 6 focus, respectively, on the rebels', the civilians', and the state's behavior, primarily using a mix of qualitative and quantitative evidence from Uganda. I also look briefly beyond Uganda in the penultimate section of each chapter. Chapter 4 focuses on Ugandan rebels' initial decisions about where to launch and how to use violence initially. It shows that initial rebel group launch is not correlated (at the subnational, county level) with factors like poverty, ethnic demography, terrain, or exclusion, which commonly feature in explanations of civil war onset. It also shows that rebels initially refrained from extensive, large-scale violence against the state or civilian targets, instead focusing on small attacks that could be used to test their adversary and spread pro-rebel rumors. Chapter 5 examines civilians' role in determining whether nascent rebels become viable. It shows how civilians' kinship network structures came about in Uganda, and why they importantly influence civilian behavior because they determine what information civilians do, and do not, receive and believe about rebels in this phase. Chapter 6 focuses on the Ugandan state and its role in addressing rebel group formation in Uganda since 1986. It demonstrates that Uganda transitioned from having numerous rebellions form and operate on its territory to relative stability today, with no rebels operating on its territory, by developing deeply penetrative intelligence institutions that enabled the center to learn about emergent local threats. These institutions allow states to defeat incipient insurgent groups and, as a result, to deter new ones from forming.

Chapter 7 examines the theoretical and policy implications of the book's findings. It focuses in particular on what this book's findings indicate for future scholarship and policy on armed conflict.

2

A Theory of Rebel Group Formation

This chapter establishes the book's theoretical foundations and builds the analytic scaffolding for the evidence presented in later chapters. In essence, its main argument is that the desire to control information flows to, from, and among civilians is what guides rebels' and states' behavior in the initial phases of rebel group formation – which gives access to civilian information networks, and the structure of those networks, a central role in determining whether nascent rebels become viable.

The chapter undertakes four tasks. First, it briefly reviews a major debate in the literature on civil conflict onset and argues that it can be greatly advanced with more explicit theory and better evidence about the very initial phases of armed conflict. Second, it defines the basic concepts at the core of the theory. It then describes and defends the key assumptions about the nature of insurgent group formation in weak states. Fourth, it turns to explaining why, given these assumptions and conditions, we should expect certain patterns of behavior from rebels, civilians, and states amid nascent rebellion. It concludes by addressing potential alternative explanations and other implications of the theory.

2.1 AN ENDURING DEBATE

Interest in the causes of intrastate armed conflict has generated an expansive body of research on its onset.[1] A major axis of debate emerging in this literature is between a family of explanation that champions factors that *motivate* people to rebel and one emphasizing factors that make rebellion

---

[1] See Blattman and Miguel (2010) for a comprehensive review of this literature.

more *feasible*.[2] Motivation-focused explanations tend to posit that conflict occurs because of group-level demands and frustrations aimed at the central government – typically driven by group-level political or economic inequality within a state.[3] Such works tend to build and test refinements of Ted Robert Gurr's classic hypothesis: "The potential for collective violence varies strongly with the intensity and scope of relative deprivation among members of a collectivity."[4] Feasibility-centered arguments, on the other hand, respond that motivation to rebel is unlikely to distinguish cases of non-rebellion from cases of rebellion because grievances are often widely held in areas where rebellion occurs *and* where it does not.[5] Furthermore, people may be coerced or financially induced to participate in rebellion, rendering an individual's frustrations toward the government (or lack thereof) largely irrelevant to understanding why they rebel.

Factors that have been associated with feasibility for rebellion include state weakness, rough terrain, poverty, prior organizational capacity, and proximity to an international border, all of which are thought to provide a military advantage for rebels.[6] Variants of these arguments stress that these factors provide a military advantage because they offer a ready pool of potential recruits with low opportunity costs of fighting[7] or material benefits, including sources of rebel finance such as lootable natural resources[8] and sympathetic external parties such as foreign governments or diasporas.[9] Empirical conflict analyses have led to few consistent findings about which family of explanation better predicts the onset of conflict or unifies them into a single explanation.[10]

---

[2] In noting this axis of difference in the civil war onset literature, I follow Collier and Hoeffler (2004), who instead of using the term "feasibility" use "opportunity."

[3] E.g. Stewart 2002; Toft 2002; Toft 2003; Østby 2008; Cederman, Wimmer, and Min 2010; Cederman, Weidmann, and Gleditsch 2011.

[4] Gurr 1970, 24.

[5] McAdam, McCarthy, and Zald 1988; Fearon and Laitin 2003; Collier and Hoeffler 2004.

[6] Herbst 2000; Fearon and Laitin 2003; Buhaug and Rod 2006; Buhaug, Cederman, and Rod 2008; Salehyan 2009; Zukerman-Daly 2012.

[7] Collier and Hoeffler 2004; Urdal 2006.

[8] Collier and Hoeffler 2004; Ross 2004; Humphreys 2005; Lujala 2010.

[9] Fearon and Laitin 2003; Collier and Hoeffler 2004; Salehyan 2009; Cunningham 2010.

[10] The most robust finding emerging from the country-level wave of conflict research in the 1990s and 2000s is that of a correlation between per capita GDP and civil conflict onset (Hegre and Sambanis 2006). Micro-level empirical research has also found support for the relationship between local income shocks and violence (or behavior associated with criminality) in Colombia and sub-Saharan Africa (Dube and Vargas 2010; Berman and Couttenier 2015; Blattman and Annan 2016). Such findings generally support feasibility-centered accounts. On the other hand, numerous more recent works spurred by Cederman, Wimmer, and Min (2010) and the Ethnic Power Relations Dataset Family

A fundamental, but rarely noted, difference underlying this debate is that each stance relies on distinct assumptions about how people initiate organized violence, and particularly about *the role of the noncombatant population where these rebellions form.* The "motivation" family of explanation tends to envision rebellion similar to that of a public protest, requiring high levels of active public participation from a large swath of a local population *prior to* rebel group formation. For example, in their influential 2011 book *Inequality, Grievances, and Civil War*, Lars-Erik Cederman, Kristian Skrede Gleditsch, and Halvard Buhaug sketch a causal pathway to organized violence that begins with group-level inequalities or exclusion, leading to politicized grievances and emotional processes among group members, culminating in mobilization of the group and then ultimately increasing the proclivity of that group to rebel. This process, as they conceptualize it, unfolds slowly: "[G]radually escalating, nonviolent conflict typically precedes violent phases."[11] An implication is that the more people in an area who are highly motivated to mobilize – often initially as part of a nonviolent movement – then the more likely it is that violence will subsequently erupt. Indeed, a more recent literature that directly examines the effectiveness of nonviolent mobilization,[12] and why nonviolent movements sometimes turn violent,[13] tends to envision a similar causal pathway. Those who characterize violent rebellion's start in this way often view it as a classic free-rider problem, differing over whether the level of motivation alone – conferred by emotional processes, community norms, or simply the severity of group inequalities – can induce mobilization,[14] or whether selective incentives are necessary.[15]

On the other hand, explanations that center on feasibility tend to sketch a pathway to conflict for which the first movers are a small group of entrepreneurial individuals; mobilization of a large group does not occur until *after* rebel violence is underway. This conceptualization is central to Fearon and Laitin's (2003) pathbreaking critique of Gurr and others. They argue, "[B]ecause insurgency can be successfully practiced by small numbers of rebels under the right conditions, *civil war may require only a small number with intense grievances to get going*" (italics

---

(Wimmer, Cederman, and Min 2009; Vogt et al. 2015) have found a positive relationship between group-level grievances and conflict onset.

[11] Cederman, Gleditsch, and Buhaug 2013, 35–51.   [12] Chenoweth and Stephan 2013.

[13] Pearlman 2011; Cunningham 2013; Cunningham et al. 2017.

[14] E.g. Petersen 2001; Wood 2003; Gurr 1970; Cederman, Wimmer, and Min 2010.

[15] E.g. Lichbach 1998; Popkin 1979.

added).[16] This theory allows for a small number of individuals forming a rebellion and initiating violence *irrespective of the preferences of the local population there.* Insurgency's start, conceived of in this manner, does not follow the logic of a gradual, widespread social movement.

Instead, these conceptualizations of rebellion and its origins are closer to the economics literature on insurrections[17] and foundational work in the coercion-as-state-building literature. Such works characterize armed group formation as a struggle for spoils and powers of extraction that is endemic to territories lacking a body that monopolizes the legitimate use of violence.[18] Some related arguments emphasize the "greedy," profit-maximizing qualities of those who initiate rebellion.[19] Others, especially in more recent literatures on political and criminal violence, underscore a connection between armed groups' violent coercion and ultimately their provision of order and governance in the communities where they operate.[20] While initial armed group formation is not the focus of these accounts, they tend to assume that the groups' leaders – sometimes cast as "bandits," "organized criminals," "specialists in violence," or "competitive state builders" – act independently of the preferences of populations from which they emerge, at least initially.

This debate about the role of the noncombatant population where rebel groups form cuts across a parallel debate about *how and why ethnic identity influences the start of conflict.* In his seminal 1985 book *Ethnic Groups in Conflict,* Donald Horowitz posits that ethnic conflict and violence grow out of domestic politics, especially groups' relative economic and political position within a state.[21] More recently, and similar to Cederman, Gleditsch, and Buhaug's (2011) theory described previously, Cederman, Wimmer, and Min (2010, 92) propose a general sequence whereby ethnic group-level exclusion from state power first generates reservoirs of grievances among excluded ethnic groups and then the path to civil war occurs when "ethnonationalist mobilization turns violent."

By contrast, for a feasibility approach that envisions rebellion as beginning with just a small group of individuals, then even ethnic grievances are not likely to distinguish areas where conflict begins from areas where it

---

[16] Fearon and Laitin 2003, 76.   [17] Grossman 1991.   [18] Tilly 1985; Olson 1993.
[19] Collier 2000; Mueller 2000; Collier and Hoeffler 2004.
[20] Bates 2008; Skarbek 2011; Staniland 2012b; Arjona 2017; Barnes 2017; Lessing and Willis 2019; Sanchez de la Sierra 2020.
[21] Horowitz 2000, 230–264.

does not; small numbers of aggrieved people can appear nearly anywhere. This latter conceptualization leaves open the possibility that those who start the rebellion may use the early stages of armed group formation to *manipulate* or *amplify* a sense of group identity or grievance.[22] Here, ethnicity can play a more subtle role as a technology of coordination, helping incipient rebels influence local perceptions and secure local support.[23]

In sum, these two families of explanation for conflict onset put forth fundamentally different conceptualizations of how conflict initially comes about and what ethnic identity has to do with it. In one, armed conflict begins like a large protest movement and ethnicity's role in mobilizing the support of large groups of people occurs *before* violence breaks out. In the other, rebellion begins with a small group of individuals and ethnicity's role in mobilization is unimportant until *after* the group has formed. The latter accounts, including the related theory I present in the following, do not preclude the importance of ethnic (or other) grievances to conflict *escalation*, since aggrieved populations can help rebel groups, once they are viable, gain the capacity to sustain themselves – for example, through motivating foot soldiers to join. Nor do these accounts deny the potential usefulness to aspiring rebels of a shared, prior sense of grievance where rebels initially form. Instead, they suggest that such prior reservoirs of grievance are not needed for rebel group formation – even for groups that are later remembered as seeking to address certain grievances.

Despite this enduring debate in the literature on conflict "onset" and "origins," few theories have explicitly probed the very initial stages of rebel group formation, when a small group of people first come together and decide to use violence to challenge a state. I aim to do so later, arguing that the latter conceptualization – one that stresses the small, clandestine nature of incipient rebel groups and how rebels' early uses of violence and rumor shapes noncombatants' perspectives – better captures how

---

[22] E.g. Laitin 2000; Brubaker 2002; Kalyvas 2008a.

[23] As Brubaker and Laitin (1998, 426–427) argue, "to the extent that ethnic entrepreneurs recruit young men who are already inclined toward or practiced in other forms of violence, and help bestow meaning on that violence and honor and social status on its perpetrators, we may have as much to learn about the sources and dynamics of ethnic violence from the literature on criminology ... as from the literature on ethnicity or [non-violent] ethnic conflict." Roessler (2016, 178–181) argues that ethnopolitical exclusion both motivates rebellion and renders it more feasible due to it increasing the pool of aggrieved would-be recruits and weakening the government's counterinsurgency and patronage opportunities in affected ethnoregions.

insurgencies begin in rural areas of weak states, which has several implications for rebel, civilian, and state behavior.

I revisit the alternative explanations posed by motivation-based theories of conflict onset, among others, at the end of this chapter. There, I build the case that motivation-based accounts, and especially those that stress the mobilization and organization of large populations, often better capture dynamics of conflict initiation in stronger state contexts and of later stages of conflict in weak states – once rebel group formation has already occurred and violence is well underway.

2.2 DEFINITIONS

I define *insurgent groups* (which I also call *rebel groups*) as non-state actors that use physical violence against government targets with the aim of challenging the ruling government's authority – through seizing control of either the central government or some of that government's territory.[24] I use *formation* to indicate the general process of building a rebel group – this includes both the actions leading up to *launch* and those leading up to *viability*, defined in the following.

To "count" as an insurgent group that has *launched*, entering into the population of interest to this book, a group had to possess a discernable leadership and command structure and it must have committed at least one act of violence on the soil of the target country – or there must be credible evidence that the group had concretely planned at least one violent attack against the target country.[25] The aim of these criteria is to isolate the groups that truly intended to build a fighting force and to attempt to use violence against the central government: to distinguish "real" rebel groups that plan to violently challenge the authority of the state from groups that were rumored but that did not truly intend and take steps to become, at a minimum, a viable fighting force. This book aims to study new rebel groups; it does not consider groups that were formed from the merger of prior, already formed rebel groups, nor does it consider those that formed via splintering off from a prior, already formed group.

---

[24] All of the Ugandan groups studied in this book, if they publicly articulated a goal, said they sought to overthrow the central government. Some occasionally also articulated secessionist or other demands. I examine the fluidity and function of rebels' stated goals in insurgency in Chapter 4.

[25] By "concretely" I mean that the group must have selected a target and gathered the resources necessary to conduct the attack. Only one group of the sixteen studied in this book, the People's Redemption Army (PRA), did not commit an attack.

I define *viability* as a threshold after which a rebel group can pose at least a minimal threat to the authority of the incumbent government. The period between launch and viability is thus an earlier phase of rebellion than most studies of conflict onset consider. I operationalize this viability threshold as occurring after a group has maintained a base on the target country's soil. In order to be considered viable, a sizable group of at least 100 rebels must maintain at least one base on the target country's soil for a minimum of three months.[26] These criteria intentionally exclude groups that may have attempted to enter the target country, even those that succeeded very briefly, if they were then promptly crushed or intimidated into moving across a border to foreign soil. Thus, these criteria distinguish groups that have achieved capacities that are fundamental to threaten the authority of the state from those that have not. A minimal level of manpower and an ability to operate on the target country's territory are essential to credibly posing a threat.[27]

This conceptualization of rebel viability joins the approach of works that stress armed groups' relationship to territory – usually the extent of the group's territorial control – in understanding their behavior.[28] Since I focus on whether armed groups survive beyond their infancy, a relatively minimal level of territorial control – sufficient to operate an initial base – is a useful threshold to study when analyzing why some groups fail in the initial phases of insurgency. Without a base, rebels cannot recruit and train even a small army, and if they cannot do that, then they cannot hope to go on and militarily challenge a government. This theory thus probes a much earlier threshold in rebel groups' trajectories than those that focus on the outcomes of rebellion, such as whether or not they win, lose, or several alternatives in between.[29]

Why not measure a rebel group's viability in terms of duration (time) or extent of violence (number of battle-related deaths), as do other important

---

[26] It is difficult to specify a precise number of troops and months on a base without introducing some arbitrary judgment; I arrived at 100 troops and 3 months in order to exclude small groups that could easily hide on a target country's territory but would not serve as a considerable threat, as well as groups that might briefly have a base in the target country but then retreat to a base across a national border. The findings of the book are not sensitive to small changes in the magnitudes of these numbers.

[27] This definition does not include total rebel control over a territory, such as provision of governance or public goods in that territory. Because this occurs after viability, this book leaves this later stage of rebellion and competition for territorial control to other works (e.g. Arjona, Kasfir, and Mampilly 2015; Arjona 2017; Kaplan 2018).

[28] See especially Kalyvas 2006; Arjona and Kalyvas 2009; Arjona 2017.

[29] E.g. Day 2011; Day 2019; Cunningham and Sawyer 2019.

works?[30] Time and violence are not necessarily related to the primary analytic target I pursue here: why only some groups become viable rebellions, having the chance to go on to bargain with or even militarily defeat a government. Small, incipient groups may survive for a long time, avoiding open confrontation with government forces – especially if they have a base across an international border in weakly governed territory – yet despite their endurance, they may fail to grow and to train a substantial group of fighters and may never become a substantial threat to the target government.

It is also well-documented that violence has myriad causes and functions in war, and it is not necessarily the case that quantity of violence on a battlefield increases in proportion to a rebel group's ability to challenge the authority of the state.[31] Lower levels of violence may indicate that rebel groups have developed such high levels of military strength that they deter attacks from the government or that the government and rebels have the discipline (or other incentives) to avoid violence. Similarly, large-scale violence may not be evidence of a militarily strong rebel group, but instead it may be an indication that a weak rebel group is trying to attract attention from international actors or is under intense military pressure from the government.

2.3 THEORETICAL FOUNDATIONS

2.3.1 Incipient Rebels: Small, Poor, and Vulnerable

What are the basic attributes of nascent insurgencies in weak states? I take the common approach of assuming that rebellion is a form of strategic bargaining; rebels are rational and seek, at a minimum, to build sufficient coercive capacity to compel the government to negotiate with them.[32] Those who choose to start an armed rebellion against a state can do so for a wide variety of motivations. I assume that any initial rebel goals – from private status or wealth to more group-oriented goals such as better public goods provision for a particular people or region – are more likely to be achieved when the group attains viability.

Recall from the discussion of scope conditions in Chapter 1 that this book limits its scope to instances of new rebel groups forming in weak states. I posit

---

[30] E.g. Cunningham 2006; Lacina 2006.
[31] Kalyvas 2006; Lacina 2006; Weinstein 2007; Stanton 2016. See also Staniland 2012b, 245–246, on the need for a conceptual distinction between control and violence in civil war research.
[32] E.g. Kalyvas 1999, 279; Roessler 2016; Webster 2019.

that in such weak state contexts, where government monitoring of its territories is limited, barriers to entry for nascent rebellions are low; one needs few resources or people to start a rebellion in environments where the government will not quickly meet the threat with intense military or intelligence pressure. Therefore, I conceptualize the initial movers who form a rebel group in a weak state to be small in number and weakly endowed; they do not need substantial material or organizational resources to get started.

Qualitative accounts of rebel group formation for a wide swath of groups are consistent with these contentions about incipient rebel groups' small size and modest resource endowments. For example, the BBC describes the Maoist rebels in Nepal as initially being "a small group of shotgun-wielding insurgents ... [they were] lightly armed and not considered a genuine military threat."[33] The Tamil Tigers also started as a clandestine group of just thirty men.[34] A scholar of Sri Lankan history describes the nascent Tamil Tigers in the early 1980s as follows: "Hideouts for the militants were few ... The 'boys' themselves were facing constant cash shortage. Arms were sparse, and it was not easy getting ammunition."[35] The National Resistance Army (NRA) rebels that overthrew the Ugandan government in January 1986 and have since governed Uganda famously started in 1981 with just twenty-six men and one gun. The Zapatista guerillas (the EZLN) began in Chiapas, Mexico, in 1983 as a group of just three people, growing to twelve members in 1986. They operated clandestinely until the group grew substantially in the late 1980s and early 1990s.[36] This description also reflects the start of several other former guerilla groups in Latin America, such as the Sandanistas in Nicaragua, the Shining Path in Peru, and Castro's guerillas.

The assertion that rebels, in their early phases, are poor – rarely having large caches of weapons or significant material resources – marks a distinction between this conceptualization of rebel emergence and that of others. In particular, in his seminal book *Inside Rebellion*, Jeremy Weinstein envisions rebel groups' production functions as being constituted of a mix of initial social and material endowments, implying that some rebel groups have a sizable material resource base early on.[37] While

---

[33] Alastair Lawson, "Who Are Nepal's Maoist Rebels?" *BBC News*, http://news.bbc.co.uk/2/hi/3573402.stm, accessed July 11, 2018.

[34] Biziouras 2012.   [35] Narayan Swamy 2003, 96.   [36] Harvey 1998, 164–166.

[37] Weinstein (2007), who builds on the prior body of work on social movements and contentious politics, emphasized how variation in groups' resource endowments explains their mobilization potential and behaviors (e.g. McCarthy and Zald 1977; Jenkins 1983; McAdam 2001).

the extent of an armed group's material resources surely influences its prospects for long-term survival as well as its capacity for violence, the presence of substantial material endowments is unlikely in the initial stages of rebel group formation. For example, even rebel groups that come to rely on high-value natural resources must first gain sufficient coercive capacity in order to overtake and control the area containing those resources and the organizational sophistication to develop networks that enable them to profit from those resources. This assertion is supported by an analysis by Michael Ross, who conducted in-depth, qualitative studies of thirteen civil wars between 1990 and 2000 for which natural resources influenced the wars' onset, duration, or intensity.[38] Ross found that the armed groups involved in all thirteen wars "never gained funding before the war broke out from the extraction or sale of natural resources, or from the extortion of others who extract, transport, or market resources."[39] In sum, even incipient rebel groups that eventually fund their war with money from natural resources do not typically have access to these funds at the *start* of their campaign.

A similar logic applies to rebel groups that come to be sponsored substantially by foreign actors. Especially since the end of the Cold War, it is unusual to find external sponsors that build proxy armies from the ground up for the purpose of destabilizing another government. Further, just as investors rarely fund start-up companies that have not yet demonstrated at least minimal competence, foreign sponsors are unlikely to finance an armed group until that group has demonstrated its basic skills and coercive capacity. For example, while the Tamil Tigers are usually associated with high levels of support from the Tamil diaspora in the Tamil Naidu region of India, they did not receive substantial support until the late 1970s, several years after the group had formed and began committing violence;[40] the same is true of Boko Haram's sponsorship by the Islamic State, Al Shabaab's sponsorship by Al Qaeda, and the Lord's Resistance Army's (LRA) sponsorship by the government in Khartoum. I more systematically evaluate these claims about low initial rebel material endowments from natural resources and external sponsors in Chapter 3, especially Table 3.2.

---

[38] These civil wars (and their start dates) are Afghanistan (1992), Angola (1975), Burma (1983), Cambodia (1978), Colombia (1984), Congo-Brazzaville (1997), Congo-DRC (1996), Congo-DRC (1997), Indonesia (Aceh) (1976), Liberia (1989), Peru (1982), Sierra Leone (1991), and Sudan (1983).

[39] Ross 2004, 50.   [40] Samaranayaka 2008, 324.

This argument about rebels starting small and with scant material resources also implies that rebels in this stage are not gaining significant resources from any other rebel groups that operate simultaneously in other regions of the target state. Seminal work on rebel group alliances stresses that such alliances largely serve instrumental purposes;[41] by this logic, it is difficult to imagine why any existing group would ally with or provide resources to a nascent group that has not yet demonstrated the ability to be a viable threat.

As a result of nascent rebel groups typically being small and poor, we can expect them to be highly *vulnerable* to defeat.[42] At a later phase, once rebel groups have developed a reasonable level of coercive capacity, they may be able to survive attacks or even the capture of top commanders. But for incipient groups – a small number of people with a small number of weapons – information leaked to the government about the rebel leaders' identities and whereabouts likely spells the end of the rebellion. This vulnerability of nascent rebel groups tends to distinguish the initial stage of conflict from later stages and has critical implications for nascent rebels' behavior – in particular, making them uncertain about their chances for becoming a viable threat to the government and making them reliant on *civilians* to withhold information about them from the government if they wish to do so. While rebels of course do not share important tactical information with those outside of their inner circle, many nearby civilians will inevitably learn basic information about rebels' existence, identities, and general whereabouts, which is sufficient to damage the rebel group if the government knew it.[43]

In emphasizing the role of civilians, this book's central argument joins decades of scholarship and observations from practitioners of insurgency

---

[41] Christia 2012.

[42] By defeat, I simply mean the end of the organized use of violence on the target country's soil. This conceptualization thus includes outcomes ranging from military devastation of the rebels to rebels voluntarily surrendering, disbanding, moving operations to another country, or merging with another rebel group. In some cases, what I consider a defeat may involve negotiations that ultimately deliver rents to certain rebel leaders, who avoid jail by providing intelligence on other rebel elements, and/or some government concessions to the communities from which the rebels emerged; this enables rebels who put down arms to save face.

[43] Civilians may do so, for example, by observing training exercises, identifying some rebels, or detecting the location of bases. Merely confirming the existence of a nascent rebel group can be valuable to the government, which, early on, may be trying to discern whether a nascent rebel organization truly exists.

and counterinsurgency that have converged on a simple tenet: insurgents cannot survive without the cooperation of the civilian population.[44] It also joins recent works in emphasizing the importance of the information environment to conflict's start,[45] and more generally of a specific form of support that insurgents need from civilians: secrecy.[46] The difference here is a focus on information in the *initial phases* of insurgent group formation.

2.3.2 Civilians as Strategic Actors

Civilians are individuals who do not participate in the military activities of a rebel group or government, and here I focus on civilians who live in the area where a rebel group forms. They typically learn about nascent rebels both indirectly through rumor and, as described previously, occasionally directly by seeing rebels move to and from meetings, trainings, or initial attacks.

Civilians do not initially play an active role in supporting the rebels, who need only a lean, intensively screened group and have not yet begun large-scale recruitment.[47] Since violence has barely begun, civilians do not yet perceive the rebels to be an immediate threat to their livelihood. Indeed, as numerous studies have shown, during the onset of insurgency individuals often fail to anticipate the duration and severity of violence that may ensue.[48]

Furthermore, with the exception of communities that have experienced violent conflict under their current government – and thus have recent,

---

[44] E.g. Leites 1970; Mao 1978; Kalyvas 1999; U.S. Army and Marine Corps 2007; Petersen 2001; Wood 2003.

[45] Webster 2019; Malone 2019.

[46] E.g. Kalyvas 2006; Berman and Matanock 2013; Berman et al. 2018.

[47] While this assertion is at odds with the common characterization of extensive social mobilization coinciding with violent conflict initiation, it is consistent with several accounts by practitioners of insurgency or counterinsurgency. For example, a United States Army Special Operations Command analysis, originally authored in 1965, stated: "During the early phase [of building an insurgency], primary attention is given to selecting a well-disciplined cadre. The essential need is for tight security; hence, recruitment is highly selective and recruits are thoroughly screened ... In later phases, as the insurgency gains in organizational sophistication, emphasis is placed on expanding the size of the multiple elements of the movement and increasing its mass support from outside" (Thompkins Jr. 2013, 7).

[48] See Kalyvas (2006, 207–208, especially fn. 45), which also notes this pattern and documents its presence in the Philippines, Kenya, El Salvador, among other cases. Several other theorists have noted the short time horizons of civilians amid insurgency, given that immediate desires for safety often trump calculations about potential long-term benefits or costs of certain actions; see especially Leites (1970, 42–44). Of course, factors such as emotions do play a crucial role in later stages of conflict, after substantial violence has occurred and thus noncombatants begin to develop strong beliefs about the combatants.

direct experience and knowledge of the government's military capabilities – civilians in weak states often have limited direct engagement with
national politics and therefore do not have strong beliefs about what level
of protection they can expect from the central government.[49]

For these reasons, I consider civilians to be instrumental actors during the
uncertain, initial phases of insurgency considered here; in responding to a
rebel group forming in their midst, they are concerned with maximizing their
well-being rather than being "true believers" on the rebel or government side.
To maximize their chance of enjoying the potential benefits of the conflict that
is beginning to emerge around them, they want to side with the party that will
win.

In sum, especially in weak states, I contend that strong preferences for or
against incipient rebels are not typically present. While weak preferences may
exist – for example, due to identity-related affinities – most people do not
offer support to new, violent groups simply because they share an identity
feature with its leaders or members, even if they share anti-government
political proclivities. Civilians want to learn more about nascent rebels'
qualities – and especially whether or not they will likely succeed in
becoming viable challengers to the government – before deciding whether
or not to help them. However, in these initial, clandestine phases, civilians are
limited in what they can independently, directly learn; they must rely on the
impressions they piece together from their trusted networks. These dynamics
change, often dramatically, after the violence of warfare is well underway.

2.3.3 The State: Weak but Motivated to End Nascent Challengers

Because of their limited presence and monitoring capacity outside of the
capital city, weak states do not possess the ability to obtain fine-grained
information about their citizens' activities. In the absence of such institutions,
it is difficult for weak states to identify the existence of nascent rebel groups
until aspiring rebels take conspicuous, typically violent, action.[50] Even then,

---

[49] E.g., as Michael Bratton explains, "As I see it, citizens in Africa have an ambivalent
attitude towards the state; they are simultaneously attracted to it and wary of it" (Bratton
1989, 414). I substantiate these arguments in a section on prewar factors.

[50] By this logic, in stronger state contexts the barriers to entry are higher for aspiring rebels
since they can expect the likelihood of detection of subversive activities to be higher. In
such contexts, only non-state groups that are able from a very early stage to repel
a government attack or to sustain losses – potentially due to superior resource access or
prior fighting experience and organizational ties – would be likely to attempt to challenge
such states. This book aims to understand insurgent group formation in weak states;

the earlier discussion implies that after violence begins, it may take time for a government to know that people committing violence aim to build an organized, armed group.

I assume that all states – even weak states – prefer to avoid rebel control of any part of their territory. While some may go on to accept rebel operations in areas the rebels have come to control,[51] I posit that at the outset of a rebellion, states will act to prevent rebel groups from forming anywhere on their territory if they have the information to do so. This is not a strong assumption if one accepts that there is a non-trivial chance that incipient rebels will become strong enough to incur significant costs to the state, or even capture the state. Because no government wants to run that risk, and because ending a rebel group in its infancy is surely less costly than battling an established, sizable fighting force, I assume that a government will respond to reports of a nascent rebellion by trying to put it down.

2.4 AN INFORMATION-CENTRIC THEORY OF REBEL GROUP FORMATION

Given these assumptions, what behavior can we expect from of nascent rebels, the civilians they operate among, and the state that aims to end them? What are the key factors that condition this behavior? The following section addresses these questions, highlighting with italicized text key empirical claims and implications that arise from the theory. After probing several of the assumptions' empirical relevance in Chapter 3, I take up these expected relationships about *rebels* in Chapter 4; about *civilians* in Chapter 5; and about the *state* in Chapter 6.

2.5 REBELS

2.5.1 The Idiosyncrasy of Rebel Launch

As established previously, I conceptualize nascent rebel groups as small and poorly resourced, and thus highly vulnerable to defeat, so their

---

I leave for future work empirically evaluating this expectation about stronger groups forming in stronger states.

[51] Cases do exist in which governments allow rebel groups, once formed, to persist on their territory. Mukherjee 2014 argues that this is the case in peripheral territories of medium-capacity states, which have the capacity to contain such armed groups; thus their persistence does not threaten the political survival of the central government.

primary concern is avoiding having the government identify and locate them. We can therefore expect that aspiring *rebels will seek to form in areas where they believe that there is a low likelihood that they will be detected and confronted by the government, and thus where they know the social and physical terrain well.*

Choosing to start an armed group requires a fairly risk-accepting[52] and status-seeking person, and one that has a personal motivation to challenge the state. Within a weak state, predicting where such individuals will emerge – or even where just a small number will be clustered together and contemplate collaboration – will not be easy using structural factors that existing research commonly associates with the onset of civil conflict, such as poverty, ethnic homogeneity, grievances, or rough terrain. Absent detailed information about individuals' attitudes toward risk, among rural regions of weak states, it will be difficult to anticipate where groups will initially form. Therefore, we can expect that in territories with minimal state penetration, the formation of rebel groups will be relatively common – more common than much of the existing literature on conflict onset tends to capture – but the *location and timing of rebel group formation will be idiosyncratic.*

2.5.2 Nascent Rebels' Limited Uses of Violence

Committing major acts of violence is not easy for small, poorly resourced groups. Furthermore, and most importantly, large-scale violence may attract unwanted scrutiny from the government during this formative phase when secrecy is vital. I therefore expect that *sporadic, small-scale violent attacks occur but large-scale violent attacks by rebels are rare in the early phases of rebel group formation*; only in later phases will rebels commit numerous attacks against the state or civilians.

Incipient rebels cannot usually move quickly past this most vulnerable stage – by, for example, quickly raising a large, well-resourced army – because of the fundamental need to maintain secrecy; each new recruit, particularly in the vulnerable initial phases, must be vetted and monitored with the utmost care.[53] Further, rapid access to weaponry would entail

---

[52] I posit that choosing to launch a rebellion takes a "fairly" – rather than "very" – risk-accepting person because in a weak state with porous borders, exit to safety is often an option if an aspiring insurgent believes that the government may be close to apprehending him.

[53] High levels of initial material endowments would likely change these and subsequent dynamics considerably, as Weinstein 2007 argues.

first acquiring a substantial pool of resources. But rebels must also make the case to would-be investors (such as foreign governments seeking a proxy) that they are a competent group. Until they successfully pull off moderate acts of violence against the state, it will be difficult to do so credibly.[54]

What strategic purpose, if any, does small-scale violence against the government serve in the initial phases? Why not avoid violence altogether? The answer I propose is twofold. First, it can allow incipient rebels to better understand their operational environment; they gain the chance to test the competence and reach of government forces in that region. Small acts of violence against easy targets – those that can be attacked without high risk of immediate harm to the rebels – can allow rebels the chance to test the government's response quietly, without risking military defeat or excessive scrutiny.[55] If they learn that the government's informational or military capabilities are high, would-be rebels can simply stop and blend in with the population or move across a border before committing more ambitious attacks. Initial, small acts of violence are thus like a pilot phase of the rebellion.

Second, early phases of violence offer an important, additional opportunity for rebels to shape beliefs among the local population. They seek to score easy victories that can demonstrate their fighting competence to nearby civilians. The need to influence civilian perceptions of them underpins another expected empirical regularity of nascent rebel groups' behavior: *rebels rarely commit violence against civilians until after they have gained substantial coercive and local intelligence capacity.* Aspiring rebels must prioritize building intelligence networks among the civilian population. Until they have local

---

[54] This implies that the rare aspiring rebel group that is able to access a large pool of highly trusted recruits and resources from an early stage could escalate violence more quickly. Such a pattern would be broadly consistent with recent work showing a relationship between areas with reservoirs of former fighters and conflict onset (Zukerman-Daly 2012; Jha and Wilkinson 2012).

[55] Here I diverge from Bueno de Mesquita 2010 on armed groups' uses of violence to mobilize civilians. One subtlety of his argument is that without the support of the civilians, vanguards cannot commit violence. Thus, he predicts selection effects: violence will occur only in communities that are already coordinated on a participatory equilibrium. By contrast, the approach put forth here assumes explicitly that the initial group of aspiring rebels forms without the prior coordination of the surrounding community. It is the response of civilians after those stages that determines whether the rebels – or the "revolutionary vanguard," in Bueno de Mesquita's terms – can later commit more frequent, larger attacks.

intelligence capacity in place, they cannot easily apply selective violence to monitor and sanction those who leak information to the government. Since harming civilians who did not leak information severely damages the rebels' credibility, doing so is quite risky for nascent rebels. Furthermore, in order to build networks that will serve later as reliable avenues for monitoring, rebels in this stage want civilians to reveal their true, private preferences about the rebellion. While other works have shown that policing plays a critical role in insurgency and the application of selective violence once violent conflict is well underway, in the early phases, rebel coercion of civilians would be unwise since it introduces incentives to misrepresent those private preferences. Until rebels have developed a local intelligence capacity, they cannot credibly threaten to punish defectors through the use of selective violence, and thus have little incentive to employ coercion. *We should therefore expect to see little violence against civilians in the initial stages of insurgent group formation.*

2.5.3 Rebels' Rumors

Because they are vulnerable, nascent rebels will want to avoid having the government learn basic information about them that could threaten them: their existence as a rebel group with the intent to violently challenge its authority, as well as their identities and location. *We can expect the initial leadership circle of rebels, therefore, to conduct themselves with secrecy*, for example meeting only in very small, inconspicuous groups. Nascent groups should also be less likely to make attention-seeking, public pronouncements than groups that are already viable. After developing basic coercive and intelligence capacity, such pronouncements can serve as a useful way to publicize their group and to legitimize their standing as national political actors. But in the early phases, such pronouncements are dangerous, since they draw attention to the nascent group before it is ready to detect and survive government attempts to infiltrate or attack it.

However, realities on the ground create a tension for the nascent rebels. Many local villagers who observe their movements, for example to and from initial meetings, trainings, and attacks, inevitably learn basic information about the rebels' identity and location. Recognizing this, and the damage to the rebellion that civilians could do by providing this information to the government, rebels wish to dissuade them from leaks by building an expectation among civilians that they will be competent and strong.

They can do so by spreading *rumors*[56] – regardless of their accuracy – about the justness of their cause, and their high levels of skill and support from the surrounding population. These rumors can also make claims about the competence or justness of the government. Further, as news of the rebels' early attacks spread, they can spread rumors characterizing those attacks as impressive early successes. In doing so, rebels aim to shape the early perceptions and narratives about them that emerge among civilians where they initially operate.

In sum, rumors that shape local beliefs about the relative threats or protection that governments versus rebels may pose to civilians play a crucial role in civilian mobilization during conflict;[57] rebels try to shape those rumors from the outset. I expect that *from the very start of group formation, incipient rebels seek to seed positive rumors about their competence and righteousness, relative to the central government, in the community where they launch.*

2.6 CIVILIANS

2.6.1 Civilian Support as Herding Behavior

In the context envisioned here in which the state is weak at the local level – recall that an itinerant military presence may exist but local security and civil intelligence institutions are scant – aspiring rebels are the first movers. Recall that I assume that because the rebels must move around a community to attend meetings and trainings, most civilians in the area where rebels form incidentally learn some basic information about rebels' existence and whereabouts that would be highly valuable to government forces; just a few information leaks could doom the vulnerable rebels. Soon after the rebels' initial attacks occur, the government sends emissaries to communities to learn whether a rebel group exists and to gather information about it. Therefore, if civilians residing in the locality where rebels launch maintain secrecy, then the rebels will substantially increase their likelihood of becoming a viable force.

Each civilian faces a strategic decision: whether to cooperate with the rebels (by *not* revealing information about the rebels to the government)

---

[56] I use the term "information" to connote verifiable facts that the government wants to learn about rebels – such as their identities or location. I use "rumors" for the unverifiable news that rebels spread about their intentions and future capabilities.

[57] Toft 2003; Shesterinina 2016.

or not (by sharing information with the government).[58] In work co-authored with Jennifer M. Larson, we formally model this decision as a coordination game and explicitly derive the expected empirical patterns I describe informally here.[59] In the model, each civilian's decision whether or not to provide information about the rebels to the government depends on the value of an offer from the government for providing information weighed against the civilian's beliefs about the expected gains from rebellion. Those expected gains can depend on expectations about the nascent rebel group's future capabilities relative to the government, about the justness of the rebels' cause, and especially about the actions of his fellow civilians. These civilians' expectations are critical because of the uncertainty that shrouds the early phases of conflict and because of the inherently unverifiable nature of these factors that matter to civilians.[60] Civilians care about relative capabilities because they know that a rebel group that becomes viable is more likely to bring benefits to its regional base of support, via bargaining with or even overtaking the government. An attempted rebel group that does not succeed may bring substantial harm to the locality – such as shame, and neglect or worse from the central government.

Importantly, civilians know that what other civilians will do is critical, since whether or not most other civilians will keep secrets from the government determines whether the rebel group becomes viable. In other words, keeping secrets is more valuable to a civilian when he expects other civilians to keep secrets too. These dynamics can produce herding; people want to do what everyone else is doing. Of course, this can also make rumors about support for the rebels self-fulfilling, if they are widely spread and believed.

---

[58] In practice, some civilians may have a third option: they may flee to a nearby town or even to the capital city, in order to avoid choosing sides. Such individuals essentially select out of the account captured here.

[59] Larson and Lewis 2018.

[60] This characterization of civilians' uncertainty about the current and future relative capabilities of warring parties represents a critical departure between this account and influential micro-level theories of violence during civil war. In particular, in explaining patterns of violence during civil war, Kalyvas 2006 finds that the degree of each warring faction's territorial control determines the level of collaboration each fighting party receives from the civilians. That argument relies on an assumption that civilians have complete information about the fighting party's relative capabilities. This assumption makes sense for scenarios in which war has persisted over several years, so that civilians have observed each side's fighting ability – but it is unlikely to hold in the initial stages of insurgency.

Note that while many classic conceptualizations of civilian mobilization for insurrection view it through the lens of a classic free-rider problem,[61] the strategic problem captured here differs in important ways. In those classic conceptualizations, the benefit of helping rebels also depends on the number of others who will help. By contrast, in a the theory put forth here, rather than exhibiting free-riding, it can be that just a few informants could do significant damage to the aspiring rebels' probability of success.[62] Knowing this, in contexts where a widespread belief emerges that the rebels are likely to succeed, an otherwise would-be informant knows his marginal damage – if he were to inform on the rebels – would be high. He may therefore prefer to keep secrets – getting a chance at a substantial benefit from a viable rebellion, rather than taking the offer from the government. If instead a would-be informant expects many others to inform, too, his marginal damage from informing will be low, which in turn increases his incentive to inform and gain the government's offer.

How does each civilian make a judgment about what other civilians will do and, therefore, about the rebels' likelihood of success? While civilians may prefer to learn about these things from direct observation of the rebels, their opportunities to directly observe rebels are limited, since the rebels are trying to avoid spreading information about their location, identities, and true fighting capacity.

Instead, civilians rely on conversations – usually face-to-face conversations, given the sensitive nature of the subject matter – with people they trust.[63] In the meantime, as discussed earlier, rebels are actively attempting to seed positive rumors about themselves, injecting rumors into civilian networks via a small number of trusted contacts in the community. Assuming that rebels successfully seed a persuasive message with an initial contact, these networks spread the rebels' rumors, touting the rebels' capabilities, virtues, and widespread support.

For example, suppose the rebels identify a trusted contact among the civilians and provide him with a framed, compelling message about the rebels, which may include goals, promises, glowing assessments of future

---

[61] Popkin 1979; Lichbach 1998; Petersen 2001; Wood 2003.
[62] In the formal model, we assume that an individual's marginal damage is decreasing in the number of civilians informing; the first person to identify a hidden rebel base to the government can be the most damaging to the rebels.
[63] A large literature documents the importance of interpersonal networks in developing countries and their ability to transmit trusted news (e.g. Fafchamps and Minten 1999; Banerjee et al. 2013; Larson and Lewis 2017).

capabilities, or arguments for why rebellion is just – and possibly negative perceptions of the government.[64] Recall that this framed account is about aspects of the rebels (or government) that are generally prospective or impossible to confirm: a rumor. By contrast, information about the rebels that the government seeks to learn is factual – for example, who and where they are. After hearing the rebels' message, each civilian forms a belief about the benefits the village would receive if the rebels are successful; that civilian then passes a rumor about the rebels' message to his neighbors in the network, who pass it to theirs, and so on. Suppose also that the farther the rumor travels through the network, the less potent it becomes. This is the case because the message may be transmitted with errors as it passes from person to person or it may be less believable as it extends farther from the source, or it may resonate less with people at greater social distance. But where rumors spread quickly among those who are at low social distance from one another, the rumors can cohere into a shared narrative about the rebellion's merit.

In sum, when rebels start a pro-rebellion rumor and their initial contacts spread it, certain network attributes can allow the rumor to reach more people and give rebels greater likelihood of control over it. With favorable networks, the number of civilians that can come to value the rebels highly and expect many others to keep quiet can be large, incentivizing wide-spread secret-keeping.

Note however that even areas with favorable networks, described next, do not always lead to widespread pro-rebel rumors; recall that this condition was contingent on rebels successfully persuading initial contacts to spread glowing news about them. If that seed or another person instead decides to spread negative rumors about the rebels, even favorable networks could work against nascent rebels, leading negative assessments of them to spread widely, resulting in numerous information leaks. Such scenarios would lead to dynamics similar to those occurring in areas with unfavorable networks; I assume that where civilians hear little about rebels (because the rebels cannot spread positive rumors), civilians judge that the rebels are not likely to become viable, and therefore should be rejected. In sum, all else equal, rebels launching in areas with favorable

---

[64] See Condra and Wright 2019 for related theory and evidence that, in Afghanistan, civilians' perceptions of the government and the Taliban's relative righteousness – specifically, each side's efforts to minimize civilian casualties – influence whether or not civilians provide information to government authorities, even when controlling for political sentiment.

networks have the best chance at maintaining the secrecy they need to become a viable force. I now turn to describing attributes of such networks.

2.6.2 The Importance of Trusted Network Structure

The previous discussion suggests a crucial role for the structure of the trusted network, since only those connected via the trusted network have the potential to hear the rebels' rumor. In particular, networks that are *fragmented* – that is, separated into multiple components – pose problems for rebels. A network's *fragmentation* is the proportion of people (nodes) outside of the largest group of people connected by the network. Civilians in components outside the reach of the rebels' message inform the government since these civilians have not heard positive rumors about the rebels. Figure 2.1 shows three hypothetical networks among twenty civilians with increasing fragmentation. In the network on the far right, due to high fragmentation, any rumor that rebels seed would necessarily fail to reach at least 65 percent of the civilians. These civilians would have an incentive to inform on the rebels; whether others would, too, depends on a second property of networks, their path lengths.

Path length, also known as network distance, refers to the number of people (nodes) that separate two people in a network. Diameter, a common measure of path length, is like asking: How many degrees of

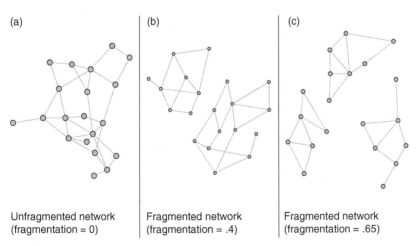

| (a) | (b) | (c) |

Unfragmented network (fragmentation = 0) Fragmented network (fragmentation = .4) Fragmented network (fragmentation = .65)

FIGURE 2.1 Example networks with twenty civilians and different levels of fragmentation

(a)   (b)

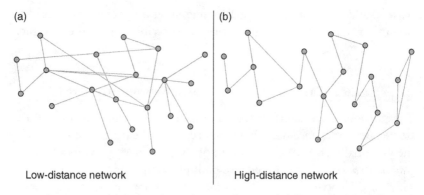

Low-distance network | High-distance network

FIGURE 2.2 Example networks with 20 civilians and different path lengths Both
networks have 24 links. Network (a) has an average path length of 2.5 and
a diameter of 5. Network (b) has an average path length of 5 and a diameter of 15.

separation are there between the two people in the network who have the
most degrees of separation between them? Note that path length is different from network *density*, a measure of the quantity of links in a network,
which features in several theories of networks' relevance to conflict
dynamics.[65] In the account advanced here, networks do *not* need to be
dense in order to be helpful to rebels. Density does not necessarily facilitate
the spread of trusted information; links in a dense network can be
arranged such that the reach of information is limited despite the number
of links being large.[66] However, residing in a lower-*distance* network – one
with a shorter path length – means that news will travel to everyone in the
network faster, and with less error, than in a higher-distance network.
There is less error because there are fewer intermediary people between
each two people in the network; as in a classic game of telephone, the more
intermediaries there are, the more likely it is that the initially seeded
message will be altered. To illustrate this concept, Figure 2.2 shows two
networks with different path lengths. Network (a) is low-distance; it has
an average path length of 2.5 and a diameter of 5. Network (b) is higher-
distance; it has an average path length of 5 and a diameter of 15.

In summary, in areas with minimal penetration of central government
institutions, if rebels can manage to convince a small number of trusted
contacts of their potential value, areas with civilian word-of-mouth

[65] Fearon and Laitin 1996, 719; Petersen 2001, 61–66; Chandra 2004, 71–72; Gubler and
    Selway 2012, 210.
[66] Atalas et al. 2015.

networks that are unfragmented and feature short paths allow for rebel success. Civilians who hear the rebels' rumor in such networks are most likely to be persuaded by it and expect the rumor to reach and persuade many others, which in turn increases the value of secret-keeping for these civilians. In this sense, the rumors coordinate secret-keeping, and do so best in unfragmented networks with short paths. Fragmented, long-path networks can even undermine the good intentions of strong rebel supporters, since even civilians who favor the rebels may prefer to inform the government if they expect many others to do so as well. Likewise, unfragmented, low-distance networks can incentivize civilians who do not genuinely support the rebels' cause to nonetheless keep the rebels' secrets – if they believe enough others plan to do so.

Certain types of networks are thus quite valuable for aspiring rebels but are potentially dangerous for civilians. Rebels with access to contacts whom they can convince to believe and transmit their message through their networks have an advantage; once in, news spreads through the network and is deemed credible. Rebels with such a contact could spread rumors in support of the rebel cause, including perceptions of injustices or other unfavorable interpretations of government actions.

Recall that such networks spread favorable news about rebels only when rebels convince their initial contacts in the community to do so. An implication of the theory is thus that networks that are good at spreading trusted information can also work against rebels. If initial seeds determine that rebels are "bad" and they spread news accordingly, then civilian populations can quickly and decisively settle on rejecting the rebels. In fragmented networks, news does not spread as widely. In sum, both lack of news about nascent rebels and bad news about nascent rebels lead civilians to reject them.

In the next section, I argue that these features of networks that allow for the possibility of good rumors about rebels – those with low fragmentation and low path length – likely underlie areas that are ethnically homogeneous.

2.6.3 Kinship Networks and Ethnic Demography

Networks of trust, however, are quite difficult to observe. What types of social features indicate the above types of trusted information networks? Theoretically, such networks could take a variety of forms – those among religious groups, or people who become close through other informal or formal affiliations. Here I focus on one particular context because of its salience in sub-Saharan Africa and other rural, weak state contexts: kinship networks.

Ethnic groups in sub-Saharan Africa and much of Asia are comprised of an underlying web of kinship ties.[67] Ties between kin are especially salient in rural Africa and beyond since they establish bonds of trust.[68] However, given the variety of kinship-based migration and familial practices that drive the emergence and spatial patterns of such ties, it is likely that *different kinship network structures underpin different patterns of ethnic demography.* Specifically, ethnically homogeneous areas more often have the types of network features that help rebels – lower fragmentation and shorter path length – than heterogeneous areas.

To understand why this is likely the case, it is instructive to consider how ethnically homogeneous areas come about in kinship-based societies: through gradual processes of migration, settlement, and marriage. Members of an extended family (known as a clan, a subgroup of an ethnic group) tend to live in close proximity to one another, in a cluster of homes, often on ancestral land. However, the common practice of exogamy – rules that necessitate that one marry outside one's own clan – typically leads to men seeking wives from areas outside their immediate home area. For patrilocal groups, wives then come to live with the husband's extended family but maintain strong ties to their own extended family and homestead. As anthropologist John Middleton explains, "[M]arriage is not merely a union between two individuals, but one between two lineages and two clusters of kinsfolk ... Throughout a marriage the ties of a woman to her natal kin are remembered and are important ... regular visits are made to see that they are well."[69] Exogamy thus generates kinship networks that span a rather large area,[70] perhaps dozens of miles. However, pressure also often exists to marry within one's ethnic group. Groups that value both exogamy and marrying within one's ethnic group thus have resulting networks with many interconnections among

---

[67] Horowitz 2000, 57.

[68] Barr 2004; Robinson 2016. Recent research demonstrates the salience of familial ties in conflict settings. For example, Seymour (2014) finds that kinship-based rivalries drove patterns of alignment in the Sudanese civil war; McDoom (2014) finds that an individual's quantity of kinship ties to killers during the Rwandan genocide had by far the largest effect on his likelihood of participating in violence; and Haim 2019 finds that local familial ties had a strong influence on counterinsurgency operations in the Philippines.

[69] Middleton 1965, 56.

[70] Evans-Pritchard 1940, 225–228; Evans-Pritchard 1951, 46–48.

clans within a given ethnic settlement area. Such patterns, over time, generate ethnically homogeneous areas – dispersed areas where most inhabitants are part of the same ethnic group, yet their marriage relations mean that they are tied in an overlapping manner to other kinsfolk. Ties overlapping in this way generate short paths through a network.

By contrast, some rural areas are quite diverse. They may be homogeneous at a highly local (e.g. village or roughly one square mile) level, but at a slightly lower level of resolution (e.g. county or district, tens of square miles), numerous, distinct ethno-linguistic groups are present.[71] Such local ethnic diversity typically comes about as a result of processes that also generate fragmented kinship networks. This heterogeneity often exists along common migration routes or regions with diverse geography or land with rich soil;[72] their diversity often comes about when several migrating ethnic groups pass through an area and some of their members decide to remain in that area. Assuming a preference to live among kin or geographically specific skills, those that stay settle close to their co-ethnics in small clusters. In these areas, familial networks can become more geographically concentrated and insular, and the kinship networks among the many ethnic groups in the region are fragmented – there are few familial ties that span the separate ethnic groups.

In sum, from this discussion of civilian behavior amid rebel group formation, networks of trust, and ethnic demography, a straightforward hypothesis emerges: *Among rebel groups that have launched, those that do so in more ethnically homogeneous areas are more likely to become viable than those that form in less homogeneous areas.*

Why, then, would rebels launch in a heterogeneous area, with networks that are fragmented? If aspiring rebels recognize an area's ethnic demography but do not fully appreciate its network structure, they could reasonably expect to build a viable rebellion in heterogeneous areas given that several potential benefits of viable rebellion are not locally excludable. Prior work on voting in Ghana shows that villagers often "cross ethnic lines" where they believe that voting for a local out-group member will bring such non-locally excludable goods to their locality.[73] Other recent, careful work on interethnic trust in Africa shows evidence of

---

[71] For example, in Uganda, while most regions are named after the ethnic group that predominates there – e.g. Acholiland is named after the Acholi people – three distinct regions have non-people-specific names. All three of these regions – West Nile in the northwest, Kigezi in the southwest, and Bukedi in the southeast – are highly ethnically diverse, and also all lie on historical migration paths.
[72] Michalopoulos 2012.   [73] Ichino and Nathan 2013.

higher levels of interethnic tolerance, and lower levels of ethnocentric trust, in ethnically diverse localities – which indicates why rebels could expect cross-ethnic mobilization on behalf of their group in such contexts.[74] Furthermore, even if the rebels knew the network structure of an area well enough to select on it, many constraints limit the practical choice of location. In particular, one key constraint is the location of trusted contacts, with whom rebels seed their rumors. If the rebels hope to win over a community and have their secrets kept, they must have a solid contact in that community. In practice, the set of options that meet this criterion may be small. Thorough knowledge of the local social and geographic terrain is also crucial to aspiring rebels, further limiting their options.

2.7 THE STATE

Given these propositions, the implications for the state are straightforward: the better the government can persuade civilians to share information with them,[75] and the greater the density of likely government informants in a given locality, the lower the likelihood of rebel group launch or viability there. This is especially true if the density of government informants is common knowledge in that area. Government informants may observe information about incipient rebels firsthand, or they may learn about the rebels from other civilians in the area. Each civilian calculates that the more informants in his community, the more likely it is that the government will obtain information about the rebels. Thus, in a community with numerous informers, a civilian will judge that newly formed rebels' success is unlikely. In such a community, this knowledge of intelligence institutions' deep penetration sets off a cascade of willingness to provide information about the rebels to the government since each civilian is more likely to provide information to the government themselves if they expect that others will. These dynamics diminish the likelihood that nascent rebels will succeed.

More importantly, knowing this, would-be rebels in a locality with a high density of government informants (or expected informants) will be deterred from attempting rebellion there in the first place. Whereas rebel

---

[74] Kasara 2013; Robinson 2017.

[75] In the formal model in Larson and Lewis 2018, this is a simple offer from the government to a civilian for providing information about rebels. The higher the value of the offer, the less likely the rebels will succeed in becoming viable.

groups that attain viability may hold some leverage in negotiations with a government, even if they do not come close to overthrowing the government, those that end early will not. Additionally, the better the government's surveillance capacity, the more likely that aspiring insurgents will be caught quickly, without an opportunity to first escape into exile. Therefore, *rebel formation will be less likely to occur in an area in which the state's intelligence institutions have deeply penetrated. If rebel group formation does occur, the group will be less likely to become viable.*

There are several implications for the behavior of government actors. First, this means that the more informants that governments have in as many communities as possible, the better. Developing extensive, local information networks that enable the state to identify potential violent challengers (or end those that do form early) is often less costly than responding with substantial military force to groups after they have already developed an army. Information networks will be particularly cost-effective in poor, rural areas of developing countries, where co-opting civilians will not be expensive, due to the limited opportunities for gain elsewhere. In some contexts, states gain access to local information through repression and fear; as Chapter 6 shows, the Ugandan state under Yoweri Museveni did so through a combination of persuasion and co-optation.

I illustrate this argument by describing Uganda's civil intelligence apparatus, and how former rebels perceive it, in Chapter 6.

2.8 PREWAR FACTORS

In seeking to explain initial rebel group formation and why some groups fail in the early stages, this theory did not stress the importance of prewar factors such as previously held grievances or ideologies, or certain prewar, feasibility-related factors such as the organizational or skill endowments of the actors. This may be surprising to some readers who may reasonably wonder: Shouldn't the political preferences, ideas, and organizations that predominated in communities *prior to* rebel group formation help to explain why rebels initially launch, and whether rebels that do launch become viable?

My response is twofold. First, the arguments I put forth earlier imply that these factors are more likely to be important to the start of organized violence in stronger-state contexts. Second, they leave open the likelihood, and help to explain why it may be, that such factors are important to the period *after* aspiring rebels have cohered into viable groups. Indeed, while several recent works on the causes and conduct of internal war have emphasized the importance of such prewar factors,[76] most either aim to explain stronger state contexts than this book or focus on later stages of conflict, well after rebel groups have cohered.

These explanations are more likely to be relevant to armed group formation in stronger-state contexts for at least two reasons. First, as argued previously, in environments where the state is weak, barriers to entry for new rebel groups are low; small, poorly armed rebel groups can and frequently do form. This suggests that where states have better penetrated their peripheral territories – and thus all actors have greater certainty that states have the capacity to learn about and end insurgencies early – barriers to entry for armed groups challenging the state are substantially higher; would-be weak groups will not typically bother to form.[77] These dynamics indicate a more important role in strong states for factors that allow aspiring rebels to mobilize and organize new, relatively capable armed groups quickly. Without such capacity, armed group formation in these contexts would be a fool's errand. A highly motivated, skilled, or ideologically committed population, or strong prior, oppositional political organizations or skills, could be a source of such capacity.[78]

Second, rural contexts are simply less likely to have highly ideological or "politicized" populations, meaning those that are deeply knowledgeable about and engaged in national politics, especially through regularized participation in opposition organizations. As Stathis Kalyvas documents, the urban bias prevalent in conflict studies tends to privilege "top-down" perspectives that emphasize "high" politics and ideological or normative motivations for warfare – whereas rural civilians often have shorter time horizons and focus on more immediate social dynamics (2006 43–46).

---

[76] See, for example, Cederman, Wimmer, and Min 2010; Cederman, Weidmann, and Gleditsch 2011; Zukerman-Daly 2012; Staniland 2014; Parkinson and Zaks 2018; Balcells 2017; Finkel 2015; Lyall 2020.

[77] Consistent with this argument, Webster 2019 finds that stronger states are less likely to face low-intensity conflicts than weak ones – but when they do, those conflicts are more likely to escalate to large-scale civil war.

[78] Zukerman-Daly's (2012) findings, for example, are generally consistent with this framework. Colombia is a relatively strong state, and using extraordinarily fine-grained data, she shows that armed groups that committed violence there in municipalities since 1964 were those that could rely on a type of organizational endowment that could be easily repurposed for rebel group formation: armed organizations that had operated there during a previous period of armed conflict. In another example Finkel (2015; 2017) shows that, when facing the extremely strong Nazi state, Jewish resistance was rare – but when it occurred, presence of people who had previously gained skills in rebellion – the "resister's toolkit" – was a crucial precondition.

The vast majority of rural households in sub-Saharan Africa are subsistence farmers, whose participation in associational life focuses on highly *local* economic, social, and political issues, traveling infrequently outside of their home ethno-region.

Careful observations of rural life in Africa support these points. For example, after using evidence from Nigeria, Zambia, Kenya, and Ivory Coast to show that the "numerous and widely scattered" nature of rural, smallholder farmers puts them at a substantial disadvantage in collective action, Robert H. Bates concludes, "Farmers thus seem to be relatively inactive in interest-group politics."[79] In another example, Michael Bratton observes that "At first glance, [rural African] societies seem to possess few intermediate organizations to occupy the political space between the family (broadly defined by affective ties of blood, marriage, residence, clan, and ethnicity) and the state. Those civic structures that do exist are typically small in scale and local in orientation" (Bratton 1989, 410–411).[80] As Bratton goes on to note, vibrant civil society organizations from trade organizations to nongovernmental advocacy organizations thrive in African countries – however, they have typically predominated in mining towns or more urban, industrialized areas.[81]

Organized, associational life is surely transforming in contemporary Africa, especially because such urbanized contexts are growing rapidly; however, even as of 2018, about 60 percent of the population of sub-Saharan Africa was rural. Almost three quarters was rural in 1990.[82] Indeed, while popular, grievance-driven political protest has occurred in Africa with regularity since the colonial period and continues to, this has been largely an urban phenomenon.[83] Building on Mahmoud Mamdani's work,[84] Adam Branch and Zacariah Mamphilly show that colonial and postcolonial authorities used distinct strategies of control and fragmentation in urban and rural Africa. They argue that this has caused a persistent divide between both the types of political grievances held in each context and the modes of contentious politics people use in each to redress them. Generally consistent with these arguments, the percent of African countries'

---

[79] Bates 1981, 87–90.   [80] Gyimah-Boadi (1997, 280) makes a similar observation.

[81] Bratton 1989, 427. As Nelson Kasfir (1998, 126) notes, patronage politics has also limited the strength of oppositional civil society organizations.

[82] In contrast, Latin America's population was about 20 percent rural in 2018 and 30 percent rural in 1990; South Asia's population was 66 percent and 75 percent rural, respectively. Data comes from the World Bank Data Bank based on the United Nations Population Division's World Urbanization Prospects data.

[83] Branch and Mampilly 2015.   [84] Mamdani 1996.

GDP composed of manufacturing and the percent of the population that is urban are both positively associated with the onset of nonviolent, antigovernment campaigns; the former is also negatively associated with civil conflict onset.[85] Thus, while rural African politics is of course complex and varied,[86] oppositional, nationally oriented interest groups that underpin social movements have historically been less important to quotidian life there – rather, their presence is more relevant to contentious politics in cities.

Even for weak state contexts, these arguments do not deny the potential importance of prewar factors to later stages of armed conflict. For example, after a rebel group is viable and the fighting is fully underway, rebels need – and are better able to absorb – large numbers of recruits and access to material resources. At that stage, people or practices from a preexisting organization, or highly motivated joiners, can be crucial. Also, once rebels are strong enough to govern residents of a given territory, prewar community structures or other attributes would likely be relevant.[87] These are later stages of conflict than those at the center of this book.[88]

Furthermore, while I have argued previously that strong, prewar antigovernment grievances among the population where rebels form are not a necessary condition for rebel group formation or even rebel viability in weak states, this does not rule out the potential usefulness of such factors. Indeed, in one important example, Phillip Roessler's work shows that ethnopolitical exclusion propelled rebellion in Darfur. I have, however, argued that such highly nationally politicized contexts are unusual in rural contexts in weak states – and that prewar *objective* levels of exclusion are generally less important than *perceptions* of them during the uncertain, early phases of conflict. Even in Roessler's account, a key factor in the escalation to civil war in Darfur was how local villagers *interpreted* local militia and armed nomad violence that

---

[85] Butcher and Svensson 2016. Additionally, Cunningham et al. 2017 find that civil society organizations are negatively associated with civil conflict onset, and positively associated with the onset of nonviolent campaigns.

[86] See especially Boone 2003.   [87] Arjona 2016.

[88] This discussion begs the question: Do strategic, would-be rebels anticipate these later stages, does this make them more likely to form in areas where these endowments are plentiful? My answer is no, for three reasons. First, would-be rebels know they may move to new locations as the conflict evolves. Second, would-be rebels know they may be able to extract concessions from the government without needing to endure for long periods or becoming highly violent; leaders of even minimally viable groups may find an audience with the government, leading to a bargain that improves upon their status quo. Third, as discussed earlier in the chapter, due to aspiring rebels' critical need – in order to become viable – to form where they know the social and geographic terrain well, their options for locations in which to form are limited.

preceded the civil war – especially how villagers interpreted the government's degree of culpability for these attacks. Notably, the nascent rebels in Darfur also attempted to shape these civilian perceptions during their initial attacks.[89]

This discussion highlights why detailed scrutiny of events when grievances became salient and prevalent in a given population, and when a rebel group formed and how it used initial violence to shape perceptions, is needed to disentangle processes of organized violence's start and escalation. Doing so has eluded recent quantitative studies of conflict onset, since they rely on measures of conflict onset that, by using the inclusion criterion of twenty-five recorded battle-deaths in a calendar year, capture conflict after rebel groups initially form and initiate violence. Without detailed evidence about the early stages of rebel group formation, it can be difficult to observe whether grievances propelled the *initial* formation of rebel groups, or the *later* dynamics of conflict escalation. Crucially, the latter channel leaves open the possibility that factors that retrospective observers believe caused a conflict in the first place were in fact subjective and generated by early violence. This is an especially high risk for factors like ethnic grievances, which we know to be endogenous to violence.

2.9 DISCUSSION

The theory presented in this chapter indicates that rebel group formation is much more frequent, and often quite different in character, than prior work suggests. While some have sought to explain a stark dichotomy – why some areas experience explosive civil war while others remain peaceful – this theory suggests that this approach risks mischaracterizing the landscape of organized, anti-state violence by overlooking numerous cases of rebel groups forming but not escalating dramatically. Such cases are not trivial from the standpoint of human suffering; armed groups that engage only in low-intensity violence can cause a great deal of disruption and insecurity for those who live among them. From a theoretical standpoint, these groups' existence implies the prevalence of low-intensity conflict escalation processes that are overlooked and not only important to understand in their own right but because doing so may improve knowledge about the processes that culminate in large-scale civil war.

I have argued that the formative, initial phases of insurgency in weak states are often shrouded in secrecy and uncertainty. As a result, initial

---

[89] Roessler 2016, 184–185.

acts of violence against the state are often small, secretive, and ambiguous, with no group claiming responsibility for them on the national stage, and few attacks on civilians. This conceptualization of insurgency formation builds on those in the conflict onset literature that have emphasized the importance of factors that render rebellion feasible, rather than emphasizing intensity of the local population's motivation. It also joins with those who have emphasized *information*, especially factors that influence the incipient rebels' ability to induce civilians to keep secrets.

My claims about the modal initial rebel groups' size, endowments, and strategies, and about the highly locally oriented nature of rural life in weak states in Africa, paint a very different picture of early-stage rebellion than is often assumed in the civil war onset literature – especially works that argue in favor of motivation-based arguments. While those arguments present a clear, important role for prior, strong, anti-state grievances, the theory presented in this chapter does not. Instead, rebel groups form due to largely idiosyncratic, individual-level factors, and the key to determining rebel group viability is whether or not nascent rebel groups generate a widespread perception among villagers that they will be just, strong, and successful, at least relative to the government.

A key implication of this theory is that studying the start of rebellion in weak state contexts is even more challenging than previously recognized, since rebel violence may simmer at a low level for months or years. The clandestine nature of rebellion exacerbates problems of observing nascent insurgency. The existence of rather lengthy, clandestine periods also suggests that acts that may retrospectively be perceived as prior to a war were in fact acts committed as part of strategic actions by newly formed, secretive armed groups. This underscores why great care is needed in disentangling whether factors are propelling the very initial stages of insurgency or are driving later escalation of conflict.

Part II of this book aims to do so, using detailed evidence about Uganda from 1986 to 2006 to show the empirical promise of the claims that emerged from this theory. The following chapters also examine systematic evidence from other countries in east and central Africa to probe whether Uganda's rebellions are exceptional or potentially representative of broader patterns. After providing evidence in Chapter 3 that supports key assumptions about the contexts in which nascent rebellions form, Chapter 4 takes up the perceptions and behavior of the rebels; Chapter 5 examines those of civilians who lived near nascent rebel activity; and Chapter 6 probes the role of the state.

PART II

UGANDA AND BEYOND

3

Context and Initial Conditions

Political power comes out of the barrel of a gun.
                                          – Mao Zedong

We felt that unless we fought, we wouldn't be recognized.
                        – Former UNRF II leader, author interview

I now turn to Uganda. This chapter provides context and description about rebel group formation there since 1986. It supports several theoretical assertions from Chapter 2 about the strategic approach of initial rebel leaders and the initial conditions they typically face in weak states. It also provides contextual background for the empirical analyses of the behavior of rebels, civilians, and the state, respectively, in Chapters 4, 5, and 6.

The chapter first sketches the key events that led to Uganda's exceedingly low state capacity by 1986, the year in which this book's analysis of rebel group formation begins. Doing so also demonstrates the uncertainty about the government that pervaded much of Uganda in the late 1980s, after the new NRM government took power in January 1986. The chapter then describes the formation of the Ugandan rebel groups after the new government took power. It describes the nascent rebel group leaders' initial stated goals, their initial lack of strong ideology or material and organizational endowments, and the clandestine nature of their early days. Looking briefly beyond Uganda to other cases of attempted rebellion in other eastern and central African states, the chapter also checks the relevance of these initial conditions of rebel group formation to contexts proximate to, but beyond the borders of, Uganda.

The descriptions of rebel group beginnings here clarify which of the two conceptualizations of conflict onset described in Chapter 2 is germane to the rebellions at the center of this book. Recall that one common approach to theorizing civil conflict onset characterizes it as a collective action problem that plays out in public with the early participation of large numbers of people; the key question for that body of work is why and how people will be motivated or induced to participate in rebellion, given free-rider problems. By contrast, this book builds on another family of theoretical arguments that emphasizes the secretive nature of conflict onset, characterizing the process as one that involves a small group of devoted individuals whose primary initial aim is to remain undetected. The evidence presented in this chapter brings into focus why the latter approach better captures the most common path to rebel group initiation in weak states, at least in eastern and central Africa. It shows that in Uganda, the national political moment when most of the rebels were "born" was one of ambiguity and uncertainty, and it was small, secretive groups of rebel entrepreneurs – not large groups of intensely aggrieved, protesting citizens – who initially formed groups that aimed to use violence to challenge the state.

3.1 UGANDA FROM INDEPENDENCE (1962) TO STATE FAILURE (1986)

By the mid-1980s, Uganda was a failed state.[1] As Ugandan scholar Abdu Basajabaka Kawalya Kasozi explains:

(I)n 1985, Uganda could no longer be described as a state. No one military or political organization commanded the legitimate use of violence in the country ... The near elimination in some places of the infrastructure that supported organized human endeavour lowered the quality of life. Violence, dishonesty, corruption, and moral degeneration permeated the whole social system.[2]

It had not always been this way. Pre-colonial Uganda was a relatively prosperous mix of both centralized, mostly Bantu, kingdoms and decentralized, predominantly Nilotic, tribes. Later, Europeans described Uganda as the "pearl of Africa"[3] for its beauty and the "cockpit of

---

[1] This section provides just a brief look at Uganda's post-independence period; I refer the reader to Kasozi 1994 and Karugire 1996 for detailed discussion of Uganda's history between independence and 1986.

[2] Kasozi 1994, 193.

[3] The description of Uganda as the "pearl of Africa" is commonly attributed to Winston Churchill in 1909. However, it appears that Churchill was using a well-known turn of phrase to describe Uganda. The phrase was used over a decade prior to 1909 by acclaimed

Central Africa" for its strategic location.[4] It was prized by nineteenth-century European explorers for its lush vegetation, its temperate climate, and, most importantly, its location at the headwaters of the Nile River and at the northern shores of Lake Victoria – respectively the longest river in the world and the largest lake (measured by surface area) in Africa. Uganda's position upstream from Egypt and Sudan made it particularly appealing to the British, who sought to increase their influence on these heavily Nile-dependent territories.

The British Empire established Uganda as a Protectorate in 1894 and ruled the country with a rather light touch relative to its other colonies, particularly Kenya and Rhodesia, where it more aggressively appropriated large swaths of land for farming and settlement. The proto-state left behind by colonists had minimal initial reach beyond the capital. Still, by the time Uganda gained its independence in 1962, many observers were sanguine about the country's prospects. In addition to a favorable climate for agriculture with two annual growing seasons, Uganda touted the most prestigious university in the region, the University of East Africa (now Makerere University), which was reportedly known at the time as "the Harvard of Africa." After independence in 1962, Prime Minister Milton Obote, from northern Uganda (the Lango region), led Uganda to relative prosperity; real GDP grew at roughly 5 percent annually.[5]

Unfortunately, a common trope of post-independence sub-Saharan African states generally captures what took place in Uganda next: a barely institutionalized proto-state gave way to power struggles, political rivalries articulated as ethno-regional divisions, and then coups, violence, and steady economic and political decline. In 1966, Obote suspended the 1962 constitution that had required him to share executive power with the king of Buganda, the kingdom that surrounds the current capital city, Kampala (as well as the seat of the colonial government, Entebbe).[6] The king of Buganda had been president of Uganda, but in

---

Victorian journalist William Thomas Stead, who also referred to Uganda as the "cockpit of Central Africa." See Stead (1898).

[4] Stead 1898, 63–64.

[5] The Republic of Uganda, Ministry of Planning and Economic Development 1987.

[6] The Baganda people have long held a disproportionately large portion of civil service positions; the British favored the Baganda because of their centralized political institutions as well as their perceived cultural superiority. Frederick Lugard, who first established Britain's official presence in Uganda in 1890, made this hyperbolic remark about the Baganda: "(I)t is of unanimous verdict of everyone, without exception, who has been brought in contact with this remarkable race, that they show a most extraordinary advance upon all people who surround their country to north, south, east or west …

abrogating the constitution Obote usurped that position and the entirety
of the power of the executive. The power-sharing agreement had been
a foundational agreement of the fledgling country; in reneging upon that
agreement, Obote set in motion the erosion of Uganda's burgeoning
democratic state and consolidated his hold on power – until 1971, when
his former ally, Major General Idi Amin, deposed him in a military coup.

Throughout the 1970s, Amin ruled Uganda with notorious cruelty,
purging potential rivals from elite levels of the government and military
through intimidation, imprisonment, and violence. While Amin used
populism to acquire support from some Ugandans that persists to
this day, he also presided over a widespread decay of national infrastructure and did devastating damage to the economy, especially in 1972 when
he expelled all Asians, who had constituted the vast majority of the
country's merchants and business owners. Further, while many observers
in Uganda and beyond have presumed that Amin's government had at
least disproportionately benefitted his home region, West Nile, careful
analyses found that in fact this is not the case.[7] In 1979, a coalition of
Ugandan rebel forces ousted Amin with the aid of the Tanzanian army.
But these parties failed to agree on a successor, and in the resulting
confusion and political struggle, six presidents led Uganda between the
end of Amin's regime and January 1986.

Elections were held in 1980 and former President Obote was declared
victorious – but amidst widespread allegations of fraud. A civil war now
known as the Bush War ensued, affecting much of the county's central and
southwestern regions from 1981 to 1985. Several rebel factions fought
against Obote's army, the Uganda National Liberation Army (UNLA),
during this war. One of these groups was the National Resistance
Movement (NRM)[8] led by Yoweri Museveni, who had come in fourth

---

They are an extremely brave race, though treacherous from our point of view, are
passionately fond of learning, and are capable of high attainments … " (Lugard 1898,
189).

[7] For example, Robert Gersony's report on northern Uganda notes that, "Except for the
installation of a communications satellite (which has long ceased to function) and a failed
project to build an international airport, Amin's home region benefited little from government programs during his regime … [M]any Ugandans believe incorrectly that the West
Nile prospered as a region as a result of Amin's favoritism" (Gersony 1997).

[8] The rebel group was in fact named the National Resistance Army (NRA), but it later
named its political wing the NRM. The NRM is now the name of the ruling party in
Uganda. For simplicity, throughout this book NRM refers to both the rebel group and the
ruling party.

in the official results of the 1980 presidential elections.[9] Much of the violence and confusion associated with the Bush War ended in July 1985 after UNLA commander Tito Okello staged a coup and peace negotiations between the new Okello-led government and the various rebel factions were initiated. However, the NRM continued recruiting soldiers throughout the negotiations and seized Kampala from the Okello-led government in January 1986. The former UNLA military disbanded – most fled to their home villages, predominantly in northern Uganda, while some sought to enter the NRM vetting system, through which they could join the new Ugandan army, the NRA. On January 29, 1986, Yoweri Museveni was sworn in as president and has remained president since.

These decades of state decay and violence from the mid-1960s to the mid-1980s exacted a considerable toll on Uganda. An estimated 800,000 Ugandans were killed as a result of political violence between 1971 when Amin seized power and the end of the civil war in 1985.[10] Hundreds of thousands more were displaced from their homes, especially in West Nile, in the years following Amin's ouster and in central Uganda during the Bush War.

By the mid-1980s, the economy was also in tatters. In 1985, income per capita was at just 59 percent of its 1971 level,[11] and inflation was over 240 percent.[12] The NRM's Ministry of Planning and Economic Development wrote in its March 1987 *Rehabilitation and Development Plan*:

The country now has to depend on imports even for simple manufactured products. The communication network, roads, railways, and telephone services are in a terrible state of disrepair. The power supply is unreliable. Water and sanitation have deteriorated very badly. Hospitals and schools are in a very poor state and are extremely short of supplies.

The NRM/NRA thus assumed power against this background of a monumental collapse ... Nearly a third of the country's most productive areas were laid to waste over the last five years. In addition, the atmosphere of insecurity which characterized the period between 1972 and 1985 destroyed peoples' confidence in the country and resulted in massive capital flight. Some people took

---

[9] Museveni was educated in the late 1960s at Dar es Salaam University alongside leading socialist intellectuals such as Walter Rodney as well as Samora Machel and Julius Nyerere, African "revolutionaries" who would also later become heads of state.

[10] The 800,000 figure comes from Tripp (2004, 4). Kasozi (1994, 3) estimates that "well over one million Ugandans were killed [between 1964 and 1985] through violence that was invoked for political purposes."

[11] Kiyaga-Nsubuga 2004, 89.   [12] Dagne 2010, 1.

a short view of life, businessmen concentrated on short-term speculative activities.[13]

Thus, in 1986 and in the years immediately following, the country stood in an uncertain position. Given the country's recent experience of state predation of its citizens – or at least, for many, the state's failure to protect them and provide basic services – skepticism was warranted. But the recollections of most civilian interviewees indicate that most Ugandans were unsure of what to expect from the new NRM government. Museveni was a Munyankole from southwestern Uganda (in an area near Mbarara municipality), an area that had not been influential in post-independence national politics.[14] His capacity to govern on a large scale, and to avoid the abuses of power that had predominated in prior regimes, was uncertain in the eyes of most citizens. This uncertainty was particularly marked in the northern and eastern areas of the country, which were not directly affected by the Bush War and thus had no direct, prior experience with the NRM. For example, while West Nilers have long held grievances against other northerners – generally the Acholi and Langi, who predominated in the UNLA military that committed violent anti-Amin reprisals in West Nile in the early 1980s – most had little direct, prior exposure to "westerners" before the NRM took power. More generally, outside of Kampala, people's lives were highly localized; most Ugandans rarely left their region – let alone the handful of villages surrounding the one where they resided – and knew few people in other regions. Weinstein[15] writes of that period that "few believed that (Museveni's) guerrilla government would survive."

Yet some Ugandans and external observers were cautiously optimistic. Reflecting back on this transition, a 1989 Amnesty International report stated: "[A]bove all the change in government was seen as a chance for Uganda to break with a 20-year history of gross and horrific abuse of human rights."[16] Among populations that came under its control during the Bush War, the NRM had developed a reputation of generally treating

---

[13] Ministry of Planning and Economic Development 1987, 2.
[14] In fact, in several interviews, Ugandans remarked that the Banyankole were generally known to the rest of the country in the early 1980s for their cattle rearing and their work in basic service jobs in Kampala such as janitorial positions. For example, one civilian interviewee from eastern Uganda remarked that until 1986, the Banyankole were known as "the toilet cleaners of Uganda." Based on the context and remainder of the conversation, I interpret this statement as implying that the NRM's competence was viewed as not assured – but that they did not seem nefarious, either.
[15] 2005, 15.   [16] Amnesty International, 1989, 1.

civilians humanely and encouraging democratic local governance.[17] An editorial in the national newspaper *The Star* on the day of Museveni's swearing-in ceremony as president on January 19, 1986, wrote:

The hopes that Ugandans have quietly nursed about the restoration of peace are at last in sight. The peace that has prevailed in the areas under control of the NRA augurs well for the future of this nation.

The administrative and government machinery in Uganda have ground to a halt. The productive and economic sectors are at a standstill ...

There is therefore an urgent need to restore the government and administrative machinery back to normality ... It will be only then that Ugandans will harmoniously work hand in hand to make this one time Pearl of Africa [sic] rise and shine again.[18]

Citing their illegitimacy and history of abuses, the NRM disbanded most former state organizations, including the military, largely starting from scratch. As described in greater detail in Chapter 6, in the months after seizing Kampala, the NRM turned to expanding the reach of the state throughout Uganda's territory up to its borders. NRM emissaries arrived in each district to set up new local government bodies. They focused especially on the gradual process of honing the state's informational capacity, their ability to monitor the local population for would-be challengers – or to end those that had already emerged.

3.2 REBEL GROUP FORMATION IN UGANDA SINCE 1986

Amidst this uncertainty, for seven months after the NRM seized Kampala at the end of January 1986, Uganda was largely free of organized political violence.[19] But in August, a new rebel group called the Ugandan People's Defense Army (UPDA) launched its first attack; this was the first of numerous rebel attacks that NRM forces would face while governing Uganda.

During the twenty years that followed, the NRM government faced some rebel groups that became particularly threatening to their control over a region of Uganda – particularly Joseph Kony's Lord's Resistance Army (LRA). However, few outside observers of conflict realize that Uganda has also recently faced numerous other rebellions – sixteen

---

[17] See in particular Weinstein 2007, 175–180, for a concise discussion of the Resistance Council system of local governance that the NRM put in place in the areas it controlled. I also discuss this system in Chapter 6.

[18] "We Commend the NRA." *The Star*, January 29, 1986, p. 2.

[19] Museveni describes "total peace" in northern Uganda between March and August 1986, Museveni 1997. Newspaper articles from this period and my interviews throughout northern and eastern Uganda generally corroborate his statement.

distinct rebellions in all – many of which are left unmentioned in recent histories of Uganda and omitted from conflict datasets. Only four of these groups – ADF, HSM, LRA, and UPA – went on to become viable, able to at least minimally threaten the authority of the central government.[20]

The groups that I count as having formed in Uganda since February 1986 are listed in Table 3.1. Recall from Chapter 1 that to be included in this list, each group needed to have at least a nascent organizational structure, such as a delineation of roles among its initial members, and to have committed or have had concrete plans to commit at least one violent attack against the state. Groups also had to form after the NRM took power in late January 1986; groups that formed prior to this date (during the Bush War) are not included.

Arriving at this list involved triangulating among interviews in areas where rebel groups had reportedly begun, newspaper articles, and government documents. Interviews were particularly crucial since Ugandan newspaper articles that reported violence against the state were often quite imprecise about who committed the violence, simply stating that "rebels" committed violence. There was also reason to believe that the NRM – which has staked its reputation on its ability to provide stability – may inflate the quantity of rebel groups that had formed (and thus that the NRM had vanquished). See Appendix A for a more detailed discussion of how I mitigated these issues and arrived at this list. I also provide evidence throughout the book and in the appendices that the analyses in the book are not sensitive to excluding the group for which evidence of its formation is most scant (especially the PRA).

3.3 STARTING SMALL, POOR, AND SECRET

All of the Ugandan groups' initial leaders were Ugandan citizens, and the vast majority of their eventual fighters were Ugandans. The aspiring rebel leaders who initiated these groups were mostly young adults or middle aged when they decided to form rebel groups. Most initial leaders were not typical villagers: they were generally better educated than the average Ugandan, having completed at least some secondary school.[21]

---

[20] Recall from Chapter 2 that I operationalize this threshold as occurring after a group has maintained a base on the target country's soil. In order to be considered viable, a sizeable group of at least about 100 rebels must maintain at least one base on the target country's soil for a minimum of approximately three months.

[21] An exception is Joseph Kony, who is believed to be only minimally educated but highly charismatic.

TABLE 3.1 *Rebel groups that formed in Uganda since February 1986*

Region	Group name[a]	Dates on which attacks occurred on Ugandan territory[b]	Leaders
Eastern	Force Obote Back Again (FOBA)	1987 to 1990	Nelson Omwero, Aggrey Awori, Charles Korokoto
	Uganda People's Army (UPA)*	1987 to 1992	"Hitler" Eregu, Musa Ecweru, Nathan Okurut
Western	National Army for the Liberation of Uganda (NALU)	1987 to 1991	Amon Bazira
	Allied Democratic Force (ADF)*	1994[c] to 2004	Jamil Mukulu
	People's Redemption Army (PRA)[d]	2001 to 2005	Unknown[e]
Northern	Uganda People's Democratic Army (UPDA)	1986 to 1988	Odong Latek
	Holy Spirit Movement (HSM)*	1986 to 1987	Alice Lakwena
	Lord's Resistance Army (LRA)*	1988 to 2006	Joseph Kony
	Ninth of October Movement (NOM)	1988 to 1990	Dan Opito
	Citizens Army for Multiparty Politics (CAMP)	1999	Smith Opon Acak
West Nile	West Nile Bank Front (WNBF)	1988, 1994 to 1997	Juma Oris
	Uganda National Resistance Front II (UNRF II)	1997 to 2002	Ali Bamuze
	National Freedom Army (NFA)	1997 to 2002	Mohammed Kiggundu
Central	National Democratic Alliance (NDA)	1989 to 1993	Sam Luwero
	Uganda Democratic Alliance (UDA)	1994 to 1996	Herbert Itongwa
	Uganda Federal Democratic Front (UFDF)	1996	Kisule

Source: Uganda Chieftancy for Military Intelligence (CMI), newspaper articles, and interviews.

Note: * indicates that this rebel group became a viable threat to the Ugandan government.

[a] Group names were often ambiguous or misreported in newspapers, and sometimes changed over the course of a rebellion. The names here reflect what I deem to be the most commonly used name for an armed group.

[b] End dates listed here are the year that groups signed peace accords, were pushed for at least five years into a neighboring state, and/or the primary leaders were captured, killed, or fled into exile. In several cases, attacks continued, and newspapers continued attributing them to the group after what I consider the end date.

[c] The ADF's initial planning began in Busereka forest near Hoima in 1994 under the name Uganda Mujahidin Freedom Fighters (UMFF); it was attacked by the UPDF before becoming viable, regrouped in DRC, and then re-formed in Bundibugyo in 1996, where it committed initial attacks, had a base, and became viable – later going on to gain support from the government in Khartoum and becoming quite violent. I therefore consider the start date as 1994, but code the area it formed (used in analyses in Chapters Four and Five) as the area around Bundibugyo.

[d] The PRA's existence is contested. I discuss this issue in greater depth in Appendix A. The analyses in this book are not sensitive to exclusion of this group.

[e] Several Ugandan military and intelligence officials stated that Samson Mande was the leader of the PRA. Mande has denied any involvement in the PRA and currently lives in exile in Sweden.

Those who closely observed these rebel groups in their infancy generally characterized their leaders as entrepreneurs in a context with an extremely weak private sector – where gaining access to the government was one's mostly likely route to status or wealth. They therefore echo Mao's words at the opening of this chapter on seeking political power using force and resemble Hirshleifer's "entrepreneurs of the conflict industry."[22] For example, when asked about why people elected to form these rebel groups, a senior military official involved in counterinsurgency against several of them explained, "One way to get [the government] to respond to you is to challenge them."[23] An intelligence officer conveyed a similar interpretation. When asked why he thought there had been several attempted rebellions in Uganda since 1986, he replied simply: "Men want to be chiefs."[24] Another intelligence officer said of that period, "Rebellion was the only way to stay relevant."[25]

In their early days, these groups shared several characteristics, which relate directly to the theory and scope conditions of this book. None benefitted from lootable, high-value natural resource wealth, including in the initial phases. Uganda has no known diamonds, and while it has substantial deposits of lower-value-per-weight minerals, such as copper, I found no evidence that they were used to finance rebel groups. Commercially viable petroleum reserves were not discovered in Uganda until 2006.

None of the groups initially benefitted from substantial material resources from an external state sponsor, either. Of the rebel groups that ended before becoming viable, none started with external, material sponsorship. Among the groups that did become viable, the HSM never made contacts across borders – and while the others did, it took them several years for those contacts to yield support. For example, while the LRA is often characterized as serving as a proxy for the Sudanese government, in the initial years, Kony had no direct connections to foreign governments. His weapons came initially from ambushes of police barracks and small military detachments, as well as from the former UNLA and UPDA fighters that eventually joined him. Kony did not move any of his forces to Sudanese territory until 1994,[26] and he received little military assistance from Sudan

[22] Hirshleifer 1994, 6.
[23] Interview with senior Ugandan military official, Bombo barracks, Luwero district, February 2009.
[24] Interview with former intelligence officer, Kampala, March 2009.
[25] Interview with intelligence official from ISO, Kampala, March 2009.
[26] Interview with Ugandan intelligence officer from the Acholi region, October 2009.

until that year.[27] One former LRA commander stated that there was no contact between LRA leaders and any leader in Sudan until 1993.[28] Khartoum appears to have wanted to support the LRA at that time in retaliation for the Ugandan government's support of the Sudanese rebel group, the Sudanese People's Liberation Army (SPLA), which began in the early 1990s, after a 1989 coup brought Islamic hardliner Hassan al-Turabi and the National Islamic Front to power in Khartoum. Later in the insurgency, especially in the late 1990s, the LRA relied heavily on fallback positions in southern Sudan.[29]

The story is similar for the ADF, another case of a rebel group that became quite violent, owing in part to sponsorship from Khartoum.[30] While the ADF went on to receive financing and weapons shipments from Sudan, it took two to four years for them to make the political connections to Khartoum to make this possible, and presumably to demonstrate that their group was a worthwhile agent.

The UPA, which launched in early 1987, based one of its leaders in Nairobi in late 1987 with the aim of acquiring weapons and ammunition from the government of Kenya. He sought to take advantage of rancorous relations between new Ugandan President Museveni and long-time Kenyan President Moi,[31] seeking assistance from Moi's associates in the rebellion against Uganda. In September 1991, three years after forming

---

[27] Interview with former LRA commander, Gulu, November 2009. Confirmed by Ugandan intelligence officer, November 2009, Kampala.

[28] Interview with former LRA Commander, Gulu, January 2010.

[29] This was the case until 2002. Under pressure from the UN and the US in the wake of the 9/11 World Trade Center attacks, Khartoum ceased support to the LRA, which had been placed on the US Department of State's list of terrorist organizations.

[30] Hovil and Werker 2005.

[31] This animosity was due to at least two factors: first, Moi's resentment that in order to capture Kampala, Museveni had abrogated a peace accord brokered by Moi in late 1985 between Museveni and then-President Okello; and second, Moi's concern that Museveni's left-leaning tendencies would lead him to ally with Soviet-aligned states, perhaps supporting leftist dissidents in Kenya against Moi's pro-market government. Their rivalry came to a head in a series of incidents in 1987 in which Kenya repeatedly closed the border with Uganda, disrupting shipments to Uganda, while Uganda shut off its power supply to Kenya. These tensions culminated in cross-border exchanges of fire in late 1987, and then simmered until the early 1990s. For more detail, see Byrnes (1990), chapter entitled "Kenya and Tanzania," available at http://countrystudies.us/uganda/67.htm. Note also that according to one UPA operative, the cross-border exchange of fire was in fact instigated by UPA rebels who sought to gain material support from Kenya by drawing Kenya into a military dispute with Uganda: The UPA rebels disguised themselves in Ugandan military uniforms and fired on the Kenyan military (Interview with former UPA operative, Soroti town, Soroti district, June 2009).

their group, the UPA finally succeeded in acquiring a large cache of bullets[32] from Kenya. However, after smuggling these bullets across the border at Busia, the Ugandan government received intelligence about the shipment. They confiscated it in Soroti in September 1991 and arrested the UPA intelligence officer that had ferried it there.[33] Following that seizure of ammunition, events began to turn against the UPA and key leaders began to defect to the government. While violence continued in the Teso region for about two more years, the group did not receive any additional support from external sources.

Beyond material endowments, few of these groups benefitted from substantial organizational endowments. Almost all of the groups' initial leaders included at least one who was a member (often a relatively senior official) of a former Ugandan government or military.[34] However, with the exception of the UPDA, all of the groups began as secretive, small groups of men – or in the case of the Holy Spirit Movement, a woman (Alice Lakwena) and several men. The UPDA was unusual among Ugandan rebels in beginning as a fairly large group, drawing in large numbers on the Obote government's UNLA military.

In contrast, most started small – usually, a group of just five to ten people – and then expanded their fighting forces in the initial months. For example, the initial UPA planners were just four people, and soon expanded to a circle of roughly two dozen trusted fighters to conduct their initial attacks. One of the initial leaders explained, "What we needed only was a few boys to start off the fighting . . . the others would just join us as we proceed. That is what it is always. You can even start with ten people."[35] Having small numbers helped these groups to remain hidden. As the same former UPA leader explained: "We were making sure that our

---

[32] Interview with that former UPA intelligence operative, July 2008. According to one former UPA leader, it was 47,000 rounds of ammunition hidden in a block of cement. Interview, Soroti town, Soroti district, June 2009.

[33] Interview with UPA intelligence operative who ferried the ammunition and former government operative who followed him, Soroti town, Soroti county, July 2009.

[34] For example, Amon Bazira, leader of the National Army for the Liberation of Uganda (NALU), was Minister of Cooperatives in the second Obote government. Aggrey Awori, leader of Force Obote Back Again (FOBA), was Ugandan Ambassador to the US under the second Obote government. Nelson Omweru of FOBA was a former NRM fighter in the Bush War, and Herbert Itongwa of the Uganda Democratic Alliance (UDA) had served in the military under Museveni. Smith Opon Acak, leader of the Citizens Army for Multiparty Politics (CAMP), was the Chief of Staff of the military under the second Obote government.

[35] Interview with UPA leader, Soroti town, Soroti district, January 16, 2011.

concealment would be good until we were a force that could be in the open." A different UPA leader remarked, "If you are careless while planning, [government] intelligence will nip you in the bud."[36] Two other leaders who were deeply involved in these pre-violence planning stages insisted that no one who was not supposed to know about the group learned about their existence and said that they did not even inform their wives about their plans until after the violence had began. One commented, "We had to maintain secrecy, so we only relied on only the most reliable people. We kept the group intentionally small ... We needed to start as a small, core group, and then slowly enlarge."[37] The UPA did rely on former Ugandan police networks for a considerable number of recruits, but after the group was viable; not until they had a well-established base and fighting was already well underway.

These rebel groups were also organizationally distinct from rebel groups that came before them – for example, those that fought during the Bush War – and from one another. Those that endured benefitted from Uganda's history of organized political violence and relative frequency of upheaval in the central government and security forces; almost all of the rebel groups that formed and endured long enough to recruit large fighting forces drew on the large pools of former fighters – from both former rebellions and former national security forces – that existed in Uganda during this period. Each rebel group had a separate command structure and while some of the rebel groups occasionally communicated with one another and discussed coordinating their arms shipments and attacks, actual acts of coordination were extremely rare. While incipient rebel leaders aimed for coordination or even merger of their groups in the future, they perceived that doing so was contingent on establishing their group's reputation as strong fighters, as well as trusted relationships with potential allies. Furthermore, the areas where rebel groups operated were quite remote from one another; while the distances between them were not great – for example, West Nile's local metropolis (Arua) and that of Acholi (Gulu) are roughly 140 miles from one another – the poor state of Uganda's road network made them quite difficult to travel between.

---

[36] Interview with former UPA leader, Soroti town, June 2009.
[37] Interview with former UPA leader, Soroti, June 2009; Interview with another former UPA leader, Amuria district, July 2009.

3.4 REBELS' STATED OBJECTIVES

For all of the groups I was able to confirm goals – all but two groups[38] –
their central, stated goal was to take over Uganda's central government.
Consistent with bargaining approaches to conflict onset, the evidence
below suggests that there is good reason to believe that the substance of
these stated goals was responsive to the rebels' strategic environment.
Aiming to take over the state has been the *stated* goal of most rebels in
Africa since independence, probably owing to the state-based context in
which rebels operated[39] as well as the weakness of the state – and thus the
relative plausibility of the goal. As Michael Bratton noted in 1989, "[(T)he
state in Africa] remains a major source of spoils, and one of the only
available channels for getting what little there is to get."[40] Like most
African rebels of this period,[41] while these Ugandan groups were political,
none were particularly ideological.

It may seem implausible that these small groups could someday succeed in
overthrowing a central government. However, most former rebel leaders said
they did believe it was possible that they could overthrow the government – or
at the very least, that they would mount a sufficiently strong rebellion to
prompt the government to negotiate with them. These accounts are generally
consistent with recent research showing – using post-Cold War data from
Africa – that the strategic context faced by militarily weak rebels challenging
states of uncertain strength leads rebels to make "unrealistically large
demands" of governments, due to rebels' needs to signal credibility.[42] Still,
Ugandan rebels defended the possibility that they could overtake governments; increased availability of arms from Europe and southern Africa at the
end of the Cold War meant that acquiring small arms in Africa beginning in
the mid-1980s was relatively cheap and easy,[43] and widespread subsistence
farming (and lack of formal employment) meant that recruiting was not
challenging. Of course, the Ugandan context is particularly relevant here:
Most former Ugandan rebel leaders I interviewed cited President Museveni's
then-recently successful rebellion in the Bush War, which was initiated with
just twenty-six men and one gun, according to well-known Ugandan lore.
Several expressed variants of the sentiment: "If Museveni could do it, why

---

[38] I consider the goals confirmed if the leaders made public statements about their goals or if
I was able to confirm them via interviews with group leaders. I was unable to interview
leaders of the PRA or NDA, and I could not identify reliable public statements of their
goals. Analyses in later chapters are not sensitive to the exclusion of these groups.
[39] Reno 2011, 3.   [40] Bratton 1989, 415.   [41] Boas and Dunn 2007, 17.
[42] Thomas, Reed, and Wolford 2016.   [43] Herbst 2000, 255.

couldn't I?" A senior military official noted, "The success of the NRA created fear, and the sense that you can start small, and then take over [the government] ... This creates militarism."[44] An official at Uganda's Amnesty Commission interpreted the prevalence of rebellion onset in Uganda in the late 1980s and 1990s similarly, saying, "After Museveni took power, it almost became a fashion [to rebel.] People thought: If you can take over power, why not us? Let us also try."[45] Several former rebel interviewees also indicated that because the new NRM government had little presence in their communities, there did not seem to be a large chance of being discovered and arrested for planning a rebellion. Furthermore, the prospect that groups could expand, getting on the radar of a state that would "sponsor" them by providing more substantial training and weaponry, seemed plausible.

Of course, ascertaining individuals' true motives for past actions via interviews is a thorny process – especially, in this case, due to the potential desire for interviewees who were former rebel leaders to shape their legacies. I attempted to mitigate this problem by informing interviewees at the outset that I would not cite them by name in my work. I also developed relationships with several rebel leaders – often interviewing them for several hours, two or more times – in order to gain a clearer sense of their personalities and ascertaining how their self-perception and current career incentives may shape their conversations with me. I cannot, of course, entirely rule out the possibility that this dynamic influenced interviewees' responses. The risk seems especially high for rebel leaders since they care about their former group's (and not just their own) legacy. In this light, it is perhaps unsurprising that when asked about why they rebelled, most former rebel leaders first spoke of causes beyond their own self-interest – typically, a need to improve conditions for their home region or their "people" via control of or improved influence over the central government. For example, one former rebel leader said, "We felt that unless we fought, [our region] wouldn't be recognized [by the NRM

---

[44] Interview with military official, Bombo barracks, Luwero district, February 2009.
[45] Senior official at Uganda's Amnesty Commission, Kampala, July 2008. Herbst 2000, 254. argues that the NRA's success inspired the creation of new insurgent groups throughout Africa: "Since 1986, inspired (and sometimes supplied) by Museveni, armies created to compete against national forces in Rwanda, Zaire, Ethiopia, Liberia, Sierra Leone, Somalia, Congo-Brazzaville, and Chad, have challenged African governments and sometimes been able to take over power."

government]."[46] Another rebel leader said that his initial plan was not to become a rebel; however, he decided to take that path because he "wanted a voice" for his community.[47] Others articulated personal frustrations with the government, based either on past personal experiences of injustice at the hands of the NRM such as being unfairly jailed, or perceptions of group-level injustices, or a combination.

Crucially, after my interviews with former rebels had progressed past an initial period when the interviewees spoke at length about their groups' stated goals, several interviewees conceded that if overtaking Kampala proved too difficult, they planned to at least extract "some little" concessions from the government. For example, while the UPA is generally known to have planned to overtake the central government in Kampala, in interviews, one leader conceded that the purpose of asserting that they would seize the government was to "interest the population" and that the group "never really wanted to take over the government." They adopted this stated goal, he indicated, because he believed it would help to convince people that his group was confident and strong. When asked about his true intentions, he said, "We wanted to keep hitting [the government] and use that as a bargaining chip."[48] In a later interview, this leader conceded that his group "misled the public" by promising that they would soon overthrow the government.[49] He indicated that he and his inner circle did so because they calculated that they could only succeed in getting their rebel group "off the ground" if they had at least the tacit support of the civilians.

Other former rebels conveyed that they had been aware that if their rebellion succeeded in persisting for several years, their stated goals could change, responding to the political and military realities they faced. One former rebel intelligence leader said that he and other nascent rebels understood that the odds were against them of overtaking the government, but on the other hand, "[their] target was to fight and grow with the challenge."[50] In another example, at one point LRA leader Joseph Kony articulated secessionist goals, but this was not until 1998 – after a decade of fighting under the banner of seizing the central government. By that time, the Ugandan government had mounted a formidable, violent

---

[46] Interview with former UNRF II rebel in Yumbe town, Yumbe district, November 2009.
[47] Interview with former NFA leader, Kampala, April 2009.
[48] Interview of UPA leader, Soroti town Soroti district, July 2008.
[49] Interview of UPA leader, Soroti town Soroti district, January 2011.
[50] Interview with former UPA intelligence officer, Soroti municipality, Soroti district, March 2009.

counterinsurgency in the mid-1990s. LRA bases were increasingly pushed into southern Sudan, diminishing the prospects that the LRA would overtake Kampala.

Another former rebel leader said that while he believed that defeating the central government was possible, he also conceded a great deal of uncertainty; that he knew little about how successful the NRM government would be at waging a counterinsurgency against his group. He said he calculated that "if we fail, at least the government will take us seriously."[51] He also suggested that, if necessary, he could safely flee to live with his contacts in Sudan or DRC. Looking back on his failed rebellion, he indicated that he believed his strategy of attempting rebellion in order to gain recognition generally worked, even though his rebellion never became viable. They failed to maintain a base on Ugandan soil; his rebel group was repeatedly pushed into southern Sudan. However, "doors are now open [to me]," he said, noting that he is in regular contact with high-level government officials.[52] He boasted that a key confidante of the president has become his personal friend, and explained that, "People expect that if the rebels [who formed in their home region] succeed, they will get power." As the discussion continued, it became clear that this man did not see overtaking Kampala as the sole measure of success. Simply mounting a viable fighting force that could lead to attention from the central government – perhaps for his community, and at least for him – would suffice.

After attempting rebellion, several of these former leaders were bought off by the government, gaining high-level official posts in the cabinet in return for putting down arms. In the case of the UNRF II, their peace agreement included offers of spots in the national military for foot soldiers, and a promise that the former leader could reside in a hotel in Kampala, funded by the government, for the foreseeable future. Other rebels live peacefully in their home villages, where they are still known as "big men" in their communities. Others are cabinet officials, appointed district-level officials, or mid-level military officers focused on managing threats emanating from insurgencies operating across Uganda's borders, in DRC or South Sudan. As described in Chapter 6, they also still submit

---

[51] When asked what he meant by "us," he replied that he was not "just in it for himself," but that he wanted to improve conditions for his ethnic group and that of other groups in the region where he was operating. Interview with former UPA leader, Soroti district, April 2009.

[52] Interview with former NFA leader, Kampala, February 2011.

to regular informal government monitoring and consultation about potential security threats emerging from those villages.

In sum, I assess that the balance of the evidence indicates that rebels' *stated* objectives arose out of leaders' strategic calculations of what would sound most palatable to the audience that mattered most to their survival.[53] Initially, this audience is usually local villagers because of their threat to the group's ability to become viable; later, for groups that do become viable, the audience become sources of funding or material support, often in foreign countries.

This discussion provides supports for my theoretical claims that initial rebel leaders are strategic, and started with small, vulnerable groups. Furthermore, for the analyses that follow, what matters most is there is ample evidence from interviews that nascent rebel leaders in Uganda were strategic actors, and that I saw no evidence that Ugandan rebel groups were substantially different from one another in their initial goals and approach. If major differences between groups existed, this could explain why some rebel groups become viable and others do not. My assessment is that the preponderance of these nascent rebel leaders were ambitious individuals acting at a time of considerable social and political upheaval. Most made ethno-regional claims, but also stood to gain, personally, from leading a rebellion if it was even modestly successful. These individuals had few other options for personal advancement or status, and were not leaders of civil society organizations that articulated clear goals.

3.5 ARE UGANDAN REBELS UNUSUAL?

The appeal of rebellion in weak state settings is not unique to Uganda. For example, as Staniland describes the context of insurgent group emergence in Jammu and Kashmir in the late 1980s: "In the extraordinarily hazy and uncertain environment of 1988–1990, success seemed likely, costs to

---

[53] This is consistent with other scholars' interpretations of rebels' stated goals and ideology as often being fluid and/or instrumental. For example, in his classic book *Ethnic Groups in Conflict*, Donald Horowitz 2000, 232, notes that armed groups' stated objectives are often responsive to the interests of surrounding international actors, and that "[Armed group d]emands can also shift from [local] autonomy to independence and back again, depending on the state of negotiations between central government and separatists." He cites examples of the Moro National Liberation Front in the Philippines, the Mizo National Front in India, armed groups in war leading up to South Sudan's independence, and the Chad National Liberation Front to support this point. See also Sanín and Wood 2014 on the need to better specify the instrumental and non-instrumental uses of ideology.

recruitment were low, and as a result a variety of social and political groupings made a bid for militancy."[54] Bose says of joining a rebellion during the same period in Jammu and Kashmir, "it was distinctly fashionable."[55] In the wake of Che Guevara's revolution in Cuba, the 1960s saw dozen of rebellions in Latin America. More recently, the rough contours of this context apply to immediate post-invasion Iraq and Afghanistan; collapsed states with a new, relatively unknown entity controlling the center, with minimal control over outlying areas.

However, it remains possible that some of the basic features of these Ugandan rebel group starts were atypical, limiting the reach of this book's findings. Since, as shown in Chapter 1, we have a selection problem with the rebel groups about which we know most, to make this judgment I use data I collected that aims to mitigate this issue.

Specifically, I use the dataset described at the end of Chapter 1 that I built with the aim of capturing – as close as possible, using newspaper articles and other publicly available reports – all instances of rebel group formation in twelve countries surrounding Uganda in central and east Africa from 1997 through 2015. As noted in Chapter 1, while data limitations mean that we surely undercounted the true number of rebel groups that formed, we were able to collect data on about three times more groups than commonly-used datasets on armed groups (UCDP/PRIO and GTD). Because of data limitations, the figures below should be taken as rough estimates that capture general patterns, rather than precise quantities. Where specific biases resulting from missingness or other measurement error are most likely, I indicate that in the discussion (especially footnotes) below. The findings I discuss here are summarized in Table 3.2 below; further detail about the data is in Appendix D.

Basic, descriptive patterns emerging from this data clearly support my contention that the conditions from which rebellion emerged in Uganda are not unusual, at least relative to surrounding countries. In particular, most rebels in this region did indeed begin secretly and with minimal initial material endowments. Of the eighty-three rebel groups identified in the dataset that my research team was able to code, the large majority started as clandestine groups (over 70 percent).[56] About 10 percent

---

[54] Staniland 2010, 295–296.   [55] Bose 2007, 125.

[56] There is high missingness on this variable; it is likely that poor documentation of groups in news media is correlated with efforts to be secretive. Therefore, the true proportion of groups that began clandestinely is probably higher. To be coded as clandestine, there had to be explicit evidence that the group initially intended to be clandestine (within the first year after forming), or other evidence allowed coders to infer it. An example of

TABLE 3.2 *Initial attributes of rebel groups forming in central and eastern Africa (1997–2015)*

	Portion of groups (%)	n
Clandestine	72	46
Oil, diamonds, gold, ivory	10	71
External sponsor	30	74
Rural	76	70
Planned inside target country	79	73
Prior civil society organization (political party, religious, or other)	18	71
Prior military organization	38	65
Prior rebel organization	22	65

Sources: Original dataset that relied on the Armed Conflict Location and Event Dataset (ACLED), news articles and other publicly available reports, and expert consultations. The dataset includes eighty-three rebel groups; the *n* provided above indicates the missingness on each variable. Countries included are: Burundi, Central African Republic, Democratic Republic of Congo, Ethiopia, Kenya, Malawi, Mozambique, Rwanda, Sudan, South Sudan, Tanzania, and Zambia. See Appendix D for more detail.

benefitted initially (in their first year) from revenue from oil, diamonds, ivory, or gold, and only 30 percent benefitted initially (in their first year) from a foreign government that materially sponsored their activities.[57]

Regarding where rebel groups initially formed, consistent with Ugandan groups and the contentions of the theory about the "typical" rebel group forming in weak states, 76 percent of these rebel groups formed in rural areas.[58] Also, the strong majority (79 percent) did not plan their initial attacks from across international borders but instead did so from within the country they planned to challenge, not a neighboring or

explicit evidence would be commentary in a news story that the group avoided telling many people who they were and what they planned to do. An example of other evidence allowing an inference of clandestineness was if civilians and the government did not appear to attribute violence to a rebel group until after the group publicly claimed it for themselves.

[57] This could include cash (over $1,000); weapons (over 50 or value of over $1,000); numerous (over 50) rebel troops trained by the foreign government; or provision of foreign government military advisers/trainers (over 10 advisers/trainers). I consider these examples of direct support; I did not count indirect foreign support, such as allowing rebels to hide on one's territory.

[58] This variable refers to the physical location of the groups' planning meetings; it is not necessarily the location of the initial attack. An area was deemed rural if the location was a village, national park, or forested area.

other foreign country. This dataset does, therefore, indicate that a minority of rebel groups in eastern and central Africa start differently; they begin with less secrecy, larger endowments, in more urban areas, and across international borders. Save for a brief discussion in the concluding chapter, I leave for future research explaining how rebel groups' early stages are different under these less common initial conditions. Instead, this book turns toward understanding modal nascent rebel groups in weak states, especially Uganda.

Turning to the groups' organizational foundations, we sought to capture whether the structure, processes, or membership of a prior formal organization were used substantially in building the rebel groups. We found that these details are quite difficult to observe, and operationalized this variable as follows: Does the available evidence suggest that more than about one-third of rebel group membership formerly – in the ten years prior to it taking up arms – was part of another organization? Here, we were coding the membership of the rebel group in general; lack of detail in our sources prevented us from capturing this information specifically for the initial phases of rebel group formation. Recall also that this study excludes rebel groups that were splinters from or mergers of prior rebel groups. Using these criteria, we found that about 18 percent of rebel groups relied on civil society organizations, such as political parties, religious groups, or other organizations such as unions or student organizations. This is consistent with the expectation in Chapter 2 that such organizational endowments do not usually underpin rebel group formation in such contexts. Interestingly, a higher percentage of rebel groups appear to have relied on prior military organizations (38 percent) or prior rebel groups (22 percent). Qualitative accounts from Uganda presented in following chapters indicate that most Ugandan rebel groups included at least one former military, police, or rebel leader in their initial group, and later drew on fighters from former rebellions and militaries since they were amply available during this period. However, in the Ugandan cases, these organizational foundations were not particularly important to the very initial phases of rebel group formation; instead, the local civilian population – most of whom were subsistence farmers, not members of an organization associated with the rebels – were their primary preoccupation. Still, these findings suggest that the issue of how presence of prior organizational roots may influence the behavior of rebel groups is an important area of future research.[59]

---

[59] See especially Braithwaite and Cunningham (2020) for newly available data on the organizational origins of rebel groups.

3.6 DISCUSSION

This chapter has described the circumstances of initial rebel group formation in Uganda during the early Museveni era, as well as the historical
context that led to Uganda's state weakness in the middle and late 1980s.
It also looked beyond Uganda, showing that Ugandan groups' initial
conditions are common in eastern and central Africa.

In aggregate, this body of evidence suggests that despite uncertainty
about what would transpire, small groups of people started rebellions
because they believed they had a reasonable chance of gaining political
power or benefitting economically from doing so – for themselves and
possibly for their communities, too. In the poor and highly weak state
context of Uganda in the late 1980 and in to the 1990s, there were limited
other opportunities to do so. They responded strategically to their political context, asserting goals that they believed would resonate with the
villagers whose allegiance they would rely on. They also recognized that
their rebellions may fall short of their goals, prompting a shift in goals – or
possibly necessitating an outcome short of their often-ambitious stated
goals.

This characterization is consistent with that of several works on rebellion, including William Reno's seminal book on rebellion in Africa.[60] It
diverges from that work, however, in eschewing a typology of these
groups. Instead, these cases – such as the LRA example above, and several
that emerge in later chapters – highlight that rebel groups' initial, stated
goals were largely instrumental, and appeals to civilians were dynamic.
This theme recurs throughout this book; I highlight its relevance to
ethnicity's role in conflict onset in Chapters 5 and 7.

Importantly, and contrary to many scholarly depictions of conflict
onset, this evidence also lends further support to Timothy Wickham-
Crowley's claim that "any attempt to understand [guerilla movements]
as social explosions in the countryside is doomed to failure from the
start."[61] While their early leaders had ambitious goals of challenging
state authority, they began not as explosive social movements but rather
as small, poorly endowed clandestine groups. They operated under
a shadow of uncertainty about their country's political future. As the
next three chapters show, this condition has important implications for
how the rebels used violence and interacted with civilians, as well as for
the behavior of civilians and the state.

---

[60] Reno 2011.   [61] Wickham-Crowley 1993, 30.

Having described the initial context and characteristics of nascent Ugandan rebel groups during the Museveni era and beyond, I now turn toward examining rebels' behavior in the initial phases of launching a rebellion – and why they differ from the subsequent phases that are the more typical target of scholars' inquiry.

4

The Rebels

... [The first phase of rebellion] is devoted to organization, consolidation, and preservation of regional base areas ... The pattern of this process is clandestine ... Military operations will be sporadic.

In the second phase, acts of sabotage and terrorism multiply; collaborationists and "reactionary elements" are liquidated.

– Mao Zedong

[At the start of the rebellion], we were making sure that our concealment would be good until we were a force that could be in the open ... [Initially,] we selected [targets] we expected would give us feedback on what would be the reaction of the government.

– Former UPA leader, Author interview (Soroti, 2011)

Armed rebellions in weak states often start not with a bang, but with a whisper.[1] That claim is contrary to the common characterization of rebellion as an "outbreak" or "eruption," yet it is at the core of the informational theory of armed conflict's start presented in Chapter 2. This chapter's aim is to show this descriptive claim's empirical promise for understanding what rebels do as they begin planning and conducting their first attacks.

Specifically, the chapter examines evidence about when and where rebel groups formed in Uganda, and why nascent rebels' initial use of violence is distinctive in its minimal nature – against both state targets and civilians. It locates the driving forces behind these actions in rebels' needs to better discern and control the information environment in the localities

---

[1] This phrasing borrows from T. S. Eliot's *The Hollow Men*, which culminates in: "This is the way the world ends / Not with a bang but with a whimper."

where they incubate their groups. I leave aside the matter of why only some nascent rebels manage to become viable until Chapter 5.

This focus on the rebels' information environment is a divergence from several prior works that focus on rebel violence as a function of rebel capabilities – especially military strength. For example, Reed M. Wood's work suggests the importance of rebel capabilities for determining the extent of their violence against civilians; he finds that rebels who are weaker, have sustained recent battlefield losses, or are getting stronger but have outside sources of support are more likely to commit violence against civilians.[2] While this may be the case once armed conflict is well underway – the period that is Wood's analytic target – the theory presented in this book proposes that, initially, building coercive power is not rebels' primary concern. Instead, they seek to avoid detection by the authorities. This is why, the following pages indicate, nascent rebels recruit slowly and carefully, in a manner that allows for careful screening for new recruits' loyalty, rather than quickly swelling their ranks in a manner that would allow them to move quickly to conduct more, larger attacks. Conducting attacks carefully – in the hopes of demonstrating competence to civilians – decreases the likelihood that civilians will be motivated to share information about the rebels with authorities.

Qualitative evidence from interviews with former insurgents, counterinsurgents, and civilians in the pages that follow supports my argument that this lack of explosive, frequent violence in the initial stages is not a mere reflection of rebels' low capabilities. Instead, rebels' desire to control the information environment shapes their behavior – particularly their need to remain clandestine, their uncertainty about the governments' counterinsurgency, and, relatedly, their strong desire to shape civilian perceptions about their group. This chapter shows that this leads aspiring rebels to launch their insurgency where they have the greatest informational advantage, which is usually in their home region.

It also shows that rebels use violence in a manner that aims to reduce these uncertainties. The rebels' initial acts are ambiguous in that the rebels refrain from vociferously and publicly taking "credit" for them, due to their desire to remain clandestine – and they serve an important purpose in gaining information about the adversary's capabilities.

Finally, this qualitative evidence suggests that incipient rebels build information networks among civilians across a fairly wide area – their planned initial area of operations – that will help them limit these

---

[2] Wood 2010; Wood 2014a, 2014b.

uncertainties, making them better able to anticipate government attacks and identify hostile individuals within the civilian population. Their initial lack of such networks greatly influences rebels' behavior vis-à-vis civilians; it limits their use of coercion to shape civilian behavior because without such networks they cannot credibly monitor civilians and thus mete out targeted punishment, or selective violence. Rebels therefore must rely largely on persuasion to induce civilian cooperation in the initial phases. It is not until after rebel groups have surpassed a threshold of minimal coercive and intelligence capacity – if indeed they survive long enough to do so – that rebels commit substantial violence against civilians or the government.

This chapter proceeds as follows. It first probes how the initial conditions of rebel group formation in weak states, posited in Chapter 2 and demonstrated in Chapter 3 to be present in Uganda in the late 1980s and 1990s, influenced Ugandan rebels' decisions about where to form their incipient groups. The key initial condition is that barriers to entry for rebels in such contexts are quite low, resulting in nascent rebels that are often small, poor, and thus vulnerable to defeat. I examine county-level evidence for my assertion from Chapter 2 that under these conditions, which are common to rural areas of weak states, it is difficult to predict where people initially come together to form armed groups and make plans to use violence against the state (recall that I term this initial step of group formation *launch*).

The largely idiosyncratic nature of rebel launch is important to an assertion that underlies the subsequent chapters: that there are few systematic differences in the initial launch of each rebel group in Uganda that could then play a role in determining their later patterns of behavior, especially why only some rebel groups became viable. The evidence presented here suggests that there is no influential selection process that determines why some groups launch in some areas and not others. This allows me to, in effect, treat cases of rebellion in Uganda as independent observations.[3]

The chapter then turns to whether and how incipient rebel groups use violence. It builds on several recent advances in the political violence literature that seek to explain levels and types of violence that rebels commit. However, while most of those prior works examine variation in rebel violence across territories[4] or across different rebel groups,[5] this

---

[3] Recall also that none of these rebel groups coordinated substantially with one another, and none formed in the same region during the same year.

[4] Kalyvas 2006.

[5] Weinstein 2007; Blattman and Beber 2013; Cohen 2016; Stanton 2016; Hoover Green 2018.

analysis focuses instead on *variations in violence committed by certain groups, across distinct phases of conflict.*[6]

In particular, it supports a key expectation of the theory: that early rebel violence against the state will be more sporadic and limited than after rebel groups become viable. Rebels aim for attacks with a high likelihood of success – achieving their aims and avoiding embarrassing losses – rather than more frequent or more daring attacks. This is the case because in the initial phases of conflict, violence's primary strategic purpose is in how it can help rebels score early victories, learn about their operational environment, and shape perceptions (among local civilians) of the group's competence at violently challenging the government. Further, this chapter presents evidence supporting my claim that rebels initially tend to be pacific toward nearby civilians for similar reasons. While a tragic reality of civil warfare is that most rebel groups attack civilians at some point,[7] this is not typically the case in the initial phases of rebel group formation.

4.1 WHERE AND WHEN REBELS LAUNCH

I turn now to examining the subnational correlates of initial rebel group launch in Uganda. Before doing so, it is worth underscoring that several *country-level* factors already identified in the conflict onset literature put Uganda at high risk for rebellion during this period: As established in Chapter 3, Uganda during this period was a weak and largely rural state, with high levels of poverty, ample unpopulated terrain, and widely available former fighters from former regimes' militaries and rebel groups that had challenged them. The fact that so many rebel groups formed in Uganda during this period is generally consistent with findings about country-level correlates of civil conflict. The following analyses join with a more recent literature exploring these theories, which also apply at the subnational level.

Figure 3.1 displays the county within Uganda where each of the sixteen rebel groups committed their first attack between 1986 and

---

[6] An important exception is Balcells 2010, who shows that violence against civilians at a given stage of civil warfare is influenced by prior war dynamics. However, Balcells focuses on explaining violence against civilians in *conventional* civil war contexts. This book aims instead to understand insurgency, or irregular warfare. As discussed in Chapter 2 as well as in Kalyvas and Balcells 2010 and Balcells 2010, insurgency and conventional civil warfare have quite different characteristics – in particular, the latter involves much higher levels of armed group control over territories – and thus requires different theoretical explanations of wartime behaviors.

[7] Stanton 2016.

2006.[8] The spatial dispersion of these rebel groups suggest that sparks of
rebellion do not occur only on the periphery, as leading theories might
lead us to expect (especially Herbst (2000)) – they occur all over the
country, even close to the capital city, Kampala. The Moran's I index of
these points is –0.01 and is far from statistical significance (*p*-value of
0.91), indicating that these points are neither clustered nor dispersed;
there is no spatial autocorrelation among them. Therefore, it appears
that it is not the case that the initial stages of rebellion in Uganda have
been contagious; that is, if another rebel group forms in a given area,
then a nearby area is not more likely to have another rebel group form
there because of its proximity.[9]

The spatial dispersion of rebel group formation displayed here is striking given the common trope of post-1986 politics in Uganda, which holds
that rebellion was endemic only to northern Uganda, and especially
among the Acholi ethnic group. That statement is accurate in the sense
that the Lord's Resistance Army (LRA) lasted by far the longest of any of
these groups, and inflicted by far the worst harm on Ugandans – both
civilians and its military. But from the perspective of where rebel groups
formed, it is not accurate; almost half of the groups formed in regions that
are unambiguously not in northern Uganda, even broadly defined.
Furthermore, among the groups that formed in what could be broadly
defined as northern Uganda, three (the West Nile Bank Front (WNBF),
Uganda National Resistance Front II (UNRF II), and National Freedom
Army (NFA)) formed in the West Nile region and one (the Uganda
People's Army (UPA)) formed in the Teso region. Both West Nile and
Teso have entirely distinct histories and ethno-linguistic groups from the
parts of northern Uganda more commonly associated with rebellion,
where the Acholi and Langi people reside.[10]

While there is no evident spatial, statistical relationship regarding
where rebel groups formed in Uganda, one pattern about the decision of
where to form a rebel group emerged from interviews: fourteen out of

---

[8] The points are positioned at the centroid of each county where groups first committed
   violence. In the case of the People's Redemption Army (PRA), which never committed any
   violence in Uganda that I could confirm, this is the county where interviewees believed
   that planning occurred.
[9] This, of course, leaves open the possibility that rebel groups that become viable could then
   influence the behavior and the conflict escalation dynamics of other, already-viable
   groups, thereby potentially creating a spatial contagion effect for rebel violence among
   groups at later stages of violence.
[10] Furthermore, Teso has long been considered – including as part of British colonial
   regional designation – to be part of Uganda's eastern region, not its north.

FIGURE 4.1 Map of initial rebel attacks in Uganda, 1986–2006
Note: Circles on the map correspond to the centroid of the county in which the rebel group committed its first act of violence against the state. PRA is located where they were reportedly planning an attack, according to government sources.

sixteen rebel groups (all but the Allied Democratic Force (ADF) and the NFA) formed *near the home of at least one of their initial leaders.* Leaders of all the groups I interviewed explained that they opted to form their groups in their home areas since they knew the people, as well as the terrain, there better than in other areas. The ADF and NFA leaders I interviewed both felt that their home areas were too urban for a rebel group (both were from the vicinity of Kampala), and opted to join forces with people they knew from other areas. These would-be rebel leaders typically began their rebellions in their home areas, often holding several clandestine planning meetings while living at home, and soon moved to

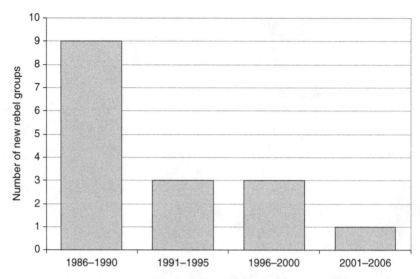

FIGURE 4.2 Number of new rebel groups launched in Uganda per five-year period

nearby forested "bush" areas – which are plentiful in Uganda – to hide as a group and use as an incipient military base.

Another clear pattern is that rebel group formation became less frequent over time. As Figure 4.2 shows, rebel group initiation was most common in the first five years after the National Resistance Movement (NRM) seized power, and then decreased until no new groups formed after 2006. As I demonstrate in Chapter 6, the best explanation for this pattern is that over this period the Ugandan state strengthened its ability to access information from localities outside the capital, allowing it to monitor threats emerging throughout its territory.

For the purposes of this chapter, I put this temporal variation aside and use cross-sectional data to examine patterns of rebel launch. I do so because the available data for most covariates change little or not at all over time. For example, geographic features and distances do not change (except perhaps for forest cover, for which unfortunately a measure on only one year is available), and Uganda's most high-quality and high-resolution demographic and poverty data (via the census) are only available in two years: 1991 and 2002. Because all but one Ugandan rebel group formed prior to 2000, adding the 2002 data would not add much information to the analysis.[11]

---

[11] Furthermore, ethnic demographic patterns changed little during this period; for example, county-level ethno-linguistic fractionalization (ELF) scores in 1991 and 2002 are correlated at 0.9.

4.1.1 Cross-Sectional Statistical Analyses

This section examines evidence for my contention that at the subnational level there are few evident, systematic relationships between the locations of these cases of rebel group launch and factors that dominant theories associate with civil conflict onset. I use logistic regression to analyze the likelihood that a given county in Uganda experienced rebel group formation between 1986 and 2006. I measure the location of rebel group launch based on the county in which the rebel group's first attack occurred. I use attacks as a proxy for rebel group formation because it was not always possible to measure where rebel planning occurred; in the cases I learned most about (the case study groups in Chapter 5 – UPA, LRA, Force Obote Back Again (FOBA), and WNBF), the planning and initial attacks occurred within a handful of kilometers of one another.

I measure covariates at the county level for several reasons. First, it allows me to capture attributes of the terrain and the community among which the rebels form. Recall from the theory presented in Chapter 2 that incipient rebels know that their primary threats are information leaks from the people among which they form. I revisit the unit of analysis issue in the next section, showing that a group-level analysis using objective measures of exclusion from the central government does not show a correlation between exclusion and rebel group formation in Uganda.

I measure at the county level – rather than using another spatial unit – because the county is the lowest administrative unit for which I could identify locations of initial rebel group attacks with relative certainty.[12] Discerning and verifying these locations involved collecting and triangulating information from interviews (with former rebel leaders, government officials, and civilians in the areas of Uganda where these groups formed), data from the government of Uganda (particularly Chieftancy of Military Intelligence responses to information requests and data from the Amnesty Commission), and newspaper articles. Second, unlike districts in Uganda, the number and boundaries of counties have remained stable over time – only one new county has been created in Uganda since the

---

[12] While it can be desirable to use more politically arbitrary, nonadministrative spatial units when examining conflict event locations (e.g. Harris 2012; Hegre, Østby, and Raleigh 2009), or have theory guide the selection of unit of analysis (Soifer 2019), using administrative units was necessary for this analysis because of its reliance on individuals' memories to identify the approximate location of events. Since individuals often associate locations with administrative boundaries, asking them in which county or subcounty an event occurred usually proved most practical.

1990s, while the number of districts has expanded from 38 in 1990 to over 100 today. There are 163 counties in Uganda, with a median size of 1,045.5 square kilometers per county – less than one-third the size of Rhode Island.

Some of the factors commonly examined in studies of conflict onset are not relevant for this analysis because they are not present in the Ugandan context and thus their general relative importance cannot be empirically evaluated. In particular, the presence of readily lootable, high-value natural resources, and the influence of a foreign government providing weapons and funds[13] to rebel groups cannot be empirically examined here because Uganda does not have known reserves of the former,[14] and none of the rebel groups there benefitted from significant resources in the initial stages. While several groups did receive material support from foreign governments over the course of their rebellion, none received substantial support until *after* they proved themselves to be a viable force.

In constructing variables to capture the potential predictors of rebel formation, I draw on the conflict onset literature summarized in Chapter 2, which tends to distinguish between proxies for motivation to rebel and feasibility for rebellion. Summary statistics and a correlation matrix for these variables are reported in Appendix C.

In the family of motivation-focused explanations for conflict onset, I use measures of local ethnic demography and of exclusion from the central government. To measure the *ethnic demography* of a county, I use 1991[15] census data to form two variables. The first is the ethno-linguistic fractionalization (ELF) score, which measures the probability that two randomly sampled individuals from a county would be from different ethno-linguistic groups.[16] Uganda's 1991 census asked

---

[13] Weinstein 2007.

[14] Oil was discovered in Uganda in 2006, but it is not readily lootable and its presence was not known during the period of my study. Uganda has substantial copper deposits, which were known about during the period of my study here, but they are not readily lootable. Uganda's primary established copper mine, Kilembe mines outside of Kasese, has been largely defunct since the early 1980s due to the instability caused by the Bush War.

[15] Ethnic demographic patterns change little over the period I am studying. For example, the ELF score of Ugandan counties using the 1991 and 2002 censuses is correlated at 0.90.

[16] ELF scores are based on a decreasing transformation of the Herfindahl Index, which is calculated as follows: Given a population composed of $N \geq 2$ different ethnic groups, let p_n be the proportion of the population comprised by group p. The ELF index value is then calculated by: $1 - \sum_{n=1}^{N} p_n^2$. Data for the census was collected by the government of Uganda in January 1991.

respondents to specify their "tribe." Tribes – a term I take to be synon-ymous with ethnic groups – are arguably the most politically salient identity-based groups in Uganda.[17] An individual's tribe in Uganda, as in much of Africa, also conveys regional information about that indivi-dual's family's home area within Uganda, where that tribe predominates. Therefore, while for the remainder of the book I refer often to a person's "ethnicity" or "ethnic group," in Uganda this ethnic identity also conveys linguistic and regional affiliations. A second measure of ethnic demogra-phy – the share of a county's total population that is comprised by the largest ethno-linguistic group in that county – is almost perfectly (nega-tively) correlated with ELF.[18] Thus, I show results solely using ELF. Contrary to the theory in Chapter 2, which expects no relationship between initial rebel group launch and ethnic demography, existing work expects that more homogeneous areas will be more likely to experi-ence rebel group launch.[19]

I measured *exclusion* from the central government using Stefan Lindemann's data for the ethnic composition of Uganda's cabinet in 1988. First, I developed an exclusion score for each Ugandan ethnic group by subtracting the ethnic group's share of Uganda's total popula-tion from its share of the cabinet.[20] I then developed exclusion scores for each county according to a weighted average based on the ethnic compo-sition of each county.[21] Negative scores indicate "under-representation" in the cabinet – meaning that on average the ethnic groups in a given

[17] I use the term "ethno-linguistic" fractionalization because one's self-identified tribe conveys information about both ethnic identity (a person's extended kinship network) and that person's language; each tribe in Uganda typically speaks a distinct language or dialect. Some tribes' languages in Uganda are more similar to one another than others; some are mutually intelligible, while others are part of entirely distinct language families, e.g. Bantu vs. Nilotic. I know of no systematic measure of the extent of these differences.
[18] The correlation coefficient for these variables is –0.98.
[19] While the expected relationship in the country-level civil war literature was that more diverse countries would be more likely to have warfare due to interethnic struggles over central power, the recent, subnational literature on conflict onset has generally hypothe-sized that locally concentrated ethnic groups, or areas that are more ethnically homo-geneous, are more likely to rebel.
[20] Lindemann 2011, 397–400.
[21] The average proportion of the largest ethnic group in a Ugandan county is 0.74, with a standard deviation of 0.20. In other words, many Ugandan counties are quite diverse. Given that most grievance-based theories assume a widespread mobilization, a weighted average of the exclusion of all ethnic groups present in a given county appears to be the best county-level proxy for the theoretical concept. In the next section of this chapter, I revisit the possibility of a group-level relationship (following Cederman, Wimmer, and Min 2010).

county are underrepresented – and positive scores indicate "over-representation." The distribution of this measure, however, is left-skewed because the Baganda are quite overrepresented – the median exclusion score for ethnic groups is –0.75, and while the lower bound of the range is –3.4, the Baganda (at the upper bound) score is 17.4. To deal with this issue, I also code a trichotomous version of ethnic cabinet representation that takes "0" if the ethnic group is underrepresented, with a score below –1, a "1" if it is not substantially over- or underrepresented, with scores between –1 and 1, and "2" if it scores above 1. Then, I again associate these ethnic cabinet representation scores with counties using a weighted average based on each county's ethnic composition. For both of these measures of exclusion, most existing theories posit that more underrepresented areas will be more likely to rebel.

To capture the feasibility of rebellion, I follow major findings in the civil conflict literature in measuring variation in terrain, distance from international borders, local development, and local state capacity. To capture variation in *terrain* that may facilitate rebel viability, I first generated an elevation variable that measures the difference between the highest and lowest point in a county, using data compiled by the US Geological Survey.[22] I also constructed a measure of forest cover, measuring the percentage of each county that has natural (nonagricultural) vegetation, such as trees and shrubs, using data from the UN Food and Agriculture Organization's (FAO) Africover project.[23] As an additional measure, and because population density is plausibly lower in thickly forested or otherwise "rough" areas that may be favorable for rebellion, I also compiled a population density variable (logged) using the complete

---

[22] I constructed the variable using ArcGIS. The data source is Digital Elevation Models, available at http://srtm.usgs.gov/index.php, accessed August 23, 2010. I also reran the analysis instead using an alternative measure I constructed using the same data source that measures the highest point in the county in which the rebels formed, and found a substantively and statistically similar result.

[23] I constructed the variable using ArcGIS. Africover uses satellite remote sensing to generate land cover maps. This data is from 2000 and 2001 images of Uganda and is available at www.africover.org/aggregation.htm, accessed August 24, 2011. The UN FAO estimates that between 1990 and 2000, net deforestation was occurring in Uganda at an annual rate of –2.0 percent (UN Food and Agriculture Organization 2005, 134). The average net deforestation rate for all African countries during that period was –0.8 percent. Therefore, while 2000/1 data is not an ideal measure of forest cover in Uganda in the late 1980s and 1990s, the extent of forest cover at least did not dramatically change over that period. Unfortunately, there is no available data that I know of that would allow me to measure whether deforestation occurred at much higher rates in some areas of the country than others.

1991 census, measuring the number of people per square kilometer. The expected relationship, based on prior work, is that areas that are more mountainous (greater difference in elevation), more forested, or less populous will be more likely to experience rebel group launch.[24]

To examine the importance of access to *international borders* with states that may be advantageous for rebels who can use the cross-border area as a fallback option, I measure the distance (as a straight line, logged) from the centroid of the county to the closest international border using ArcGIS. As a second measure, in order to capture the possibility that what matters to nascent rebels is having direct access to an international border, rather than relative proximity, I create a binary variable to indicate whether or not a county is on an international border.[25] The expected relationship, based on prior theories, is that the closer a county is to an international border (or if it is contiguous with a border), the more likely it is to experience rebel group launch.

To measure the extent of local *development* in a given area, I use a county-level 1992 measure of the percentage of a county's population living below the poverty line,[26] obtained from the Ugandan Bureau of Statistics report, "Where Are the Poor? Mapping Patterns of Well-Being in Uganda."[27] I also use a measure of the poverty gap, which measures how far (as a percentage) below the poverty line is the average consumption of poor people (those living below the poverty line), providing insight into how deep poverty is in a given county. However, this measure is almost perfectly correlated (0.96) with the former poverty line measure, and thus the results of the below analyses are quite similar using either measure.

---

[24] These measures are not highly correlated: The correlation between forest cover and elevation range (distance between highest and lowest point) is 0.41; the correlation between forest cover and maximum elevation is 0.37; the correlation between population density and elevation range is −0.13; the correlation between forest and population density is −0.44. See also the correlation matrix in Appendix B.

[25] This measure is somewhat correlated with the distance from the capital measure; the correlation between the two measures is −0.66. Based on my interviews, I learned that there were weakly governed areas across all of Uganda's borders, so for simplicity I treated all borders equally. For example, in the late 1980s and early 1990s, eastern Ugandan rebel groups viewed western Kenya as a fallback option. I only considered land borders – I did not count lakes as international borders since large bodies of water do not offer rebels an appealing fallback option, and I did not learn of any cases of rebel groups hiding in, or smuggling weapons via, boats.

[26] The poverty line used is the official one adopted by the government of Uganda, according to the methodology in Ravallion 1994. For basic information about Uganda's poverty line, see Emwanu et al. 2003, 13.

[27] Emwanu et al. 2003.

I show only results for the poverty line measure in what follows. While there are several theoretical perspectives on why poverty influences conflict onset, all would expect a positive relationship between poverty and rebel initiation.

These poverty measures are based on county-level estimates of household consumption information collected in Uganda's 1992 Integrated Household Survey, combined with information from Uganda's 1991 census.[28] These measures provide the best available estimates of poverty in Uganda's counties in the early 1990s. One potential problem with this measure is that several rebel groups formed prior to 1992 and local consumption is likely highly responsive to violence; but unfortunately, reliable local economic welfare data on 1980s Uganda does not exist. This measure will capture any increases in poverty that occurred as a result of violence in areas where rebels formed prior to 1992, therefore biasing results in favor of finding a stronger relationship between poverty and rebel formation than the "true" relationship.

Following Collier and Hoeffler (2004) and others (e.g. Do and Iyer 2010; Thyne 2006; Walter 2004), I also compiled county-level literacy rates using the 1991 Uganda census. Literacy rates are an alternative proxy for living conditions or the opportunity cost of participating in rebellion.[29] The correlation between percentage of people living below the poverty line and literacy is −0.57. Most existing theories expect that in areas with higher literacy rates, individuals will be less likely to rebel, because of the higher opportunity costs of rebelling implied by a literate, and thus employable, population.

To measure potential spatial variation in *state strength*, I create a binary variable measuring whether or not the county was under NRM control during the Bush War. Because the NRM controlled some parts of

---

[28] This estimation (rather than a direct poverty measure from the household survey) is necessary because the household survey, which is the only one conducted in the early 1990s in Uganda, was designed to be representative only at a higher level (regions). The results of the survey are therefore not representative at the county level (there are 4 regions and 163 counties in Uganda). However, using Small Area Estimation techniques with information from variables that were directly measured in both the household survey and the census, the Ugandan Bureau of Statistics (in collaboration with the International Livestock Research Institute) generated the estimates of county-level poverty I use here. For more information about how this measure was compiled, see Emwanu et al. Ibid., especially Appendix 1, and Okwi et al. (2003).

[29] I note that some analyses, such as Thyne (2006), interpret the significance, and negative effect, of educational attainment variables in models of civil war onset not as evidence of opportunity costs, but rather that a lack of education generates grievances and thus motivates people to rebel.

central and western Uganda during the Bush War and developed local political institutions in the areas it controlled, the state may plausibly have had higher capacity to respond to potential threats in those areas. Additionally, because the capital, Kampala, was the institutional center of the state and the military when the first anti-NRM rebel group formed in August 1986, I create a second measure of state capacity: logged distance from the capital. The distance is measured (using ArcGIS) as a straight line from the centroid of each county to the center of Kampala. Most extant theories would expect that the further a county is from Kampala, the more likely it is to have a rebel group form there.

To control for possible regional effects, I also include regional dummies in all model specifications. I cluster standard errors by region.

Table 4.1 displays the results of logistic regression analyses with robust standard errors clustered by region. The main finding of this exercise is that there is no strong, statistically significant pattern that is consistent with prior theories of conflict onset – with the exception that rebel groups are more likely to launch in counties that are on an international border.[30] An additional finding is that there is some evidence for a *positive* relationship between literacy and rebel group launch, which is contrary to common theoretical expectations.

Model 1 shows the full model, which includes measures for each of the variables discussed earlier. I include all measures of the terrain and development variables in the full model since they measure different types of rough terrain, and the measures are not highly correlated.[31] I only include one measure of proximity to international borders, state capacity, and exclusion in the full model since in these cases the alternative measures capture a similar concept. Models 2 and 3 check whether the results of the full model hold when using alternative measures of these three variables. Literacy is significant and positive in all models, although only at the 5 or 10 percent levels,

---

[30] As further evidence of a lack of a clear relationship between these variables and rebel group launch, none of these variables are statistically significantly related to rebel launch (at the 10 percent level) in bivariate logistic regression analysis, with the exception of the binary variable which indicated whether a county is on an international border, which is significant at the 1 percent level.

[31] Furthermore, the results do not substantially change, and none of the terrain variables become statistically significant, when including just one of them in any model. I discuss the development measures at greater length in the text and examine their relationship in models 6 and 7. Multicollinearity does not appear to be a major problem; in addition to a lack of strong bivariate correlations, the covariates do not appear to be linearly related to one another. For model 1, the tolerance scores of all of the covariates are all well above 0.1; the lowest tolerance score is 0.32.

TABLE 4.1 *Correlates of rebel launch in Uganda (county level)*

	1	2	3	4	5	6	7
MOTIVATION							
Exclusion							
Cabinet rep.	0.02		0.05				
	(0.20)		(0.15)				
Cabinet rep. 2		−0.40					
		(0.78)					
Ethnic Demography							
ELF	0.24	0.21	0.58	0.37	−0.23	−0.23	0.47
	(1.86)	(1.92)	(1.60)	(1.60)	(1.43)	(1.43)	(1.29)
FEASIBILITY							
Terrain							
Elevation (km)	0.54	0.53	0.46	0.42	0.32	0.32	0.45
	(0.71)	(0.58)	(0.75)	(0.65)	(0.67)	(0.67)	(0.70)
Forest	−0.02	−0.02	−0.01	−0.02	−0.02**	−0.02**	−0.01
	(0.01)	(0.01)	(0.01)	(0.01)	(0.01)	(0.01)	(0.01)
Population density (log)	−0.25	−0.24	−0.27**	−0.13	−0.13	−0.13	−0.30**
	(0.19)	(0.24)	(0.09)	(0.21)	(0.14)	(0.10)	(0.10)
International Borders							
Distance to border (m) (log)	−0.47	−0.63		−0.34			
	(0.36)	(0.45)		(0.22)			
Contiguous with border			1.55**		1.37**	1.36**	1.65**
			(0.59)		(0.51)	(0.46)	(0.54)
Development							
Poverty line	0.03	0.03	0.02			0.00	
	(0.04)	(0.04)	(0.04)			(0.03)	
Literacy	0.06*	0.06†	0.06**				0.06**
	(0.03)	(0.03)	(0.02)				(0.02)
State Capacity							
Prior NRM institutions	−0.58	−0.69		−0.71			
	(0.50)	(0.81)		(0.49)			
Distance to Kampala (m) (log)			−0.06		−0.10	−0.11	0.02
			(0.10)		(0.04)	(0.11)	(0.04)
Region dummies	X	X	X	X	X	X	X
N	161	161	161	161	161	161	161

DV is a dichotomous measure of whether a rebel group committed their first attack in the county.

All models estimated using logistic regression with robust standard errors, clustered by region (central, northern, western, eastern), reported in parentheses.
† $p < 0.10$, * $p < 0.05$, ** $p < 0.01$

and its substantive effect is not large; for example, in a simulation using model 3, holding all other covariates at their means and increasing the literacy variable from its 25th percentile to its 75th percentile raises the likelihood of rebel group formation by 4.6 percentage points. Contiguity with an international border is significant in model 3 and has a large substantive effect; in a simulation using model 3, holding all covariates at their means while changing the contiguous border variable from zero to one yields a 14.6 percentage point increase in the predicted probability of a rebellion occurring in that county.

In models 1, 2, and 3, all measures of ethnic demography and exclusion, terrain, and state strength are insignificant in all models, with the exception of population density's significance in model 3 only. Most of the variables do, however, take the sign anticipated by existing theories: conditional on the other variables, ELF is negatively related to rebel formation; change in elevation is positively related; population density is negatively related; measures of state strength are negatively related; distance to international borders is negatively related; and poverty is positively related. One exception is percentage of forested area, which we would expect to be positively related to rebel group formation but comes through here as negatively related – however, the substantive influence of this negative relationship is quite small.

Another exception in which a variable does not take the expected sign is the first measure of ethnic exclusion, for which counties are coded according to a weighted average of their ethnic composition, based on each ethnic group's over- or underrepresentation in the cabinet. Excluded groups take negative values. The coefficient on this covariate is positive, contradicting conventional wisdom that less-excluded groups would be less likely to rebel. This result is likely due to the influence of the counties with a large portion of Baganda, who are much more overrepresented than any other group is; three of the sixteen rebel groups formed in majority-Baganda areas. Comparing model 1 and model 2 makes this clear; the coefficient on exclusion switches signs when substituting the original exclusion measure for the second measure, which dampens the influence of the Baganda's extreme overrepresentation by making extent of ethnic exclusion a categorical (three-category) variable.

Models 4 and 5 address the possibility that poverty, education, and exclusion are influenced by some of the other factors which also have a direct influence on rebel group formation, and thus those other factors' relationship with rebel formation would be attenuated or exaggerated in models 1, 2, and 3. For example, it is possible that being closer to the capital, or having been occupied by the NRM during the Bush War, would make it less likely that a county would be poorer, less educated, or under-represented in the cabinet. This might be the case if we believe, for example, that employment and educational opportunities are positively correlated with proximity to the prior presence of NRM local institutions, and if areas more proximate to the capital or that had an NRM presence prior to 1986 are better able to pressure the NRM governments into including their representatives in the cabinet. If these conjectures are correct, then models that include, for example, both distance from Kampala and exclusion from the cabinet covariates would dampen (bias downward) the effect of distance from Kampala on rebel group formation. Comparing model 4 with model 2, and model 5 with model 3, respectively, shows that the absolute value of the magnitude of coefficients increases, so the above intuition may be correct.

In model 6, I probe the influence of poverty and literacy, since it is plausible that literacy has a direct influence on both poverty and rebel formation, including it along with poverty may attenuate the effect of the poverty variable. In model 7, I check the possibility that poverty is attenuating the coefficient on literacy. However, in models 6 and 7 the substantive and statistical significance of the variables changes little from prior models.[32]

In sum, the incidence of initial rebel group launch in Uganda appears to be rather idiosyncratic, or at least its spatial distribution is not consistent with most existing explanations. An exception is that this analysis finds that counties that are contiguous with an international border are more likely to experience rebel group formation – or at least to have a new rebel group launch its first attack there – than those that are not contiguous with a border. This finding, combined with the lack of significance of the distance to a border measure, suggests that would-be rebels calculate that being very close to a border might make the risks of attempting rebellion worthwhile, since they can easily escape across the border if the government identifies them as aspiring rebel leaders in the initial phases. Indeed, rebel groups that formed in Uganda were generally more enduring if launched near a border; for example, groups like the UNRF II never maintained a base on Ugandan territory and never became viable, but existed for five years due to their ability to easily slip across the border to weakly governed areas of Sudan.

---

[32] For both models 6 and 7, these results remain substantively and statistically similar when including either measure of exclusion.

Another finding of note, although the relationship is not particularly strong or certain, is that literacy is positively related to rebel group formation. This finding contradicts most existing explanations, which consider literacy to be a proxy for development and to indicate individuals' opportunity costs for participating in rebellion.[33] As discussed in Chapter 3, most nascent rebel leaders were reasonably well educated. This implies that rather than proxying for the opportunity costs of rebellion, higher local levels of literacy may indicate a concentration of people who have higher capacity for taking on the complex, risky enterprise of forming a rebellion.

This analysis generally supports a contention of the theory from Chapter 2: rebel groups' location of initial formation is difficult to predict at the subnational level, since it is due to largely idiosyncratic, individual-level factors. Also, for the purposes of the next chapter, the main potential issue that these findings raise is the possibility that patterns affecting the area where rebels initially launch could influence the subsequent stages when they attempt to become viable – that is, if certain types of rebel groups are more or less likely to form on borders or with a more literate population, then that difference in type could be the reason why only some rebel groups become viable. I address this possibility with a paired comparison research design in Chapter 5, which helps to hold such factors constant.

4.2 DO EXCLUDED ETHNIC GROUPS REBEL?

While the regression analyses in the prior section did not find a relationship between ethnic group exclusion and rebellion launch at the county level, given the prominence and importance of works using *group-level* data that find evidence for this association, it is worth revisiting its potential relevance to Uganda with group-level data here.

To identify ethnic groups in Uganda, I use all ethnic groups listed in the 1991 Ugandan census that constituted at least 1 percent of the Ugandan population. This approach is consistent with Fearon's (2003) approach to measuring socially relevant ethnic groups in sub-Saharan Africa. Although this means that several small ethnic groups are included, given that several rebel leaders were members of small ethnic groups and that

---

[33] One exception to this conventional interpretation is Sambanis (2004a, 264), who argues that education could be positively associated with war onset, particularly since nationalism is often taught in schools.

individuals from small ethnic groups held positions in the cabinet, I see no
compelling reason to exclude them. In addition, to avoid post hoc, subjective coding of whether groups were excluded from power – susceptible
to conflation with distrustful actions that arise out of violence – I use
a direct, quantitative measure of a given group's proportion of the total
1988 cabinet seats. This approach to determining which groups to include
and measuring their exclusion is different from that of the Minorities at
Risk Project and the Ethnic Power Relations data family; I revisit why my
data differs, and the broader implications for the study of ethnicity and
conflict onset, in Chapter 7.

I operationalize whether a group launched a rebellion by measuring
whether or not the group had a leader in the initial core of the rebel group.
This approach is necessitated by the fact, posited in the theory and
supported in Chapter 3, that these rebel groups started as very small
groups, not as movements of already-mobilized groups. That descriptive
finding alone indicates a mismatch with those who have articulated group-
level theories and actual processes of rebellion initiation, at least in
Uganda. Still, it is worth examining the relationship of the ethnic groups
of the initial rebel leaders and those groups' level of exclusion. The
resulting data is displayed in Table 4.2, with groups listed in ascending
order by status, measured as the difference between a group's population
share and its share of cabinet seats.

The most revealing column of Table 4.2 is the "Status" column; *no
group appears to be markedly underrepresented* in the NRM's 1988
cabinet – measured as the difference between a group's population share
and its share of cabinet seats. Therefore, evidence is rather weak for the
conventional wisdom that northern Ugandan ethnic groups were underrepresented in the central government when the LRA and other rebellions
initially formed; the margin by which northern groups were underrepresented is quite small. Furthermore, no group is overwhelmingly overrepresented except for the Baganda, which – contrary to expectations of
a link between exclusion and rebellion – served as the ethnic base of three
distinct attempted rebellions.

An additional pattern evident in Table 4.2 is that there is no clear
positive relationship between group status and initiating a rebellion.
Although it is of course difficult to identify general relationships with
so few observations, these data indicate that a weak relationship, if any,
existed between exclusion from the cabinet and rebellion in Uganda. Of
course, there is a crucial difference between actual exclusion and *perceived* exclusion. Consistent with this book's core theoretical claims, for

TABLE 4.2 *Ethnic group cabinet representation and rebellion in Uganda*

Ethnic group (All groups listed in 1991 census with more than 1% of the population)	Population* share (% of total population)	Representation* (% of cabinet seats in 1988)	Status (Difference between representation and population share)	Rebelled? (Had a leader in a rebel group)
Banyankole/ Bahima	9.9	6.5	−3.4	Y
Iteso	6.0	3.2	−2.8	Y
Langi	5.9	3.2	−2.7	Y
Alur/Jonam	2.4	0	−2.4	N
Bakonjo	2.2	0	−2.2	Y
Karimojong/ Dodoth/ Tepeth/Suk	2.1	0	−2.1	N
Basoga	8.2	6.5	−1.7	N
Bagwere	1.7	0	−1.7	N
Banyole	1.4	0	−1.4	N
Acholi/Labwor	4.4	3.2	−1.2	Y
Lugbara/Aringa	3.5	3.2	−0.3	Y
Banyoro/Bagungu	3.0	3.2	+0.2	N
Batoro/Batuku/ Basongora	2.9	3.2	+0.3	N
Banyarwanda	2.0	3.2	+1.2	N
Bakiga	8.3	9.7	+1.4	N
Badama/ Japadhola	1.5	3.2	+1.7	Y
Bagisu/Bamasaba	4.5	6.5	+2	N
Samia	1.1	3.2	+2.1	Y
Madi	1.1	3.3	+2.2	N
Baganda	18.1	35.5	+17.4	Y

Source: Representation data comes from Lindemann 2011, table 2; population data comes from the 1991 Uganda census; rebellion data comes from a variety of sources, primarily interviews with Ugandan government officials and former rebels.
* These columns total to 90 and 97 percent, respectively, and are less than 100 because of the groups that constitute less than 1 percent of the population, which are not shown here.

which I show evidence in Chapter 5, it is possible that in homogeneous areas rebels are more successful at generating perceptions that favor nascent rebels. I revisit the importance of this finding to the study on conflict onset, including contrasting my evidence and findings from Uganda with those of Cederman, Wimmer, and Min's (2010) ground-breaking study, in a section in Chapter 7 on disentangling the role of ethnicity in conflict onset.

To those familiar with Ugandan history, the data in Table 4.2 about the Acholi may be especially striking. The Acholi have played a central role in Ugandan history due to their dominance (along with the Langi) in the military in several pre-Museveni governments, and their tragic suffering for almost two decades due to the LRA conflict. Their prominence in Ugandan history has greatly outmatched their relative population size; they are about 5 percent of Uganda's population. Furthermore, while some Acholi have voiced disappointment or outrage at grave problems with the NRA's counterinsurgency response at points of the LRA conflict, we see here that at the outset of the LRA rebellion, the Acholi people were not dramatically underrepresented in the central government. Human rights reporting from this period notes that the local population in northern Uganda initially welcomed the NRA when they first arrived after seizing power.[34]

A key takeaway of this evidence is that the Acholi were not, objectively, excluded from the central government when the LRA (and other Acholi-based rebels) formed. To the extent that grievances propelled armed conflict in this ethno-region, it was more likely due to people's *perceptions* of exclusion, or their interpretations of what early NRM actions – such as calling members of the prior national military (the Uganda National Liberation Army (UNLA)) back to their barracks after they had fled[35] – meant for their group's future treatment. In my view, the uncertainty that characterized this period presented an opportunity for rebel entrepreneurs to manipulate these perceptions. I take this up again in the case studies presented in Chapter 5 – and address the implications for the government's behavior in Chapter 6, and for scholars and policymakers in Chapter 7.

---

[34] Amnesty International 1989, 24.
[35] See, for example, Day 2011 for an interpretation of how the UPDA rebels used this event to generate and amplify "status-reversal grievances" among the Acholi toward the new NRM government.

4.3 USING VIOLENCE DURING NASCENT INSURGENCY

I now turn to examining how rebels used violence in the initial stages – after bringing together their small, initial membership core, but prior to maintaining a base and developing substantial coercive capacity. Because groups that did not become viable were often "nipped in the bud" before committing more than a small handful of attacks, only the four groups that did become viable (ADF, Holy Spirit Movement (HSM), LRA, and UPA) present an opportunity to examine these arguments. Because among these four groups I was able to collect the most detailed and reliable information about the UPA rebellion, the following analysis centers primarily on them. I also briefly describe the LRA's early uses of violence – a challenging case for the arguments here, because it is known for its extreme violence and indifference to civilians' well-being.

In addition to extensive interview evidence, in the pages below I also make use of a complete set of newspaper articles on armed conflict in Uganda since February 1986, which I collected from newspaper archives in Uganda and the US Library of Congress. These articles, like all newspaper articles, suffer from likely problems of undercounting violent events – especially in the earliest stages of conflict, when armed groups' existence has not yet been noticed by the state or news organizations. In many cases, articles attributed violent events to unnamed armed groups or "bandits." I am able to mitigate some of these problems with knowledge from interviews about which rebels operated when in which areas – and thus can attribute some accounts of violence by unnamed rebels to specific groups. Still, given known biases of newspaper articles on armed conflict,[36] the following figures should be taken as general indications of trends in violence rather than precise quantities.

4.3.1 Launching Rebellion in Eastern Uganda: The Uganda People's Army

The UPA rebellion lasted only from 1987 to 1992, but during those years it presented a fierce challenge to the Ugandan government. At its height in 1990, the UPA had well over 1,000 men (up to 1,500 by one estimate), organized into eight brigades covering different portions of the Teso region in eastern Uganda, an area of approximately 4,300 square

---

[36] See e.g. Hug 2003.

kilometers.[37] According to one news source, about 13,000 people were displaced over the course of the UPA conflict.[38] The UPA had at least two bases on Ugandan soil, each of which operated freely without significant challenge from the government for approximately six months. Between late 1987 and 1989, numerous villages in the Teso region were under contested control, with the government decisively controlling only the urban areas. After that time, the conflict continued, but the group operated using mobile forces, losing ground to the government until several leaders were captured or surrendered in 1991. A negotiated settlement was reached in 1992.

The group was conceived in December 1986 when two individuals from Teso who had served as military and police commanders for the Obote regime – respectively, Francis "Hitler" Eregu and Nathan Okurut – began to discuss the possibility of forming an armed rebel group. Eregu had been the leader of the Training and Special Operations unit of Obote's military during the Bush War, and had also been a commander of the forces that fought and ousted Amin. Okurut had been commander of the Special Forces Police College in Naguru, Kampala. Both men came from the Teso region: Eregu from Arapai subcounty of Soroti district, and Okurut from Gweri subcounty in Soroti county. They had previously considered targeting the government of General Tito Okello after his coup d'etat in July 1985 that ousted the UPC government of former president Milton Obote, who the vast majority of Teso had supported. But after Museveni seized power from Okello six months after Okello's coup, in January 1986, they launched a rebellion against the new NRM regime.

Soon after these December 1986 conversations, Eregu and Okurut reached out to and joined with a handful of men who would form the Command of the UPA.[39] The initial priorities of these aspiring rebel commanders were to identify a core group of military leaders that would be responsible for different areas of Teso, and, crucially, to set up intelligence networks across a dispersed area. Former UPA leaders

---

[37] Interview with UPA commander, Soroti, July 2008, confirmed by lead UPDF intelligence officer during that insurgency.

[38] "Uganda offers rebels some carrots – and lots of stick." *Africa Analysis*, March 31, 1989. However, several interviewees agreed that most people who were displaced returned to their original villages in the years after the war.

[39] Peter Otai, former minister of defense for Obote, became the "political spokesman" for the group, and his nephew Sam Otai became Eregu's deputy. Others in the initial leadership core were traders or farmers.

reported that setting up these networks for future use trumped other priorities. The people who they quietly sought out to join these networks were often relatives or former colleagues from a given area to oversee intelligence collection in that area.[40] With respect to recruiting this core of initial leaders and intelligence operatives, one of the UPA founders said, "I needed people I knew and who were loyal ... and who had good combat skills. I was thinking through: How can we be sure that the rebellion won't be a disaster? We needed quality people with commitment ... We needed to be sure our intel was right."[41] He also stressed the slow, careful nature of this effort.

In order to build this information network, this initial core of leaders contacted individuals in most villages in the areas close to Gweri – Okurut's home subcounty, in which the group would establish its first base – with the purpose of receiving and disseminating information from those areas. One leader explained:

> We started with the most trusted people ... The first group had to be cleared with me ... It was a network of moles. Most of them had a personal understanding with me ... I would tell one of them: "Make sure you watch [another one of the initial moles]. Be sure they don't let us down."

One of the individuals tasked with setting up the UPA intelligence network in Gweri subcounty explained that the UPA's information network included two types of intelligence officers who were located throughout the subcounty: those whose role in the rebellion was known to and shared openly with the villagers, and those whose affiliation with and work for the UPA was conducted secretly. Villagers who had useful information were expected to provide it to the publicly recognized intelligence officers, while the secret officer watched both the behavior of the public and that of the known intelligence officer in the area. The identity of the covert officer was not known to the public officer. The intelligence officer who provided this information was confident that this system had been effective in enabling the rebels to manage potential threats from the civilian population. He said that these people "told us who was good, and who was bad."[42] This system of spies was then slowly spread across much of Teso.

---

[40] Interview with former UPA leader, Soroti town, July 2008.
[41] Interview with former UPA leader, Soroti town, July 2008.
[42] Interview with former UPA intelligence officer, Soroti county, Soroti district, February 2011.

In addition to collecting information for the rebels, these information officers would also convey information about the rebels directly to the people – the UPA did not make use of intermediaries such as traditional clan leaders.[43] In selecting these information officers for the area around Gweri, this intelligence officer said that about half were former business contacts – he had been a cattle trader – and the other half were his relatives.[44] Just as the military commanders had not wanted to expand the military leadership too quickly, this intelligence officer said, "We used the few we trusted most first. We didn't want to enlarge too fast." A different UPA intelligence officer explained that different commanders could influence different communities, based on their familial connections to those communities.[45]

The fledgling rebellion pursued these goals throughout January and February 1987. During this period, Eregu and Okurut could meet in broad daylight just a few kilometers outside of Soroti town because there was little National Resistance Army (NRA) presence in the area, and because local civilians did not yet know what they were planning. To a passerby, they would have simply appeared to be two men sitting under a tree and chatting.

4.3.2 UPA Violence against the State

The first acts of violence that the UPA committed occurred on January 20, 1987. That day, the UPA conducted two simultaneous attacks targeting NRA officers who guarded two railway stations.[46] One UPA leader stated that a small number of NRA deaths occurred in these attacks and that the UPA collected about eleven guns during the operation. The UPA did not publicly claim credit for these attacks, and Ugandan newspapers did not cover them. Underscoring the ambiguity that surrounds the early steps of rebel group formation even in the historical record, even detailed qualitative accounts (e.g. Jones 2008) as well as Ugandan newspapers instead

---

[43] Interview with former UPA intelligence officer, Soroti county, Soroti district, February 2011. Corroborated by several interviews with civilians, Soroti county, Soroti district, February 2011.

[44] Indeed, the three civilians I interviewed who confided that they had served as UPA intelligence officers explained that they had been recruited by relatives (interview, civilian, Mukura subcounty, Kumi district, April 2009).

[45] Interview with former UPA intelligence officer, Soroti municipality, Soroti district, March 2009.

[46] One station was in Kaibermaido (Lwalwa) and the other was in Soroti (Amurgaru).

cite February 1987 as the date of the UPA's first attack. These likely refer to several small UPA attacks that occurred at dawn on February 19, 1987. These attacks were similarly modest in ambition, targeting a few military officers on the outskirts of the NRA's barracks, as well as the few who were guarding Soroti's flying school.

According to former UPA leader interviewees, these initial attacks were designed specifically to avoid attracting substantial attention. At this point, the rebels were not seeking to engage in open confrontation with the government forces, but were rather "testing the enemy," gaining information about their military strength and resolve, and "grooming units" to later face the NRA in more substantial battles. The purpose of these initial attacks, according to one leader, was to wait and to observe the reaction of the government. "We wanted to test the ground and see what would they [the government] do," he explained. At that time, very few people knew about the rebellion, and the rebels did not publicly claim credit for the attack, nor did they refer to themselves by the name "Uganda People's Army," or any name, for that matter.[47] The UPA was not named in Ugandan newspapers until nearly six months later.

Immediately following these initial attacks, UPA leaders made an effort to control the narrative about the attacks among civilians. As one leader noted, "The civilian population is more important than guns or manpower."[48] Another leader explained that after the initial attacks, "The next step was to draw the attention of the public ... The message [that a new rebel group had formed] had spread everywhere." Yet another explained, "This attack [in February 1987] showed [the local people] we were serious ... everyone [in the area of the attacks] now knew: there's a rebellion in Teso."[49] Similarly, yet another former UPA leader said: "We needed to draw the attention of the public, and get the message spread [throughout Teso] that we were a serious group ... Soon, everyone knew."[50]

In spreading information through the civilian population, the rebels clearly sought to persuade local civilians that they were serious, capable fighters who would serve the community well. "We needed to show that we were not just thugs," one former leader said. "We needed to sell our image."[51] Another stated: "It is important to create the impression of

---

[47] Interview with former UPA leader, Soroti town, June 2009.
[48] Interview with former UPA leader, Amuria district, July 2009.
[49] Interview with former UPA leader, Soroti town, July 2008.
[50] Interview with former UPA leader, Soroti town, June 2009.
[51] Interview with former UPA leader, Soroti town, June 2009.

strength."[52] Yet another explained that when starting a rebel group, "You are most careful not to antagonize the locals ... Your own people should know you as a good boy."[53]

One emphasized the importance of displaying military strength, especially in the earliest stages of the rebellion, saying, "It's good for people to see government soldiers killed by rebels." The UPA also employed other strategies to ensure that the local civilians would believe in their powers. One commander told me that while he did not believe in witchcraft, he allowed UPA leaders to participate in public ceremonies using a type of animal witchcraft involving a ram known as "ausi" as a means to "boost morale" of the civilian population. When asked why he allowed this tactic to be used if he did not believe in it, he shrugged and replied: "It was something the people enjoyed believing in."[54]

After seeing that the government did not have the capacity to identify who committed these attacks in early 1987, the UPA leaders resolved to slowly expand their fighting efforts. The series of attacks that the UPA committed over the following months had two goals: to score victories that would lend credibility to their cause as word spread about the rebellion and to acquire weapons and ammunition. With respect to the latter, doing so was necessary because they had started with only a modest quantity of both and because they did not have an external source of materiel.[55]

Increasing their coercive capacity was, naturally, also a concern; the UPA's tactics in these early years demonstrated that they aimed to minimize their casualties and use of their scarce ammunition. For example, they would identify a trench of NRA soldiers at night, and throw a single grenade into that trench, alarming the soldiers by its explosion. Then, the UPA would throw numerous pieces of fruit into the same trench. Upon being showered by what they assumed was a barrage of grenades, the NRA soldiers would scramble quickly out of the trench, often leaving behind some weaponry. Using this tactic, the UPA repeatedly gained weapons while sacrificing just one grenade.[56]

By June 1987, the UPA had succeeded in committing several small attacks and had gained weapons from attacking an NRA training camp

---

[52] Interview with former UPA intelligence officer, Soroti county, Soroti district, February 2011.
[53] Interview with former UPA leader, Kampala, July 2008.
[54] Interview with former UPA commander, Soroti town, Soroti.
[55] Interview with former UPA leader, Soroti town, June 2009.
[56] Interview with former UPA intelligence officer, June 2009.

in Serere.[57] It was around this time, according to a former UPA rebel leader, that "the government realized we were a serious rebellion. Before they thought: were we thieves or thugs?"[58] It was at this time – in summer of 1987 – that the UPA established an initial base in Gweri subcounty of Soroti county, not far from Okurut's home, in a forested area between a few villages. The primary aim, according to former UPA leaders who established the base, was to keep the base secret except to the immediate surrounding communities, and to use the base to train an initial core group of recruits. One of the leaders recounted: "At that stage, we did not want to control territory. Occupying an area is very difficult. We did not have enough supplies. It is too expensive."[59] He also stressed the risk of information leaks to the government during this fragile phase. Members of a focus group in one of the surrounding villages explained that while the nearby civilian population was aware of the rebel base, the government was not aware of the base for three or four months.[60] A UPA leader and government military officer confirmed this account.

The base allowed the UPA to begin training an initial cadre of troops, and, thus, thanks to the effective information networks they had established, secrecy about the base for several months allowed the UPA to develop substantial coercive capacity. It was in the following months, this leader explained, that the group became known as the UPA, and began initiating larger, more violent attacks. "Our quality had improved by then," a former UPA leader explained. This allowed the group to develop further, pulling off more frequent and larger attacks. A UPA commander reflected that the group's initial actions paid off: once "open war" began in early 1989, with several armed confrontations per month, the UPA was well prepared. The sporadic nature of this early violence, and the shift to more frequent attacks, are generally borne out in newspaper reporting in Uganda during this period, as shown in Figure 4.3.

As the violence of the Teso rebellion became more severe in 1989 and 1990, civilians took shelter in numerous IDP camps.[61] By mid-1991, the government began to make substantial military gains against the rebels.

---

[57] This interviewee also said that 200 NRA soldiers and "a few" UPA soldiers were killed in the assault.

[58] Interview with former UPA rebel leader, Soroti, January 2011.

[59] Interview with former UPA leader, Soroti town, Soroti county, February 2011.

[60] Focus group, Gweri subcounty, Soroti district, April 2009. A former UPA rebel leader also recounted that the government did not learn about this base and seek to "flush it out" for at least three or four months.

[61] According to one local leader, there were eleven camps: ten in Kumi and one in Bukedea.

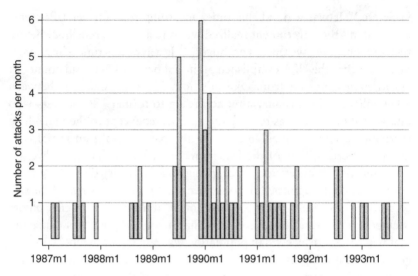

FIGURE 4.3 UPA anti-state violence
Data Source: Ugandan newspaper articles

The rebellion began drawing to a close after it suffered major setbacks in late 1991, when key agents were captured and the rebellion was running low on ammunition. Leaders negotiated a settlement with the government in 1992, although occasional violence continued at the hands of UPA rebel remnants who disagreed with the terms of the settlement.

4.3.3 Lack of Initial Violence against Civilians

When asked about rebel treatment of civilians in general, several civilians in interviews volunteered painful stories of suffering they had endured at the hands of rebels. However, when asked about how the rebels *first* approached them, before much violence had occurred, civilians almost unanimously reported a variant of the sentiment that "the rebels at first were good to us." In Teso, of the thirty-four civilians I interviewed, thirty-two (91 percent) agreed that the rebels were initially "good," not threatening or committing violence against them.[62] After I asked this question, numerous interviewees added, unprompted, that this changed once time

---

[62] Specifically, I asked in the structured portion of the interview: "When you think back to the start of the rebellion, before the violence between the UPA and the government became very severe, were the rebels bad, meaning threatening or violent to you – or were they good, approaching you in a good way?"

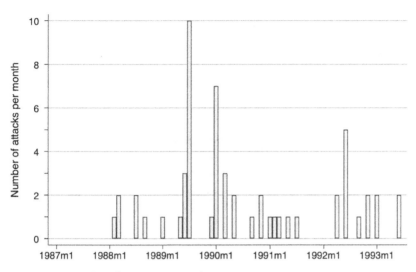

FIGURE 4.4 UPA violence against civilians (1987–1993)
Data Source: Ugandan newspaper articles

passed, with some volunteering as to how coercive the rebels became. Former rebels and local government officials corroborated this pattern.

This finding is quite striking, especially because it is widely accepted that the Uganda People's Army (UPA) became quite violent against civilians. As one civilian explained: "Once the rebellion was well underway, life was at the mercy of the rebels. If anything leaked, you don't survive. The government had not spent the time to build systems to reach the people."[63] Another civilian explained similarly about the UPA's recruitment process, "Initially, recruitment was voluntary – they wouldn't beat you if you refused them. Later, they became harsh."[64] A UPA leader corroborated these accounts about the evolution of their treatment of civilians with surprising frankness. He said, "We started with our own people, and tell them [the rebellion] is for their benefit … Anyone seen as being anti UPA gets punished. But that comes in later."[65] Indeed, when talking about 1989, when attacks and large-scale UPA-government violence were underway, he said: "We would execute people who provide information [to the government]."[66]

These patterns are also generally reflected in newspaper accounts of violence against civilians during the UPA rebellion. As Figure 4.4 shows,

[63] Interview with former UPA intelligence officer 1, Soroti, January 2011.
[64] Interview with civilian, Mukura subcounty, Kumi district, December 2009.
[65] Interview with former UPA leader, Soroti county, Soroti district, January 2011.
[66] Interview with former UPA leader, Soroti county, Soroti district, January 2011.

violence against civilians was quite limited in the initial year of the rebellion, increasing substantially in the second half of 1988 and 1989, once the war was well underway.

Ultimately, civilian information leaks to the government led to the UPA's demise. For example, one former government intelligence officer who was from Teso and served there during the rebellion said, "People were so cooperative at first in gathering intelligence for the rebels ... but then things changed ... hope subsided."[67] Rebel leaders also agreed that information leaks ended their insurgency, leading to informational gains for the government that resulted in military gains for them, ultimately compelling key rebel leaders to negotiate their surrender.

4.3.4 Early Uses of Violence by the Lord's Resistance Army

Even beyond the UPA, looking at other rebel groups in Uganda, similar patterns are evident with respect to rebel violence against the government and civilians. Rather astonishingly, even the LRA – which went on to become notorious for its cruelty and extreme violence – engaged in more limited violence in its early years. The LRA began in the late 1980s as a small band that committed only sporadic, small-scale violence, but went on to commit horrific violence in Uganda starting in the mid-1990s until 2006, when it retreated to neighboring countries and ceased attacks on Ugandan soil. Over these nearly two decades, the LRA's cumulative violence in Uganda included abduction of tens of thousands of children, leading at one point to about 1.8 million people – roughly 90 percent of civilians in affected areas – displaced and living in camps rife with poverty and disease.[68] Several works have analyzed patterns of LRA violence,[69] but none have closely examined how the LRA used violence in its initial years.

The LRA began in what is today Atanga subcounty in western Pader district, in the Acholi region of northern Uganda, when soon after joining

---

[67] Former NRA intelligence officer during UPA rebellion, Soroti town, Soroti district, July 2008.

[68] Civil Society Organizations for Peace in Northern Uganda, "Counting the Cost: Twenty Years of War in Northern Uganda." February 2006. Note that estimates on numbers of abducted youth vary widely, with one estimate reaching more than 66,000. See J. Annan, C. Blattman, and R. Horton, 2006. The State of Youth and Youth Protection in Northern Uganda: Findings from the Survey of War-Affected Youth. Kampala: UNICEF Uganda.

[69] See especially Stanton 2016 and Wood 2014a.

the UPDA as an adviser, Kony broke away, deciding to form his own group.[70] The LRA and UPDA did not much overlap in time or membership; the UPDA put down its arms and negotiated with the government to end its rebellion just weeks after Kony formed his distinct group. According to some, Kony sought counsel from another rebel, Alice Lakwena, and informed her of his plans to launch a rebellion. She warned him against doing so, these interviewees reported. But it appears that Kony was determined, and he brought a small handful of devoted followers, from his home area of Odek, to "the Bush." Most of the initial core of Kony's group was reportedly made up of his schoolmates and friends. Prior to this time, Kony had worked as a traditional healer, and in that work he had built a network that he then used to inform people about his new rebel group.

This network appears to have been effective: One soldier who voluntarily joined the LRA in the initial months said that people would receive notice from their relatives before Kony would arrive in their village, hearing that "the most powerful one is coming."[71] One military officer from Acholi who had operated as a counterinsurgent there commented, "He was good at [communicating with people] in the area."[72] A local NGO leader who had long worked in Acholi remarked about the importance of the LRA's success at getting people to believe that their group was powerful, stating: "What moves the world is belief."[73]

The LRA's initial attacks were infrequent and not highly lethal, leading the government and many other observers to dismiss its power in the early years. An editorial in the government-sponsored *New Vision* newspaper in 1989 read, referring to rebel activity in Acholi: "Some foolish people think that these rebels will rise again ... There is no way that these people can be a long-term security threat to the government."[74] It was not until the early 1990s, after the LRA received substantial support from the

---

[70] Gersony 1997, confirmed in interview with former UPDA leader, Gulu, December 2009. The UPDA was dominated by senior ex-army officers – that is, officers from Obote's UNLA who fled Kampala when the NRA seized power. Because its membership came from UNLA ranks, UPDA was a strong, disciplined army with strong relations to the Acholi community. However, the leadership of this group was apparently ready to settle once the new NRA government demonstrated an ability to inflict casualties and to offer them a deal: in 1988, the Pece Peace Agreement marked the end of the UPDA. The leadership was largely absorbed into the ranks of the central government or the NRA.

[71] Interview with former LRA soldier, Gulu town, Gulu district, March 2009.

[72] Interview with military officer, Gulu town, Gulu district, March 2009.

[73] Interview with local NGO leader, Gulu town, Gulu district, March 2009.

[74] "Gulu Peace Must Now Be Assured." *The New Vision.* April 21, 1989.

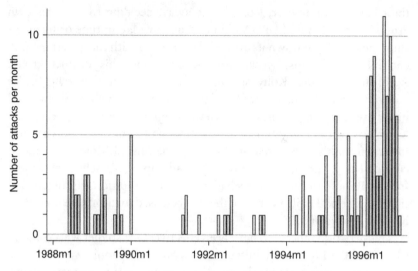

FIGURE 4.5 LRA anti-state violence (1988–1996)
Data Source: Ugandan newspaper articles

Sudanese government in Khartoum, that the LRA rebellion became quite violent, toward both the government and civilians.[75] These patterns are evident in newspaper accounts, tabulated in Figure 4.5.

Today, given the cruelty that Kony inflicted on the Acholi people over the course of the rebellion, several observers characterize Kony as a madman or an opportunist. However, the picture of Kony that emerges from civilian accounts in Lacekocot, a community near where the LRA initially had a base, is of someone who was working to build credibility among a population. A member of the community who lived there for decades explained during a focus group that when Kony arrived in their community, he encouraged people to come to be with him for singing songs and praising God. He told community members that he would overthrow the government and be president. All of his followers (approximately two dozen) at the time were voluntary, and according to one observer in Lacecokot, "they seemed like good people." Most of the others in the focus group agreed. In another focus group about 20 kilometers away, citizens said that Kony at first "gave them hope." One person commented:

---

[75] Gersony 1997, 36. Corroborated by interviews with Ugandan intelligence officer, Kampala, November 2009, and with former LRA commander, Gulu, November 2010. The Ugandan military describes this commander as Joseph Kony's most senior advisor.

"He was an orator. He was so convincing." At that time, people said, they believed they would be victorious against the NRA government. A current local leader in yet another area of the Acholi region reported that Kony seemed quite reasonable in the early years of the insurgency, and that he had seemed to have a vision for the Acholi region.[76]

While it is difficult to trace how Kony and his initial leadership circle used violence to shape civilian impressions of his rebellion,[77] it appears that in the early stages of the insurgency, he traveled personally to meet with villages. Then, after some time getting to know a community and generating a widespread perception of his competence, he would appoint a local to serve as a "coordinator," or information officer for his rebellion. Eventually, the LRA would have a coordinator embedded in almost every village in the area.[78]

Soon, a widespread perception of Kony as a powerful – even magical – fighter emerged. Civilians in one focus group reported that Kony did not ask them for information because "he seemed to already know every time an attack would come." These community members provided him with food because after seeing that he seemingly had powers that enabled him to anticipate attacks, "they believed in him." In another focus group, a woman said of Kony: "He was fearless. He used spiritual powers, and so the government could never locate where he was."[79]

The LRA was perhaps most notorious for its widespread forced conscription – abductions of individuals, particularly children, who then became foot soldiers for the LRA army.[80] Blattman and Annan (2008) assert that, "The LRA's almost total reliance on forced recruitment distinguishes it from the majority of rebel movements in Africa and elsewhere."[81] However, in the initial years, the LRA was not as reliant

---

[76] Interview with local officials and a former UPDA and HSM fighter, Mucwini county, Kitgum district, January 2010.

[77] Likely due in part to the relatively recent nature of the atrocities that the LRA committed in Uganda, and thus the sensitivities surrounding the rebellion, former LRA leaders – even those who have received amnesty – were hesitant to speak to me for more than a fairly brief interview, which precluded uncovering some of the more fine-grained information I was able to learn about the UPA.

[78] Interview with government intelligence officer from the Acholi region, Kampala, October 2009.

[79] Focus group, Lakwana subcounty, Gulu district, December 2009.

[80] For an empirical analysis of the LRA's later-stage industrial organization and abduction tactics, see Beber and Blattman, (2010).

[81] Blattman and Annan (2008) "On the nature and causes of LRA abduction: What the fighters say." Working paper available at: http://chrisblattman.com/documents/research/2009.Nature&Causes.LRAbook.pdf

on child soldiers.[82] One Member of Parliament from Acholi said that at first the LRA was quite disciplined, not engaging in practices such as forced recruitment or rape until "things really got going."[83] According to participants in one focus group in a community close to where Kony began, the vast majority of Kony's followers in his initial years of rebellion were voluntary. In another focus group, individuals reported that Kony came to "beg for their help, and if they refused, he would not disturb them."[84]

When Kony did begin abducting civilians, initially at a slow pace at the end of 1988, he usually abducted adults in small numbers, focusing in particular on "clever and bright people who could give him good advice."[85] The LRA's large-scale abductions of children remained only sporadic until an intense round of negotiations with the government collapsed in 1994, after which they became frequent.[86] In sum, in the initial years of the LRA, the horribly coercive techniques that came to define the LRA were not nearly as dominant.

Interviewees' recollections of minimal violence against civilians in the LRA's initial months are generally supported by the Ugandan newspaper accounts, shown in Figure 4.6.

The LRA's behavior changed dramatically after it became a viable group. In the early 1990s, after it had maintained bases in Acholi for well over a year, the LRA engaged in more intense battles with the NRA. As casualties mounted, civilian support for the LRA waned. According to several interviewees, Kony only began to use coercion against civilians in the early 1990s, after they began "refusing him" in large numbers.

---

[82] The first report of LRA forced recruitment in Ugandan newspapers that I could identify is on October 5, 1989.

[83] Interview with MP from Acholi, Kampala, March 2009. Several other interviewees corroborated this account and, in fact, did not place the initial incidents of violence against civilians until approximately 1992.

[84] Focus group of civilians in Opit, Gulu district, January 2010.

[85] Focus group of civilians in Opit, Gulu district, January 2010. The first report of violence against civilians I could identify in Ugandan newspapers is from "Gulu Peace Must Now Be Assured." *The New Vision*, April 21, 1989. The article reads, betraying the pro-government slant of the paper: "These so-called rebels are no longer attacking the NRA. They only rob civilians and hack them to death."

[86] "Counting the Cost: Twenty Years of War in Northern Uganda." Civil Society Organizations for Peace in Uganda, February 2006.

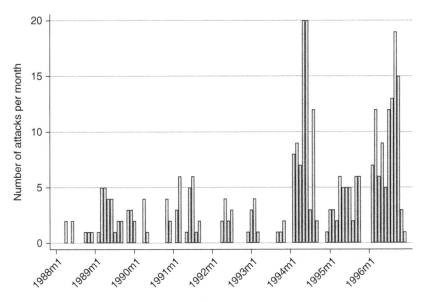

FIGURE 4.6 LRA violence against civilians (1988–1996)
Data Source: Ugandan newspaper articles

4.4 BEYOND UGANDA

Evidence from beyond Uganda suggests that these patterns of limited violence during the early phases of insurgency are relatively common to rebel groups forming in this region. In the dataset aiming to capture all rebel groups that formed in central and eastern Africa from 1997 through 2015 (described at the end of Chapters 1 and 3 with further details in Appendix D), just 23–29 percent of rebel groups committed at least one substantial attack – resulting in at least twenty-five recorded battle-related deaths – against the state in their first year.[87] Between 21 and 42 percent of these groups committed violence against civilians resulting in at least one recorded battle-related death in their initial three months; 30–58 percent did so in their first year.[88]

[87] Based on our coding protocol, here, "in the first year" means the year following when the nascent rebel leaders held their first meeting to plan the formation of a rebel group. In the case of a group that initially formed as a nonviolent group, we sought to code the year that they met with the plan of becoming a rebel group.

[88] I present intervals throughout this paragraph to account for considerable missingness on these variables; I am missing data on 18 percent of observations for the substantial anti-state attack variable and on 50 percent for the anti-civilian attack variable. The upper bound of these intervals represents percentages based on the rebel groups the research

Evidence from detailed qualitative accounts of rebel groups suggests similar patterns of early rebel violence in Africa and Asia. For example, the Maoist insurgency in Nepal is also well known for the intense violence it inflicted, especially in the early and mid-2000s; more than 13,000 deaths can be directly attributed to this war.[89] However, less often remembered about this conflict is that its explosive violence was preceded by over six years (February 1996 to November 2001) of several small, violent attacks on soft targets – "isolated, poorly armed police posts" – before the rebels initiated major violence against the state.[90] Robert Gersony explains: "Through trial and error during the six-year period, the Maoists sharpened their recruiting strategy, political messages, military training systems, attack plans, ability to use explosives, and other technical elements of their overall program." Indeed, detailed violence data reveals that the Maoists' violence did not result in over 100 battle-related deaths until their fourth year of operating, and 1,000 battle-related deaths until the sixth year.[91]

Similar patterns are apparent in accounts about the lead-up to civil war in Sudan and Sri Lanka. Roessler notes that early rebel formation in Darfur took place in secrecy, and that the rebels' early attacks "were against police posts or poorly defended army garrisons ... with the goal of testing the waters and obtaining weapons from the government."[92] A similar pattern also seems to characterize the start of the Tamil insurgency in Sri Lanka. A small group of Tamil militants committed only small attacks for several years throughout the 1970s until violence began to escalate in the early 1980s. While documentation of this period of Tamil militant activity is sparse, histories and Sri Lankan newspapers suggest that during the 1970s most attacks involved killing a small handful of police officers and local political figures such as the mayor of Jaffna and Tamil Members of Parliament who had voted for the deeply unpopular 1972 constitution. Militant groups throughout this period were clandestine – the LTTE did not publicly claim responsibility for any attacks until

---

team was able to code; in some cases, it was possible to surmise that groups had formed and committed minor violence, but not substantial violence against the state nor any violence against civilians. The lower bound presents the possibility that all observations with missing data should be coded as zeros; that is, that violence could not be coded because violence did not occur. Recall that newspapers represented the primary source of information for codings. Given that it is exceedingly difficult to find evidence that violence did *not* occur, missingness is likely correlated with absence of violence; the lower bound of these intervals is probably closer to the true number.

[89] Do and Iyer 2010, 737.   [90] Gersony 2003, 28.   [91] Do and Iyer 2010.
[92] Roessler 2016, 185.

1978 – although the LTTE or their predecessor groups likely committed most attacks against policemen and local political actors.[93]

Patterns of initially avoiding violence against civilians are also apparent in other cases of rebel groups that became known for their cruelty and violence: Even the Khmer Rouge, known for its gruesome mutilations and other violence against noncombatants, did not begin by treating civilians so atrociously. Its early leaders built up the rebel army slowly throughout the mid- and late 1960s, as sporadic violence occurred in northwestern Cambodia. Gersony explains of this period:

> [The Khmer Rouge's] extreme transformational program, and the intention to achieve it through widespread violence, were deeply embedded in plans known only to the leadership for years before they were first implemented in 1973 ... In earlier years, Khmer Rouge cadre were instructed to interact harmoniously with the populations ... concealing the intentions which they implemented so violently beginning in 1973 once they had sufficient power to do so.[94]

In sum, while the evidence needed to scrutinize patterns of initial rebel violence in a cross-national or cross-rebel contexts is not available due to the clandestine and often unclaimed nature of these actions, several qualitative accounts suggest that patterns from Uganda were present elsewhere. This is the case even for rebels are remembered for their (later) high levels of violence against the state and civilians.

4.5 DISCUSSION

Studies of civil conflict onset often ask why these conflicts "erupt," implying that they start suddenly and escalate quickly. While it may be the case that insurgencies reach an inflection point after which they escalate rapidly, the analysis in this chapter suggests that it would be a mistake to assume that such a point typically occurs immediately after an armed group forms. Instead, the initial stages of insurgency often involve an incubation period that is shrouded in secrecy and rumor, and during which the violence is sporadic and ambiguous. Prior theories of civil conflict that aim to explain the rapid mobilization of people for high-risk warfare therefore do not capture common dynamics of incipient insurgency in weak states. This chapter has aimed to do so, especially by illuminating the nature and extent of rebel violence against the state and civilians in the initial stages.

---

[93] Ponnambalam 1983, 324. [94] Gersony 2003, 86.

These findings also have important implications for how we study conflict. Because in the initial stages of insurgency violence against governments is limited and ambiguous, and violence against civilians is rare, reporting on these phases of conflict is likely limited and does not associate violent events with a particular rebel group. This exacerbates the problems noted in Chapters 1 and 2 of omissions in existing histories, documentation, and datasets that seek to capture insurgency onset. Of particular importance to recent literature on conflict onset is that, if the logic put forth here is correct, then there is good reason to believe that these phases of armed group formation are systematically omitted (or at least violent acts go unattributed to rebels) in news accounts, upon which many analyses of armed groups rely. Future theories and data collection efforts will therefore need to consider the clandestine and ambiguous nature of initial rebel violence when strategizing about how to capture the logic of, and evidence for, rebellion onset.

Additionally, the findings in the first piece of this chapter show that there probably is no influential selection process that determines why some groups emerge and others do not – or why some groups emerge in a different manner than others. Save for the important background conditions that persist in fragile states, to which I return in Chapter 6, structural factors are trumped by more idiosyncratic matters such as individual histories, proclivity, and judgment in the decision of whether or not to form a rebellion. Most former Ugandan rebel leaders said that they opted to begin their rebellion in their home area, where they knew the physical and human terrain well, but the home area of the individuals who decided to rebel was unrelated to factors such as the location of mountains, distance from borders, or the extent of exclusion from the central government in those areas. An exception was that counties contiguous to borders were more likely to host new rebel groups forming; I interpret this finding as suggesting that aspiring rebels from areas in the vicinity of the border anticipate the later benefits of proximity to a border. They thus elect to launch initial attacks in the county that has the best access to a border. As such, the following chapters treat cases of rebellion in Uganda as independent observations that do not differ in kind substantially from one another – and for the paired comparison analysis of rebels in Chapter 5, I take pains to match cases on their access to borders. With this understanding of the conditions of nascent insurgent groups, in Chapter 5 I turn to the question of why these similarly initiated rebel groups had different fates soon after they formed, with some becoming viable while others ended early.

5

Civilians

At the outset, the essential task of the guerrilla fighter is to keep himself from being destroyed ... In order to do all this the absolute cooperation of the people and a perfect knowledge of the ground are necessary ... [I]ntensive popular work must be undertaken to explain the motives of the revolution ... and to spread the incontrovertible truth that victory of the enemy against the people is finally impossible.

– Che Guevara

Information moves like wild fire in the bush.

– Former UPA intelligence officer

Why do only some newly launched rebel groups go on to become viable? This question motivates this chapter. I make the case that the behavior of civilians plays a central role in nascent rebels' fate.

As I argued in Chapter 2, because nascent rebel groups in weak states are typically small and vulnerable, their core challenge is to persuade local civilians to keep quiet about their existence and location; information leaks to the government about incipient rebels' identity and whereabouts can be devastating.

The theory shows why each civilian's decision to provide information about the rebels to the government depends on his expectations about the nascent rebels' future capabilities relative to the government, about gains from a successful rebellion, and about the expectations and actions of his fellow civilians. To form these expectations, civilians draw on rumors that reach them through their established networks of trust – their extended family.

The theory also proposed that rumors started by aspiring rebels aim to cast the early rebellion in a favorable light. When these rumors reach enough people quickly, they can convince civilians both that the rebels are worthy of support, and that others will keep quiet to make secrecy valuable. Civilian kinship networks with certain properties – low fragmentation and short paths – facilitate this process, providing rebels with a shield of secrecy behind which they can attain viability. When applied to the setting of rural societies in weak states, the most common setting for insurgency, these results have important implications for our understanding of the early stages of civil conflict – and especially for the role of ethnicity.

In Chapter 2, I drew on the work of ethnographers and historians to argue that in rural sub-Saharan Africa, kinship networks that form in homogeneous areas tend to feature low fragmentation and short paths, while those that form in heterogeneous areas do not. Due to this difference, I argue, attempts at organized rebellion are more likely to succeed when they occur in homogeneous areas; in heterogeneous areas, civilians have greater incentive to provide information to the government about the vulnerable rebels forming in their midst, leading to the rebels' demise before they present a substantial threat.

This argument, and the evidence presented below that supports it, aims to advance a new understanding of how ethnicity influences conflict onset, showing that ethnic grievances need not be the initial impetus for rebellion in a given community in order for the ethnic composition of that community to influence the trajectory of nascent rebel group. While a basic correlation between ethnic homogeneity and rebel viability is not surprising – it echoes the empirical findings of a growing body of literature that also links geographic concentration of ethnic groups with civil war onset[1] – the argument advanced here about *why* this is the case differs. Many accounts tend to assume that co-ethnics share common preferences over whether to rebel or not, often because they are excluded or otherwise mistreated by the central government. This chapter aims to illustrate how local ethnic demography can influence the initial stages of internal conflict, *irrespective of the preferences of the local population.* While others have similarly emphasized ethnicity's role in making rebellion more feasible, the evidence presented here – unusual in its scrutiny of oft-overlooked early stages of rebel group formation – offers a rare, micro-level look inside the "black box" of this process.

---

[1] Toft 2002; Laitin 2004; Weidmann 2009; Cederman, Weidmann, and Gleditsch 2011.

This chapter explores what happened when nascent rebel groups attempted to become viable in Uganda. I start by examining all sixteen groups I identified as forming in Uganda since 1986, showing that only those that formed in ethnically homogeneous areas became viable.[2] Next, in order to examine in greater depth the mechanisms underlying this correlation, I turn to two paired comparisons of rebel groups. In one pair, both groups formed in eastern Uganda;[3] the other pair formed in northern Uganda. Examining why only one group in each pair became viable provides support for several of the theory's key claims, and shows some of the inner workings of rebel–civilian interactions at the dawn of a new rebel group forming. Then, I describe experimental evidence that also offers useful support in favor of the mechanism advanced here about the role of kinship networks in spreading rebels' rumors.[4] Finally, I consider alternative mechanisms that could explain the link between ethnic demography and rebel viability in Uganda.

5.1 WHICH GROUPS BECOME VIABLE?

As an initial cut at examining evidence for the expected, positive relationship between ethnic homogeneity and rebel viability introduced in Chapter 2, I turn to evidence from all sixteen rebel groups that formed in Uganda since 1986. Recall that only four groups became viable: HSM, UPA, LRA, and ADF. Additionally, recall that I define *viable* rebel groups as those that challenged the authority of the central government, which I operationalize as groups that maintained an operational base on the target country's soil with at least 200 individuals for at least three months. The analysis here is not sensitive to these precise thresholds; for example, most groups I studied that did not become viable had bases that lasted for one month or less.

The unit of this analysis is the rebel group. However, many of the variables I seek to measure across rebel groups for this analysis are distributed across space, such as the ethnic demography of the area in which rebels operated in the initial stages. Therefore, for each rebel group, the area where rebel groups operated during the period when they sought to become viable must be defined systematically. In order to do so,

[2] Some of the evidence presented in this section of the chapter also appears in Lewis (2017).
[3] Some of the evidence presented in this section of the chapter also appears in Lewis and Larson (2018).
[4] This experimental evidence is discussed in greater detail in Lewis and Larson (2017).

I identified the county (or counties) where nascent rebels went during the initial stages of their emergence for the purpose of (1) attempting to establish a base or (2) interacting with and seeking material support (money, food, or recruits) from civilians.[5] I consider the initial stages to be the period between the inception of the insurgent group, when planning begins, and when a group achieves viability or is defeated, ceasing to attack the Ugandan government. This typically occurs following a negotiated settlement or following the capture, exile, or death of one or more top leaders.

The initial activities of four rebel groups (ADF, HSM, UFDF, and CAMP) were clearly associated with a single county, so geographic variables associated with those rebel groups correspond to that county. However, several rebel groups (UPA, LRA, NFA, WNBF, UNRF II, NALU, and FOBA) initially spanned two, three, or, in one case, four contiguous counties. For those groups, the variables were measured using data from all relevant counties. For example, the ethnic demography and population density measures for FOBA were derived using census data for all individuals living in both Tororo and Samia-Bugwe counties, and the highest elevation reported is the highest point present in either county.[6] Finally, for five rebel groups (NOM, UPDA, PRA, NDA, and UDA), it was not possible to reliably discern in which county, or counties, they operated during the initial stages. In all of those cases, it appeared that the group operated in at least one out of three to five counties, so for all spatially measured variables, I averaged the values of those three to five counties. That is, if I assessed that a rebel group operated in at least one out of three counties but I was not certain of which one(s), to arrive at a value measuring that rebel group's distance from an international border, I would average the distances of each of those three counties.

Several measures I compile for this analysis are the same as those used for the analysis of rebel group launch in Chapter 3. To measure ethnic demography, I use 1991 census data to construct an ethno-linguistic

---

[5] I do not include locations of attacks in this definition because those locations are typically determined by where government security forces are located; rebels travel there (typically under the cover of night) to commit an attack, and then quickly retreat to the area where they are based and/or receiving cover from civilians.

[6] Further, the binary "distance-to-border" measure is a "1" for FOBA since Tororo county borders Kenya, even though Samia-Bugwe does not; the continuous measure of distance to the border is the average of the distance between each county's center and the closest border. Because poverty measures are not available at the individual level for the early 1990s, the poverty measures analyzed here were averaged across counties.

fractionalization (ELF) score of the area where each rebel group operated in the initial stages. ELF measures the probability that any two randomly sampled individuals from a given population are members of different ethnic groups.[7] It thus constitutes a useful approximation of the central concept of ethnic demographic patterns discussed earlier by measuring the extent of ethnic diversity in a given area. If the earlier logic is correct in associating ethnic homogeneity with unfragmented networks with short path lengths, then higher ELF scores should indicate more fragmented, higher-path-length networks.[8] None of the results presented here are substantially changed when using an alternative, common measure of ethnic demography: the percentage of the total population of the area comprised by the largest ethnic group (see discussion, correlation matrix, and results in Appendix B).

The use of 1991 census data is necessary because reliable census data at the county level are not available prior to 1991; however, this introduces potential measurement error for the nine rebellions I examine here that began before 1991. Violent conflict can lead to migration, plausibly making an area increasingly more homogenous in the period after conflict begins, potentially biasing my results in the direction that favors my hypothesis. However, this issue affects areas with different baseline demographic patterns similarly, limiting the potential biases of inferences about the effects of *differences* in ethnic demography across areas on rebel viability – unless we believe that the groups that became viable were more likely to induce local homogeneity. It is difficult to rule out this possibility; however, six of the nine insurgencies that began prior to 1991 took place in regions I study in greater depth later in this chapter, where I present ample historical evidence that ethnic demographic patterns in these regions have persisted for decades – long before these rebellions

---

[7] ELF scores are based on a decreasing transformation of the Herfindahl Index, which is calculated as follows: Given a population composed of $N \geq 2$ different ethnic groups, let p_n be the proportion of the population compromised by group p. The ELF index value is then calculated by: $1 - \sum_{n=1}^{N} p_n^2$. Data for the census was collected by the Government of Uganda in January 1991.

[8] By using census data, I rely on the Government of Uganda's enumeration of ethnic groups. If anything, doing so biases the analysis against the expected relationship because in the West Nile region – where three groups attempted rebellion but failed to become viable – the census did not allow one group, the Aringa, to identify as a separate group. Instead, they were forced to identify as Lugbara, a group that the Aringa descended from, but generally consider themselves to be entirely distinct from. Thus the ELF score for the three groups that launched in West Nile underestimates the actual heterogeneity of those areas. I do not know of any other areas of Uganda affected by this type of undercounting of ethnic groups in the Ugandan census.

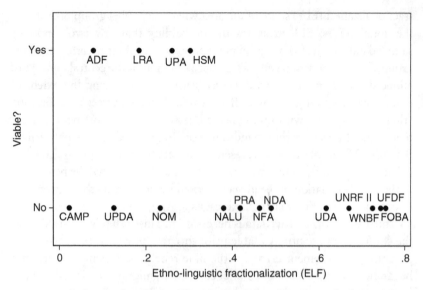

FIGURE 5.1 Scatterplot of ethno-linguistic fractionalization and rebel viability

began. To ensure that any potential biases affecting the remaining three insurgencies – NOM, NDA, and NALU – are not driving the results presented here, I re-run the analysis without these three observations, and find that they do not substantially alter the results.[9] Furthermore, Uganda's demography does not tend to change dramatically over time; the ELF score of Ugandan counties using the 1991 and 2002 censuses is correlated at 0.90.

The scatterplot in Figure 5.1 shows the relationship between the ELF of the area in which each rebel group initially operated and whether or not the group became viable. The twelve groups that did not become viable take a value of zero and are broadly distributed across the range of ELF scores for the rebel groups (between 0.02 and 0.75), while the ELF scores of groups that became viable are all below the mean and median of ELF scores (0.40 and 0.39, respectively). Attempted rebellions that failed to become viable had a mean ELF score of 0.47, while those that succeeded had a mean ELF score of 0.20.

Consistent with the theoretical account presented in Chapter Two, while not all rebel groups that formed in homogeneous areas succeeded

---

[9] See also Appendix C, in which I re-estimate the model dropping each observation.

in becoming viable, no rebel group that attempted to form in a heterogeneous area (above the mean) became viable. Regarding groups that form in homogeneous areas but do not become viable, recall from the theory that the rebels' ability to access a contact to seed their positive rumors plays a powerful role. If the rebels' contact, for example, chooses to spread negative news, perhaps because they determine that the rebels are incompetent or unsavory, then it will be extremely difficult for the rebels to become viable. If we assume that negative news is worse than no news, then this scenario can make rebels even worse off than if they had launched in a heterogeneous area. Evidence from the few interviews I was able to conduct in the locality where CAMP formed (near Lira, in Lango region) support this account; local journalists recalled that locals "seemed to immediately reject" the rebels, due to a sense that they were incompetent and taking the community in a direction that would not benefit them. This was striking, since the community where they formed is the home ethno-region of Milton Obote, who was twice President of Uganda, including in the 1980s until he was ousted in 1985. The leader of CAMP, Smith Opon Acak, had been Army Chief of Staff under President Obote until Obote was overthrown in a military coup by a predominantly Acholi brigade. One might expect that an ethno-region that had previously controlled the central government would be eager to coalesce behind a prior military leader in order to take back the center. Instead, information leaks led the NRM to learn about the rebellion, find Acak, and kill him, thereby ending the rebellion.[10]

Of course, many other alternative explanations could confound this correlation, plausibly driving variation in both ethnic demography and rebel viability. Existing scholarship on conflict onset puts forth several factors that could account for rebel group viability in some areas and not others. Most of these works take "conflict onset" or "civil war onset" as their explicit analytic target, not rebel group viability – but because rebel groups are often a primary protagonist in these conflicts, most conflict onset theories make reference (at least implicitly) to how certain factors favor rebel group emergence.

---

[10] I was unable to identify reliable sources of information about initial civilian beliefs about NOM or UPDA, and the extent to which information leaks led to their demise. NOM was from Lango and UPDA was from Acholi, therefore common tropes about ethnic exclusion or loss of power in Uganda would suggest that these communities should have been highly motivated to rebel.

Some of these factors can be discarded for the purposes of this discussion because they are not present in the Ugandan context and thus their relative importance cannot be empirically evaluated. As discussed for the spatial (county-level) analysis of initial rebel launch in Chapter 4, presence of accessible, high-value natural resources,[11] and presence of a foreign government providing weapons and funds[12] cannot be empirically examined here because Uganda does not have high-value, lootable resources, and none of the rebel groups there benefitted from significant foreign resources in their initial stages.[13] This literature suggests numerous other variables' relevance to the opportunity and motivation for conflict initiation, which I also considered as correlates of rebel launch in Chapter 4, and which also warrant consideration here: *terrain* such as mountains or forest, which favor insurgents in an asymmetric war;[14] *proximity to international borders*, which could lead to improved access to safe havens;[15] *low levels of economic development*, which could motivate or lessen the opportunity costs of participation in violence;[16] *exclusion* from the central government, which could motivate rebellion;[17] and *state strength*, which could deter rebel group formation.[18]

To probe the possibility that the relationship between ethnic demography and rebel viability is confounded by one of the above factors, I run trivariate regression models at the rebel group level ($n=16$), with each model holding constant one of the variables described earlier.[19] Using OLS and logit, in all of the models except one, the coefficient on ELF is significant at least at the 90 percent level, whereas none of the other covariates are statistically significant. The results are shown in Appendix C, along with several other sensitivity tests. For example, these results also hold when dropping the one rebel group about which

---

[11] Collier and Hoeffler 2004; Lujala 2010.   [12] Weinstein 2007.
[13] However, as discussed earlier in this chapter, there are clear theoretical reasons to believe that it is very difficult for nascent groups with little coercive capacity to control natural resources and to attract external sources of finance.
[14] Fearon and Laitin 2003; Buhaug, Cederman, and Rod 2008.
[15] Salehyan 2009; Cunningham 2010.
[16] Collier and Hoeffler 2004; Dube and Vargas 2010.
[17] Cederman, Wimmer, and Min 2010.   [18] Fearon and Laitin 2003.
[19] I add only one covariate (beyond ethnic demography) in each model due to the major degree of freedom problems posed by regression analyses with an n of 16. While naturally these analyses are problematic due to this issue, they provide some reassurance that the correlation may not be spurious.

information is weakest, the PRA.[20] Additionally, when dropping all three observations about which we may be particularly concerned about measurement error on ELF due to the use of 1991 data – NOM, NDA, and NALU – as described earlier, the basic result is attenuated but still holds; ELF retains significance throughout all models at least at the 15 percent level.

Naturally, the results of any regression analysis with so few observations must be interpreted with extreme caution. However, the fact that ELF is statistically significant in almost all of the models and withstands several sensitivity tests provides useful support that is consistent with a central hypothesis of the theory. Furthermore, in light of the substantive and statistical non-significance of the control variables, it is unlikely that the correlation between ethnic homogeneity and viability is spurious. Since rebels are constrained by where they have sufficient local knowledge to launch, as shown in Chapter 4, some are forced to form in heterogeneous areas – and are apparently at a major disadvantage. The following case studies show why.

5.2 EVIDENCE FROM TWO PAIRED COMPARISONS

To examine the processes underlying this relationship between ethnic demography and rebel viability, I turn now to comparing two pairs (four cases) of rebel groups that formed in the late 1980s: the first pair is the Ugandan People's Army (UPA) and Force Obote Back Again (FOBA); the second is the Lord's Resistance Army (LRA) and the West Nile Bank Front (WNBF). These rebel groups are paired on a number of dimensions, including the region of Uganda (northern, eastern, central, or western) in which they operated: UPA (which became viable) and FOBA (which did not) formed in eastern Uganda; LRA (which became viable) and WNBF (which did not) formed in northern Uganda. These regional distinctions hold great importance in Uganda's history: Recall from Chapter 3 that a major trope of Ugandan postcolonial politics is that northerners ruled the country until 1986, when westerners allied

---

[20] As discussed in Chapter 3, there has been controversy in Uganda about whether or not this rebel group truly existed with the intent to overthrow the government, and if it did exist, precisely where in Uganda it sought to gain material support. I drop it in one iteration of this analysis to ensure that it is not driving the results, and find that the results are not changed; all coefficients take the same sign and level of significance.

TABLE 5.1 *Case-study rebel groups*

Region of Uganda	Rebel group name	Subregion name *ethnic demography*	Became viable?
Eastern	Uganda People's Army (UPA)	Teso *homogeneous*	Yes
Eastern	Force Obote Back Again (FOBA)	Bukedi *heterogeneous*	No
Northern	Lord's Resistance Army (LRA)	Acholi *homogeneous*	Yes
Northern	West Nile Bank Front (WNBF)	West Nile *heterogeneous*	No

with elites from central Uganda seized control, and have been ruling ever since.

However, within each of these regions, the population's ethnic composition varies a great deal. One of each of these pairs of rebel groups initially operated in a homogeneous area, while the other initially operated in a heterogeneous area. Within eastern Uganda, the UPA launched in the Teso subregion, home primarily to the Iteso people, while FOBA operated in the Bukedi subregion, home to several ethno-linguistic groups such as the Iteso, the Japadolha, the Basamia, the Bagwere, the Bagwe, and others. In northern Uganda, the LRA formed in the homogeneous Acholi subregion, while the WNBF began its insurgency in the West Nile, a highly diverse area that is home to the Lugbara, the Aringa, the Madi, the Alur, and the Kakwa, among others. These basic patterns among the case study rebel groups are summarized in Table 5.1.

While these subregions are of little administrative significance in Uganda currently, the names of these areas and their locations are well known to Ugandans. Colonial administrators conferred these names to the districts of their Protectorate of Uganda,[21] which was part of the British Empire from 1894 until independence in 1962. The boundaries and names were based on the kingdoms (e.g. Buganda, Bunyoro, Toro) or peoples (e.g. Teso, Karamoja, Lango) that the British encountered in each area.[22] Today,

---

[21] Kasozi 1994, 48–49.

[22] In the decades leading up to European presence in Uganda, western and central Uganda were dominated by kingdoms (e.g. Ankole, Buganda, Bunyoro, Busoga, and Toro), in which authority was generally centralized and hierarchical. In contrast, northern and eastern Uganda – the regions where the case studies in this chapter took place – were dominated by tribes in which political authority was decentralized; while clan leaders would sometimes coordinate, none were subject to an overall authority. For a discussion

these areas are still generally considered to be the provenance of the people who have long resided there; for example, Ugandans continue to refer to Buganda as the region of the Ganda people, and Lango to describe the land where the Langi people predominate.[23] The subregions where the four case study rebel groups operated are highlighted in Figure 5.2.

5.2.1 Case Selection

The analysis presented in the remainder of this chapter employs a straightforward application of the comparative method; cases were selected with the aim of matching cases as closely as possible on multiple factors that could plausibly influence the outcome of interest, rebel viability. Cases vary in the factor of which I seek to understand the effect: the extent of ethnic homogeneity.[24] This approach of conditioning on several factors that could have potentially influenced the likelihood of these four rebel groups becoming viable helps me to better discern the impact of ethnic demographic patterns, limiting the potential influence of variables that pose alternative possibilities for why some rebel groups become viable. The variables "held constant" in each of these pairs, of which I discussed the theoretical significance in Chapters Two and Three, are: (1) external material support, (2) terrain, (3) proximity to international borders, (4) development, and (5) state strength. I summarize each of these factors in Table 5.2 and discuss them in the text that follows.

Additionally, beyond these readily quantifiable factors, I discerned no difference in the military or strategic skill level of any of these four groups' initial leadership cadre. Initial rebel leaders from all groups had some prior military experience, but none had experience in launching a prior rebellion. Local government and military officials who were knowledgeable about all rebel groups did not report a difference in the quality of each group's leaders. In addition, all four groups stated in the early stages that their aim was to

---

of these institutions in different areas of pre-colonial Uganda and how they evolved, see Kasozi 1994, 17–21 as well as Kizza 1999, Chapter 2.

[23] Only three subregions – Bukedi, Kigezi, and West Nile – are not named after an ethnic group, because no single group was numerically dominant when the British arrived there.

[24] For clear discussions of the method of paired comparison in comparative politics, including its strengths and weaknesses, see Lijphart 1971; Tarrow 2010. This design is also known as a "most similar" systems research design or a "controlled case comparison." See (Przeworski and Teune 1982, 33) and (George and Bennett 2005, 59).

FIGURE 5.2 Map of Uganda's subregions
Areas where case study rebel groups initially operated are highlighted.

overtake the central government. I interpret these statements as largely
strategic outgrowths of the fact that, given the recent history in Uganda
and surrounding states, overtaking the central Ugandan government in the
late 1980s and the early 1990s would have seemed ambitious, but plausible,
in the eyes of Ugandan villagers. I refer readers to Chapter 3 for a more
comprehensive discussion of Ugandan rebel leaders' stated objectives.

With respect to the first factor listed in Table 5.2 – external material
support – the commonalities among these four cases are straightforward:
No group received material support from sources external to Uganda in
the initial stages.[25] Instead of accessing external resources, all groups

---

[25] In fact, none of the sixteen rebel groups that launched in Uganda after 1986 initially
benefitted from foreign support, although some – particularly the LRA and the ADF, and
to some extent the WNBF and the UNRF II, did at the later stages of the rebellion.

TABLE 5.2 *Summary of paired comparisons:*
Four Ugandan rebel groups that formed in the late 1980s

	Eastern Uganda		Northern Uganda	
	UPA Teso region	FOBA Bukedi region	LRA Acholi region	WNBF West Nile region
External material support	Minimal	None	Minimal (until 1993)	Minimal (until 1994)
Terrain	Flat, semi-arid savannah	Somewhat hilly and forested	Forested and some small mountains	Forested and some small mountains
Proximity to international borders	No international border, 120 km to western Kenya	Borders western Kenya	Borders southern Sudan	Borders southern Sudan and eastern DRC
Development (Emwanu et al. 2003, 1991 census data)	77.4% living below poverty line; 51.5% literate	57.7% living below poverty line; 53% literate	77.8% living below the poverty line; 46% literate	73.4% living below the poverty line; 29.6% literate
State strength *year of rebel formation*	Low *1987*	Low *1987*	Low *1988*	Low *1988*
*Ethno-linguistically homogeneous?** (1991 census data)	*Yes* *ELF score of .26; largest ethnic group is 85% of pop.; 1 language and 3 dialects in Teso*	*No* *ELF score of .76; largest ethnic group is 38% of pop.; 3 languages and 10 dialects in Bukedi*	*Yes* *ELF score of .18; largest ethnic group is 90% of pop.; 1 language and 4 dialects in Acholi*	*No* *ELF score of .72; largest ethnic group is 33% of pop.; 9 languages and 23 dialects in West Nile*
Did the rebellion become viable?	*Yes*	*No*	*Yes*	*No*

*ELF score comes from 1991 Uganda census data. Language and dialect data comes from Ethnologue (ed. Lewis 2009)

initially relied on arms that were already available in their regions. Groups tended to receive arms from individuals, particularly those who had served in former regimes' national militaries or police forces, and attempted early in their insurgencies to attack government targets that would enable them to acquire more weapons.

With respect to terrain and borders, the variation that exists among these cases goes in the opposite direction of that anticipated by existing theories. Uganda sits astride the equator, and its landscape is mostly tropical savanna. Much of the country is semi-forested and hilly; most of the geographic variation is simply the extent of the forest cover and hills. While Uganda is bordered by two mountainous areas on its eastern and western flanks, neither is located close to, or played a significant operational role in, the initial stages of any rebellion studied in this chapter.[26] Some areas of Uganda are flatter and less thickly forested than others; of the four groups, the UPA – one that became viable – formed in the area with the least favorable terrain, since it is the most flat and has the least forest cover. Regarding international borders, WNBF and FOBA, the two cases that did not become viable, both formed closer to an international border than LRA and UPA, which did become viable.[27]

The final factors, state strength and development, require more discussion. The key determinant of economic welfare and state capacity in Uganda in the decade leading up to 1986 – warfare – did not directly affect any of the regions where these four rebel groups formed, with the partial exception of West Nile. The Bush War of the early 1980s, which led to the NRM's ascendance to central power, was fought exclusively in

---

[26] Mount Elgon, which is 4,321 meters (14,177 feet) at its highest point, is approximately sixty kilometers from the area where FOBA operated and approximately 110 kilometers from the area where UPA launched. The Rwenzori mountains are 5,109 meters (16,761 feet) at the highest point, and are approximately 370 kilometers from the area where WNBF and the LRA operated. The area north of the Acholi region on and over the border with Sudan does have about seven small mountains – ranging from about 1,000 to 3,200 meters tall – but the LRA did not make use of them until the mid-1990s.

[27] Recall from Chapter 3 that rebel groups are more likely to form in counties that rest on international borders. This finding suggests the attractiveness of borders for nascent insurgents. It also implies the possibility that weaker rebels will start on a border, since the expected costs of entry are presumably lower there. Post hoc assessments of such quality are very difficult, given retrospective knowledge about which groups became viable. I did not, however, find any evidence that the WNBF and FOBA were initially weaker, or less skilled groups than the others; all were small groups of lightly armed men, only some of who had prior military experience.

central and western Uganda.[28] Thus, the northern and eastern regions studied in this chapter escaped the direct effects of war, particularly war-related deaths, destruction of infrastructure, and population displacement.[29] The exception is West Nile, which, while unaffected by the NRA's[30] violence, suffered from a separate confrontation with Obote's military. This led to a great deal of violence and displacement in the early 1980s. However, the group that formed in West Nile – the WNBF, discussed later – is a case of a rebel group that did not become viable.

While reliable measures of economic well-being for these areas do not exist for the years immediately prior to these rebellions, measures from the 1991 census are available. As current theories may predict, the areas in which groups became viable were somewhat poorer than those where groups did not become viable: the percentage of individuals living below the poverty line was 77.4 and 57.7 for the UPA and FOBA, respectively, and 77.9 and 73.4 for the LRA and WNBF. However, because this data was collected about two years after the start of these rebellions, it is likely that events occurring in the initial stages of these rebellions drove at least some of this variation. Literacy rates may be a better proxy for a state's level of development since they are less responsive to violence, and indeed respective literacy rates for these areas suggest that areas that spawned viable groups were similarly literate, or more literate, than areas that did not: literacy rates in the areas where the four rebel groups formed, respectively, are 51.2 and 53 for UPA and FOBA, and 46.1 and 29.5 for LRA and WNBF. Thus, while two years after rebellion began the areas where groups became viable were poorer, they were similar in literacy rates, or more literate, than the areas where rebel groups did not become viable.

[28] Furthermore, the army of Ugandan and Tanzanian forces that ousted Idi Amin in 1979 entered from Uganda's southwestern border with Tanzania and followed the corridor along Lake Victoria north to Kampala.

[29] For example, both a US diplomat who had worked in Uganda throughout the 1980s and a senior Ugandan military official agreed that because northern and eastern Uganda were largely untouched by prior years of war, the roads of those areas were of much higher quality in the late 1980s than those of central and western Uganda.

[30] The current ruling party of Uganda, the National Resistance Movement (NRM), has ruled Uganda since 1986; it came to power in 1986 as a victorious rebel group, which was called the National Resistance Army (NRA). Until 1995, the national military of Uganda was known as the NRA.

Regarding state capacity, as a part of their war-fighting efforts in central and much of western Uganda, the NRA developed significant local institutional capacity. In particular, they had developed extensive local government structures that assisted the NRA rebel group in obtaining information about government troops. Thus, these institutions were already in place and were absorbed into the national government structure when the NRA took over Kampala in early 1986. However, by the time that the rebellions began in northern and eastern Uganda in 1987, the NRM government had only recently begun setting up similar local governance institutions throughout northern and eastern Uganda, appointing Special District Administrators to organize those local governments and hold local elections. Thus, throughout northern and eastern Uganda, where all of the rebellions examined here formed, the central government had very little institutional reach, and thus very low capacity to detect nascent rebels; this low capacity was common to all areas where these four groups formed.

In sum, I selected these four cases of rebel groups with the aim of "holding constant" factors other than ethnic demography that we may expect to influence rebel viability. There appears to be no compelling reason to believe that any of these factors are strongly associated with rebel viability in these cases in the direction anticipated by existing theories.

The next section presents evidence from case studies of rebel groups formed in Uganda in the late 1980s. First, I compare the trajectory of two rebel groups that formed in two areas of eastern Uganda: UPA, which became viable, and FOBA, which did not. Then, I conduct a similar comparison, in somewhat less depth, between the northern Uganda cases of LRA and WNBF. The latter pair serves as a check that some of the patterns observed in the UPA/FOBA comparison extend beyond those cases.[31] The UPA was introduced at length and the LRA's start was briefly described in Chapter 4; while those accounts focused on the *rebels'* decisions and behavior, here I emphasize that of the local *civilians* during these groups' formation.

---

[31] The latter comparison is more brief due to space constraints as well as fieldwork challenges; due to on-going political sensitivities related to the treatment of former rebels in both Acholi and West Nile, it was more challenging to find former rebels and civilians willing to speak openly about their experiences in the initial stages of the rebellion than it was in eastern Uganda.

5.2.2 UPA: Eastern Ugandan Group that Became Viable

Like all four of the groups examined here, the UPA emerged following two decades of Ugandan state decay and upheaval from warfare and over-throw of central leadership. Although the warfare of the late 1970s and early 1980s did not reach Teso, its aftermath brought about a great deal of uncertainty as all Ugandans tried to discern whether this period of bloodshed was truly, finally over. "There was a collapse of authority in Teso after [the Obote regime] left," one local leader who had served as UPA intelligence said.[32] Of particular concern were the intentions of the new NRM government, and whether they would take retributive action against those who had fought against them during the Bush War.[33] In late 1986, the central government sent representatives to Teso – as it did to all regions unaffected by the war – to set up new local government structures, but these representatives came from western Uganda. Teso, like the rest of northern and eastern Uganda, had been a stronghold of Obote's UPC party.

The UPA launched in early 1987 and became viable later that year, when it had several hundred fighters on at least two bases on Ugandan soil, operating without significant challenge from the government for approximately six months. Later, at its height in 1989 and 1990, the UPA recruited well over a thousand men, organized into eight brigades covering different portions of the Teso region, an area of approximately

[32] Interview with former UPA intelligence officer, Soroti, January 2011.
[33] Many Iteso who were part of Obote's police Special Forces fought against Museveni's NRA in the Luwero Triangle area of central Uganda during the Bush War. Recall from the discussion in Chapter 2 that following nine relatively stable years following Uganda's 1962 independence, Ugandan Army Commander Idi Amin, who was from West Nile, seized power from President Milton Obote, who was from Lango, in a military coup in 1971. Amin ruled until April 1979, when he was ousted by a number of armed Ugandan groups assisted by the Tanzanian army. Then three different individuals and one commission comprised of another three individuals held the Ugandan presidency until December 1980, when Milton Obote regained the presidency through national elections, amid accusations of electoral fraud. Beginning in 1981, in what became known as the Bush War, numerous armed factions formed seeking to overthrow Obote – including the NRA, led by current President Museveni, who had come in fourth in the 1980 elections. General Tito Okello, who was from Acholi, then seized power in a July 1985 military coup (with the assistance of Bazilio Olara-Okello, who technically held the presidency for three days), and signed a peace accord with the rebel factions, including the NRA, who had been fighting against Obote in the Bush War. However, in January 1986, the NRA abrogated the peace accord, attacking and swiftly overtaking Kampala. Okello fled to Kenya and his UNLA military fled back to their home regions, predominately in the north but also in the east. Since 1986, Museveni has remained President of Uganda.

4,300 square kilometers. Fighting between UPA and the government forces became intense, presenting a fierce challenge to the Ugandan government and leading to over a thousand battle-related deaths while displacing about 13,000 from their homes. The rebellion eventually unraveled and ended with a peace agreement in 1992.

Teso is a gently sloping, grassy savannah that is intermittently swampy and dusty, depending on season and location.[34] The soil is not particularly fertile relative to the rest of Uganda, but with two rainy seasons, it supports subsistence agriculture, and since the arrival of the British, cotton production. It has also allowed for extensive rearing of cattle, the primary means of wealth storage and transfer among the Iteso people.[35] The Iteso are a Nilo-Hamitic group, along with the Nandi, the Turkana, and the Karamojong, who also reside in nearby areas of Uganda and Kenya, and are said to have migrated to Uganda as pastoralists from Abyssinia (today Ethiopia) in the early eighteenth century.

In addition, Teso has long been quite ethnically homogeneous. The 1948 census found that only 9 percent of inhabitants in Teso district were not Iteso. In 1964, Fred Burke observed that Teso "is one of the most homogeneous districts in Uganda."[36] He traces the sense of tribal identity there to the early twentieth century, with the arrival of the British. Today, while small minorities of Kumam and Bakenye live in the Teso region, it remains a highly homogeneous area. The Iteso are 6.4 percent of the Ugandan population, according to the 2001 census, the fifth largest ethnic group in Uganda.[37] Yet having never seized control of the central government, nor having played a dominant role in any colonial or postcolonial governmental or military unit (save for the police Special Forces under Obote), the Iteso's role in Uganda's colonial and postcolonial politics was peripheral relative to many other groups.

The history of how Teso became so homogeneous reveals the unfragmented, low-distance nature of kinship networks in the region, particularly of the primary tribal subgroup there: clans (or *atekerin* in Ateso). Clans in Iteso culture represent lineages, or proximate lines of ancestry – all Iteso people believe that they descend from a common ancestor if one

---

[34] Today, the Teso region is compromised of the districts of Soroti, Ngora, Kumi, Amuria, Kabermaido, Katakwi, Bukedea, and Serere.
[35] The Iteso are also concentrated in northwestern Kenya, and small numbers have migrated south of Teso to southeastern Uganda.
[36] Burke 1964, 127.
[37] Groups larger than the Iteso, in descending order of size and also using 2001 Census data, are the Baganda at 16.9%, Banyankole at 9.5%, Basoga 8.4%, and the Bakiga at 6.9%.

reaches far enough back in the lineage. Members of each clan gather regularly for meetings and rituals.

When the nomadic Iteso first reached the area now known as Teso, it was relatively unoccupied. As Burke explains, "As plenty of land was available and no outside threat existed, the initial [land] holdings were large and scattered."[38] Upon reaching this land, the pastoralist Iteso gradually became accustomed to settled, subsistence agriculture. At first, they lived clustered by kinship group in areas called *etem*, but mobility and voluntary migration within Teso became common for several reasons. First, the plentiful land in Teso made this possible; also, the pastoralist heritage of the Iteso likely predisposes them to mobility; and finally, the custom of primogeniture – the firstborn male inheriting the family's entire wealth – means that excluded siblings often migrated to new land to seek wealth (Uchendu and Anthony 1975, 16, 19, 23).[39] Furthermore, polygamy is permitted and relatively common, and clans are patrilineal and exogamous, meaning that one must marry outside of one's own clan, and wives become part of, and go to live with, the husband's clan. Of course, due to a combination of shared culture, language, and pressure, most Iteso marry other Iteso – so spouses usually come from villages a handful of kilometers away in Teso, not another region of Uganda. Wives move to the husband's home village, but strong ties remain between the wife and her original clan; she will continue to visit them regularly, and her children will often also come to see her clan as kin.

Over time, as people continually migrated within Teso and married outside of their clan, numerous members of one clan would have many clan members in other areas of Teso, and be related by marriage to numerous members of other clans.[40] These patterns have generated a dispersed patchwork of overlapping, extended family ties that comprise

---

[38] Burke 1964, 128.

[39] Evidence from numerous other studies of areas throughout Teso shows similar patterns of and motives for migration. For example, Okalany (Webster et al. 1973, 120) found that the primary reason for migration to Mukongoro from within Teso has been "search for fertile and vacant land," finding that, typically, small groups of one clan would break off from the larger clan and migrate together. Writing about the Kumi area of Teso, Emodong finds that migration to Teso occurred "because of economic reasons and particularly the search for better farming land" (Webster et al. 1973, 91).

[40] These marriage ties have long had an important impact on social and political relations in Teso. As Emodong explains: "In the nineteenth century and earlier when there was no political authority accepted by all Iteso and therefore relations amongst them might be dangerously inflammable, good relations were promoted by a web of marriage ties" (Webster et al. 1973, 94–95).

the Iteso tribe; extended families in Teso "have a wide geographical distribution as well as a marked geographical concentration in any area" (Uchendu and Anthony 1975, 19). As Burke similarly explains, "Members of the same *ateker* are distributed throughout Teso, though there is a slight tendency for the members of a given clan to concentrate in certain areas."[41]

Still today, bonds among kin appear to hold a level of trust in Teso that do not exist as commonly between individuals in Teso who are not relatives. For example, consider the following narrative and question that I posed to interviewees:

Imagine there's a man named Nathan, who is [clan name of the interviewee] and who wants to buy a bicycle very badly. But he is having problems finding a good bike in [insert name of subcounty in which the interviewee resides]. But then, Nathan is contacted by a man named John, who is a [insert other clan name] who lives in [insert name of subcounty that is adjacent to the subcounty where the interviewee resides]. John says that there is a very good bicycle for sale in [insert John's subcounty name] for a good price. However, John says that if Nathan wants this bicycle, he has to give John the money for it today – there is no time for Nathan to come view the bicycle for himself before buying it. John promises that it is a very good bicycle. Do you think that Nathan will buy the bicycle? What if John had been from the same clan as Nathan?

Of the thirty-four individuals in Teso to whom I asked this question (via a single translator for all interviews to ensure consistency of narration), eighteen (53%) said that they would buy the bicycle if John were a member of their clan, whereas only two (6%) said they would buy the bicycle if John were not a member of their clan. This is consistent with the long-standing observation of outsiders visiting rural sub-Saharan Africa about the importance of and trust conferred by family ties. And, crucially, these familial networks appear to have become important conduits through which information about the rebellion traveled when rumors began to spread after the violence began.

As soon as the UPA's initial attacks began in February 1987, rebel leaders sought to shape civilians' perceptions of them (as was detailed in Chapter 4) and their capabilities relative to the government – and news about the group spread rapidly among civilians throughout the region. As Ugandan scholar and Teso native J. Epelu Opio observed about the start of the rebellion, "There was widespread rebel propaganda amongst the population ... The population believed what the rebels told them."[42]

[41] Burke 1964, 132.   [42] Epelu-Opio 2009, 36–37.

It is difficult to overstate how often former UPA rebels, along with government military and intelligence officials, local leaders, and civilians who were exposed to the UPA, reported in interviews that when the UPA first committed these early attacks, rumors about the group spread rapidly throughout the region, and that people trusted what they heard from their kin. One former rebel leader explained the initial spread of news about the UPA: "information moves like wild fire in the bush ... "[43] Another said of spreading the word about the rebels: "The news went like a flame ... "[44] An indication of the speed and ease of rumor flow in such contexts is that twenty-eight out of thirty-four (82 percent) civilians I interviewed in the villages adjacent to the initial UPA base said that they learned about the existence of the rebel group for the first time through being informed by another person, rather than through directly observing rebel activity, a rebel meeting, or news media about the rebels; rumor spread faster than people could even come to learn information about the rebels through other means.[45]

These rumors shaped civilians' impressions of the rebels. Several rebel leaders emphasized the critical importance of shaping civilian perceptions about their strength during this critical period, while conceding that the fledgling group was, at that point, small and poorly armed. Indeed, civilian statements indicated that soon after first hearing about the rebels, they believed that the rebels would have substantial military capabilities. Members of one focus group reported that most people in their community seemed to initially support the rebels, since they believed in the rebels' promise to take over the government, and to "help the people" when they did so. Members of the focus group also agreed that most people in their community initially believed that the rebels would succeed. Individuals in a focus group in a different district also said that their first impression of the rebels was positive. Many people in a third focus group in a different district of Teso agreed that, at first, most people "thought [the rebels] were good boys" and they "believed that they could win." It was not until later, this group agreed, that they came to fear and doubt the rebels.[46] Over half

---

[43] Interview with former UPA leader, Amuria district, June 2009.

[44] Interview with former UPA intelligence officer, June 2009.

[45] See Appendix A for a discussion of how I identified these individuals for semi-structured interviews. While they do not constitute a random sample, there was balance among interviewees on factors most likely to be related to opinions about the rebels, such as age, sex, prior participation (or not) in the rebellion, or current party affiliation (pro-NRM or not).

[46] Focus group in Mukura subcounty, Kumi district, November 2009. This initial support for and belief in the UPA among the Iteso population, and that it waned as the violence intensified, is also stressed in Epelu-Opio 2009, 36–37, 104.

(eighteen out of thirty-four, 53%) of the civilians interviewed who had lived in villages adjacent to initial rebel bases during the rebellion agreed with the statement that "in the beginning of the rebellion most people [he/she] believed that the rebels would succeed in capturing Kampala." Given that we would expect responses to be systematically biased against agreeing with this statement – since everyone knows today that the rebels failed to reach Kampala – this number is rather high. Furthermore, interviews included open-ended questions about whether and why they initially supported the rebels. In response, villagers often volunteered their early expectation of rebels' success. They did not initially mention that they were related to rebels, or knew them well, or that they had strong grievances against the government.

From the perspective of the counterinsurgents, these dynamics of generalized belief in the incipient rebels created an impression that almost every villager in Teso was supporting the rebels in the early stages of the war. A military officer who led the counterintelligence effort against the UPA rebels in Teso said that his biggest challenge was overcoming how successful the rebels were at "convincing" people that they were strong. "It was tough; people were brainwashed," he said.[47] For example, in December 1987 the government dropped leaflets, trying to encourage people to defect to the government side, but this effort was a total failure.[48] Another senior military officer from the Teso region who served in the Uganda military's counterinsurgency operations against the UPA said:

> The UPA was very successful at mobilizing people ... [the people of Teso] were told lies and they believed them ... Once you get a war in an area, the area is filled with rumors.

According to accounts from rebels, former military officers, and civilians, information leaks about the rebels were extremely rare in these initial months. A local paper reported about Teso that "Especially during the first year of rebellion ... This was the height of the 'mam ajeni' (I don't know) chorus response from the Teso peasants whenever NRA soldiers asked for the whereabouts of the rebels."[49] A former UPA intelligence officer agreed, "Information leaks were rare ... The NRA tried to infiltrate us, but were unsuccessful."[50] A former local police officer explained that it

---

[47] Interview with Brigadier in the Ugandan military, July 2009.
[48] Interview with UPA leader, Soroti town, Soroti district, July 2008.
[49] "Letting the dogs loose on Teso rebels." *Weekly Topic.* Week ending July 12, 1989.
[50] Interview with former UPA intelligence officer, Soroti town, Soroti district, June 2009.

was very difficult for his forces to penetrate Teso and obtain information about the rebels, making it seem that "everyone was a rebel."[51] Further, a focus group in the subcounty where the UPA had their first base recollected that the UPA could gather citizens freely in the early stages of the rebellion, several people at a time meeting in broad daylight, without the government becoming aware of the meetings. They explained that while the locals knew about the rebel base near their community, they refrained from telling the government about it. The government did not discover the base for months.[52] Another UPA intelligence officer remarked that the government "just didn't have penetration to reach the community."[53] Without such secrecy, the UPA would have struggled to become a viable force. As yet another former UPA intelligence officer said: "We had to keep our secrets early [in the rebellion] in order to gain strength, and to attract soldiers ... to collect guns and become strong. Once we had collected enough, we could attack them."[54]

Later, as the war progressed and the level of violence increased, the civilians' initial belief in the rebels diminished. The theme of growing civilian disappointment in the rebels, and the violence that came to Teso as a result of them, was a common theme in interviews. As one civilian from Teso, who later joined the NRA as an intelligence officer in the Teso region, said, "People were so cooperative at first in [helping] the rebels ... but things changed when the government began to bring more and more troops. People wanted to be protected from the violence ... "[55] Another added that support for the rebels waned and information leaks to the government became common as time passed and "the rebels seemed to become weak."[56] In 1991, amid this waning support, government forces intercepted a major shipment of ammunition from Kenya, and arrested several key UPA operatives. This spelled the beginning of the end for the UPA; several leaders turned themselves in, and others fled into exile.

---

[51] Interview with former police officer who was stationed in Teso, Tororo district, June 2009.

[52] Focus group in Mukura subcounty, Kumi district, November 2009. The fact that the base was not discovered by the government for months was corroborated by rebel leaders who set up the base and numerous surrounding villagers.

[53] Interview with former UPA intelligence officer, Soroti town, Soroti district, July 2008.

[54] Interview with former UPA intelligence officer, Soroti county, Soroti district, February 2011.

[55] Interview with NRA counterinsurgent, Soroti district, July 2008.

[56] Focus group in Gweri subcounty, Soroti district, December 2009.

5.2.3 FOBA: Eastern Ugandan Group that Did Not Become Viable

In contrast to the serious problem that UPA posed to the Ugandan government, FOBA – despite aiming to overthrow the government and successfully killing several local government officials – never became a considerable threat. During its height, its members killed numerous local government officials and military and police officers in Bukedi. But, despite several attempts, FOBA never sustained a base on Ugandan territory for more than a few weeks. Their sole base was located in Kenya, about 5 kilometers over the border from Uganda. While accounts vary widely, at its height, FOBA probably reached 300–500 fighters.

Like Teso, the Bukedi area where FOBA formed has not played a prominent role in Uganda's political dramas over central power. It had a sizeable number of residents who served in Obote's military, but it was not known for dominating the central government or any security institution during the colonial or postcolonial era. It is an area of about 1,750 square miles, and is hillier, more fertile, and more forested than Teso. In fact, one UPA leader remarked about the UPA disadvantage relative to FOBA with respect to terrain, stating that "the forest [in Bukedi where FOBA formed] is ideal for war. During our rebellion, I would look there with envy."[57]

Bukedi is located south of Teso on a well-worn migration path between eastern Uganda and western Kenya that is bounded by Mount Elgon to the north and Lake Victoria to the south. As a result, Bukedi has long served as a place of confluence, where Nilotics migrating south from Sudan to Western Kenya mixed with Bantus migrating eastwards from western and central Africa. Besides traveling through Bukedi, the only other route from Uganda eastward to Kenya (other than going all the way around massive Lake Victoria via Tanzania) is to travel around the northern side of Mount Elgon. But doing so would mean traveling through Karamoja, the area of Uganda with the harshest terrain. Likely because of Bukedi's temperate climate, its relatively fertile land, and its proximity to the abundant water source of Lake Victoria, numerous groups on transit migration through this area opted to stay. As historian Samwiri Karugire explains:

Bukedi itself, lying on one of the major corridors of migration, was to receive a heterogeneous collection of ethnic groupings and its population still reflects this ... The result of this criss-crossing was that Bukedi had among its population Bantu ethnic groups (the Banyore, Bagwere, Bagwe and Samia), Nilotic Padhola,

---

[57] Interview with former UPA leader, Soroti town, Soroti district, July 2009.

Nilo-Hamitic Iteso, and the Bankenyi ... This diversity of ethnic groups in an area so small reflects the different migrations at different periods of peoples whose paths crossed here.[58]

Similarly, Fred Burke contrasts Teso's homogeneity in 1964 with Bukedi's "bewildering variety of traditional organization, reflecting the cultures of the many tribes inhabiting the area."[59] Burke explains that colonists had had to coax Bukedi's six small tribes into the single local political entity of Bukedi district, and states that:

British administration has attempted, in Bukedi, to develop a heterogeneous complex territory and people into a unified local government area. Outwardly the local political system resembles that of ... tribally homogeneous Teso. But local government and politics in Bukedi have also been shaped by the welter of traditional cultures and social systems which characterize this problematically complex district. In Bukedi the crucial variables are those associated with the multiple, traditional tribal-kinship systems, with authority and solidarity clustering at levels lower than the district.[60]

Today, in contrast to the just one dominant language and about three different dialects of Teso, Bukedi has roughly ten dialects of three distinct ethno-linguistic groups.[61] The districts of the Bukedi region – Busia, Butaleja, Pallisa, and Tororo – are today still listed in Uganda's constitution as "Bukedi," a word that means "land of naked people" in Luganda, the language of the Baganda people of central Uganda.[62] Commenting on Bukedi's diversity, one local leader referred to it as "The United States of Uganda," another said that it was "like the UN"[63] and two different interviewees used the word "cosmopolitan" to describe the area.[64]

While the distance between the two primary areas of Bukedi where FOBA launched – Mella and Busitema subcounties – is only about 50 kilometers, the area around Mella town is quite homogeneously Iteso, while the area around Busitema town is largely Basamia, with a sizeable Bagwe minority. There are also areas dominated by the Japhadola tribe nearby, particularly in neighboring Osukuru and Iyolwa subcounties. While the Basamia and the Bagwe speak similar languages, and intermarriage between them is relatively common, their Bantu-based language and culture are quite different from that of the Nilotic-based Iteso language, and both of those languages are quite different from the Luo-based

[58] Karugire 1980, 9. [59] Burke 1964, 224. [60] Burke 1964, 222. [61] Lewis 2009.
[62] Burke 1964, 204.
[63] Interview with local leader, Busia town, Busia district, June 2009.
[64] Interview with local leader, Tororo town, Tororo district, June 2009.

Japhadola language. Intermarriage between these groups is quite rare, and thus there is very little overlap in any of the kinship groups that exist within the ethno-linguistic clusters in Bukedi. In sum, the kinship network structure of this area is quite fragmented.

Yet despite the diversity of people living in Bukedi, a large majority of them had been united by the support of Obote's regime. Results from the 1980 elections show that 76.4 percent of votes from Bukedi supported Obote's party, the UPC. One group of local elders described Bukedi as a "UPC stronghold."[65] Thus, as one local leader said: "There was confusion in the east beginning in 1985 [when Okello ousted Obote]."[66] Another local leader said of the late 1980s in Bukedi, "It was a state of fear and uncertainty."[67]

Like the UPA, the FOBA conflict began in 1987 with the actions of a small number of individuals. One local leader explained that FOBA was initially "not a big uprising, but a clandestine network."[68] In early 1987, a man named Nelson Adula Omwero began gathering individuals near his home village of Namuwo and encouraged them to join him in a forested area in a part of Bukedi that is now known as Busitema forest in Busia district. Omwero had been a sergeant in Obote's army during the Bush War and was then integrated into the NRA, but then deserted the NRA in August 1986.[69] Soon, with the help of prominent politicians and businessmen from the Busia area, Omwero made links with other former leaders and members of Obote's UNLA military from the Bukedi area. These men also became part of FOBA's core leadership that was based about thirty-five kilometers away in a swampy area outside of Malaba, a town at the Uganda-Kenyan border.

FOBA's initial priority was to shape the perceptions and thus secure the support of the local population. One former FOBA leader said that, "When forming a rebel group, the first thing is the support of population ... [This is] more important than weapons."[70] Similar to the UPA, FOBA tried to spread news about their rebellion across the area between what is now Busitema forest in Busia district (where Omwero

[65] Group interview of three local leaders, Tororo town, Tororo district, June 2009.
[66] Interview with a local leader from Bukedi who served as the Special District Administrator for the area in the late 1980s and early 1990s. Busia town, Busia district, March 2009.
[67] Interview with local official, Tororo Town, Tororo district, July 2009.
[68] Interview with local official, Tororo town, Tororo district, July 2009.
[69] Asuman Nakendo. "Busitema rebel captured." *The New Vision*, September 21, 1988
[70] Interview with former UPA leader, Tororo town, Tororo district, July 2009.

initially operated) and the Mella area along the Kenyan border (where others in the initial leadership core operated).[71] Like the UPA, FOBA lacked significant weapons. But thanks to former members of Obote's army, they had enough to begin their rebellion, and planned to obtain more through successful attacks on the NRM. They also hoped to gain support from sympathetic Kenyans – both exiles from Obote's regime and from members of the Kenyan government.

In an apparent effort to demonstrate their ability to inflict harm against the government, FOBA's first attacks in early 1987 targeted local officials, who had been recently installed by the NRA government . These attacks against new, locally appointed officials continued throughout 1987. By September 1987, one report indicated that twenty-nine local officials in the Busia area, in communities bordering Kenya, had been killed.[72]

FOBA attempted to spread the word of these attacks as a great success – and thus that the group would become a formidable challenge to the NRM. "We had to convince the boys," said one local leader who had helped lead FOBA.[73] For example, one villager said that the rebels "were humble at first, trying to convince him that they could overthrow the government."[74] A former FOBA fighter said that the leaders tried to "register with the population" by sharing their vision of these attacks with their local contacts.[75]

However, the fragmented nature of local kinship networks appears to have prevented FOBA from spreading their message widely. Compared to individuals interviewed in Teso about UPA, a smaller portion of the individuals I interviewed in Bukedi had first learned about FOBA via other civilians – more first learned about the existence of a rebel group in their territory when seeing direct evidence of the rebels, such as seeing members of an armed group moving around their community. In Bukedi, about half (sixteen out of thirty-one, 52%) of individuals to whom I asked this question first learned about FOBA from rumors, rather than direct evidence. In contrast, recall that in Teso, significantly more people had

---

[71] It is difficult to trace how FOBA sought to devise communication networks because many of the key operational leaders were dead or unwilling to be interviewed. This account is pieced together with some information from former FOBA leaders, but primarily from interviews with civilians and local leaders.

[72] Sam Serwanga. "Rebels sneak in from Kenya." *The New Vision*, September 18, 1987.

[73] Interview with local official, Malaba town, Tororo district, June 2009.

[74] Interview with citizen, Mukura subcounty, Kumi district, December 2009.

[75] Interview with former FOBA soldier, Mbale town, Mbale district, July 2009.

learned about the rebels via rumors (twenty-eight out of thirty-four, 82%).

It appears that the rebels, unable to rely on dispersed communication networks to spread rumors about their group, instead often personally traveled throughout the region to directly communicate with the people. One former rebel explained, "We had to move village to village, explain why we were rebelling, and ask for support."[76] The way rebel leaders had to shape perceptions of their group has two implications. First, this suggests that the structure of trusted networks was not conducive to spreading rumors widely and quickly in general. Second, this may have made coordinating on secrecy, even for those who favored the rebels, more difficult because they were not sure that others had heard the same rumors and planned to behave similarly. Indeed, several villagers who identified as having supported FOBA also recalled concern at the outset of the rebellion that many others did not.

That communication networks were not conducive to the effective spread of rumors is further corroborated by accounts suggesting that the news that civilians did receive about the rebels was rather incoherent. Among civilian interviewees, individuals from different areas had different impressions about FOBA, including who led the group, what their objectives were, whether or not the group had a particular ethnic base, and how militarily strong they were. One local leader remarked that "FOBA was not properly politicized ... it seemed that their objectives changed."[77] All of these factors, of course, bear on an individual's assessment of the group's competence and strength, and this incoherence is further evidence of the fragmented nature of communication networks in Bukedi.

Numerous sources also suggested the problem of information leaks in Bukedi as the key cause of the rebel group's demise. A local leader said, "But when we first heard about FOBA, it looked like a joke ... I didn't take it seriously ... No one was certain about the new government, but no one expected [the rebels] to last .... The public was responsible for the break up [of FOBA], always reporting suspicious activities to authorities."[78] While FOBA repeatedly attempted to hold meetings to mobilize civilians in Bukedi, when they tried to do so, information about the time and place of the meetings would be leaked to the

---

[76] Interview with former FOBA leader, December 2009.
[77] Interview with former local leader, Busia Town Council, Busia district, June 2009.
[78] Interview with local leader in Tororo, Tororo Town Council, July 2009.

government.[79] One former FOBA leader lamented the difficulty of keeping secrets in Bukedi. He added, "To win, we would have needed more community support."[80] A former FOBA leader conceded, "It was difficult to keep secrets."[81] A UPA commander that tracked FOBA's formation and demise observed that information leaks appeared to be more common in Bukedi than Teso, stating, "[The military] infiltrated [FOBA] quickly ... they didn't know how to keep their secrets."[82]

Both rebels and military officials attributed these leaks to a lack of support. One FOBA fighter agreed: "People here didn't much support the rebels ... the rebels had nowhere to go. The President was very wise, and had many informants in the area."[83] A local official offered a similar account when asked why the rebels were not more successful, stating that "they lacked local support ... so they could not expand in territory and force size."[84] Another military leader familiar with the rebel group explained of the group's demise: "the local population was not supportive."[85]

Despite numerous attempts, the FOBA rebels were unable to maintain a base in Uganda; they instead targeted government officials in the night and then went back to their base in western Kenya by dawn. Many other civilians – even those with family members fighting on behalf of FOBA – reported that they freely provided the government with information about the rebels. This type of disclosure among interviewees from Teso was quite rare.

In the early 1990s, having never sustained a base on Ugandan soil or served as much of a threat, FOBA disbanded. One former leader, who fled into exile and later joined the NRM government, said simply that he saw that "the military solution was not working."[86] Leader Nelson Omwero was captured and jailed by the NRA in September 1988,[87] never to be

---

[79] Focus group, Malaba Town, Tororo district, December 2009, corroborated by interview with local official, Buteba subcounty, Busia district, November 2009, an interview with intelligence officer who worked in Bukedi, Kampala, August 2009, and an interview with local official, Tororo Town Council, Tororo district, July 2009.

[80] Former FOBA commander, Tororo district, December 2009. Interestingly, in comparing the outcome of the UPA and FOBA rebellions, a UPA commander agreed that FOBA failed because they were "quickly infiltrated" due to a "failure to keep secrets."

[81] Interview with former FOBA leader, December 2009.

[82] Interview with former UPA leader, Soroti town, July 2008.

[83] Interview with former FOBA fighter, Busia Town Council, Busia district, June 2009.

[84] Interview with local official, Busia town, Busia district, July 2009.

[85] Interview with a senior military official, Kampala, June 2008.

[86] Interview with former FOBA leader, February 2009.

[87] Asuman Nakendo. "Busitema rebel captured." *The New Vision*, September 21, 1988.

released alive, soon after another leader had turned himself over to the authorities. The group continued to commit some violence through 1989 and 1990 from their base in Kenya, but they did not gain ground in forming a base or advancing to Kampala. Beginning in late 1988, news reports suggested that the remaining rebels hit fewer political targets, and increasingly resorted to armed robberies.[88] FOBA leader Aggrey Awori surrendered himself to the NRA in 1991. He was later appointed to Uganda's Constituent Assembly in 1993 and served as Minister of Information and Technology from 2001 to 2008. A former Ugandan intelligence official argued that the rebel group was not defeated, but beheaded, and then it "melted away" into the civilian population.[89] While some former soldiers of the group continued criminal acts of theft and banditry into the early 1990s, by the turn of the decade, FOBA no longer existed as an organized, coherent group aiming to overthrow the government.

5.2.4 LRA: Northern Ugandan Rebels Who Became Viable

Like Teso, the Acholi region where the LRA formed is highly homogeneous; according to the 1991 census, the Acholi comprise 90 percent of the population there. While Acholis descended from three distinct linguistic groups and internal factions exist,[90] a dominant, relatively unified Acholi identity in the region very likely existed before Uganda's independence. According to historian Ron Atkinson, for centuries, social and political life there has been kinship based. He explains that despite the importance of local chiefdoms, "common social beliefs and practices shared over wide areas, and the need to marry women outside of one's own lineage ... promoted ties extending beyond [each village]."[91] Atkinson finds that the Acholi identity has slowly emerged, reaching a "broad unity" and shared language in the second half of the nineteenth century that distinguished it from neighboring tribes. While the precise processes through which a shared language in an area comes about are not well understood in the field of sociolinguistics, a high degree of interaction, and thus social, economic and/or kinship networks, likely must be present throughout the area for several generations.

---

[88] "Curb insecurity, RCs urged." *The New Vision*. October 4, 1988; "Rebels Attack Police Unit, Murder 5 RCs." *The Guide*, Vol 1, No 72, Week Ending May 24, 1989.
[89] Interview with former lead intelligence officer, NRA, August 22, 2009.
[90] On this point see especially Branch 2013.   [91] Atkinson 1999, 70–71.

The Acholi region also has several features that predispose it to the low-distance, unfragmented kinship network structure similar to that of the Teso region. In particular, it has long had low population density and thus abundant, available land. Further, the Acholi people are exogamous, patrilineal, and patrilocal, promoting similar migration patterns within Acholi to those of Teso, leading different areas of Acholi to be connected to one another by marriage and extended family networks.

While it is difficult to trace precisely how rumors and kinship networks spread the news of the LRA's emergence, there is considerable evidence that the LRA worked to spread positive news about itself – and negative perspectives on the government – and managed to secure broad support from local Acholis in the initial year or two of its operation.[92] As described in Chapter 4, the LRA apparently attempted to spread news using a mix of kinship networks as well as those based on Kony's former Christian networks. In doing so, the LRA was apparently effective at reaching civilians; local leaders I interviewed generally agreed that Kony's message was quite persuasive in the early years of the insurgency.[93] USAID contractor Robert Gersony remarked that the LRA "at the outset reportedly enjoyed some popular support."[94] This public support is rather striking given that two prior insurgencies (the UPDA and HSM) had recently formed in Acholi and failed.

Much of the LRA's support apparently derived from a widespread belief in the Acholi region that it would succeed in overtaking taking over the government. A government intelligence operative who was from this region, as well as community leaders and a former LRA commander all stated that in the early years, most people in the region believed that the LRA would make it to Kampala.[95] A former LRA commander also commented on the importance of belief. He said: "People want to

---

[92] Behrend 1999, 68–71. This sense of broad initial support for Kony was corroborated in numerous interviews. Note that not every rebel group launched in this region received civilian support: numerous interviewees stressed that the UPDA was reportedly less supported by the population. Consistent with the discussion in Chapter 4, interviewees suggested that individuals judged that the UPDA would not be a successful group, and thus opted not to support them.

[93] Interview with Mucwini local official (LC3 chair) who was a former rebel (UPDA and HSM) fighter, January 2010

[94] Gersony 1997, 31.

[95] Ugandan intelligence officer born in Acholi region, October 2009. Local leader, Pader district. Local leader, Odek subcounty, Gulu district, January 2010. Civilian, Lakwana subcounty, Gulu district, January 2010. Interview with former LRA commander, Gulu, November 2010.

believe in things which they believe will help get them out of their situation. Mobilization in Acholi was easy."[96] Similarly, an NGO worker who
had lived in northern Uganda during the early years of the LRA said his
impression was that the Acholi civilians he knew "expected that one day
[the LRA] would take over the government."[97] One military official from
Acholi agreed that in the initial years of the LRA rebellion, "[the LRA]
thrived on mythical belief."[98] The rumors that the LRA apparently spread
varied widely; some stressed Kony's supernatural powers, others the
NRA's nefarious plans for Acholi, and others were mysterious planes
dropping massive stocks of weapons to the rebels.

During these initial years of the LRA rebellion, the NRM government
struggled to penetrate the local population. One senior military officer
commented, "In the beginning, in Acholi there was a high degree of
support [for the LRA]. [The civilian population] had no vehicle to communicate to the government."[99] The NRM sent a representative to serve
as the District Administrator of Gulu, as they did to the rest of the country,
in order to develop "allies from within."[100] The district administrator's
main tasks were to convince the Acholi people that the NRM had their
best interests at heart, and to cultivate informers among the community.
Coming to Acholi to support the mission of the district administrator, the
Director for Mass Mobilization for the NRM traveled to Acholi and
reportedly said:

We have come to tell the people of Gulu what the NRM government stands for.
We shall tell them that the system is an exemplary Democratic System which
enables them to participate directly in their own affairs. We have come to tell
them to come to our side, and once we have won them on our side then the rebels
will be isolated and eventually weakened.

Despite these efforts, the NRA had trouble identifying any LRA bases for
years after the rebellion formed – information leaks from civilians were
rare.[101]

---

[96] Interview with former LRA leader, Gulu town, January 2010.
[97] Interview with NGO leader, Kasese town, Kasese district.
[98] Interview with military official, rank of major, Gulu, March 2009.
[99] Interview with senior military official, Bombo barracks, Luwero district, February 2009.
    A journalist from Acholi agreed that a major problem in the initial stages of the LRA
    rebellion was that the government lacked channels to communicate with civilians, who
    all gained information primarily from other villages and kinsmen.
[100] Interview with one of the initial architects of the RC system, November 2009.
[101] Interview with local official, Kitgum district, December 2009. Corroborated by military
    official who operated in Acholi, Kampala, October 2009.

Meanwhile, the government attempted to downplay the significance of the threat posed by the LRA. Local officials representing the central government were tasked with dispelling rumors: In one focus group, civilians reported that the NRA had told them that the LRA "had no capacity."[102] A government-owned newspaper heralded the end of the rebellion in 1987, just as the rebels were gaining ground against the government. It reported: "A reliable source in the Ministry of Defense said that the rebels were being combed out of Gulu, Kitgum, Apac and Lira and that those areas were now peaceful. He said that the war in the north is almost over ... "[103] By 1990, when the LRA was reportedly at least a thousand fighters strong, the president declared publicly that "the rebel remnants had now been reduced to small, isolated, nomadic groups."[104]

The LRA became viable, maintaining a base in Uganda within about a year of launching, and then became a formidable fighting force by the late 1990s. The LRA later became by far the largest and most violent Ugandan rebel group. While the LRA rarely engaged in open combat with the Ugandan government, they committed massive violence, and advanced toward Kampala as far as Teso in the early 2000s, until they were repelled and forced to fall back to bases in Sudan. Sudanese support – which had started in the early 1990s – subsided beginning in 2002, leading to substantial military gains for the Ugandan military. The last LRA attack on Ugandan territory occurred in 2005, months before the International Criminal Court issued a warrant for Kony and other leaders' arrests. Negotiations between the LRA and the Ugandan government ensued but then broke down. Kony and remnants of the LRA are thought now to move in small groups between eastern DRC, South Sudan, and the Central African Republic, occasionally continuing to commit brazen acts of violence against civilians in those countries.

5.2.5 WNBF: Northern Ugandan Case of a Group that Failed Early

The WNBF formed in the late 1980s in West Nile, the birth area of Idi Amin, a military officer from the Kakwa tribe who gained power in a 1971

[102] Focus group in Mucwini subcounty, Kitgum district, December 2009.
[103] "Rebels defeated in Soroti." *The New Vision*, July 17, 1987
[104] Elizabeth Kanyogonya. "Museveni reaps rebels in north." *The New Vision*, May 30, 1990. A local leader confirmed that the overriding sense in the region at the time was that the government was making the case that the LRA rebellion was weak.

coup and ruled until he was ousted by an alliance of Ugandan exiles and the Tanzanian army in 1979. The WNBF was led primarily by former members of the Ugandan national military who had fled to Sudan after Amin lost power. Like the LRA, the stated goal of the WNBF was to overthrow the government in Kampala,[105] and the conflict that ensued in West Nile resulted in widespread violence against civilians.[106] However, while the WNBF repeatedly tried to sustain bases in West Nile, it never managed to do so.

The leader of the WNBF, Juma Oris, was a member of the Alur ethnic group in Nebbi district of West Nile. Oris had served as Information Minister under Idi Amin in the 1970s. Oris's second in command, Colonel Abdulatif, was a commander in Amin's national army.[107] Oris was part of the initial group of men who decided just months after Museveni took power that they would fight to overthrow him.[108] Also like the LRA, WNBF benefitted from support from Khartoum, but not until the mid-1990s. Oris appears to have had deeper connections to Sudan than Kony; for example, Oris fled to Khartoum when Amin was ousted in 1979. However, the actual level of military support provided to WNBF from Sudan, particularly in the initial years, was rather limited.[109]

The physical and political geography of the areas where the LRA and the WNBF formed have a great deal in common. Both areas, Acholi and West Nile, respectively, are roughly equivalently forested and hilly, and the two areas have a similar climate – drier than Uganda's southern regions, but still quite suitable for cultivation of many crops and with

---

[105] All of the rebel leaders I interviewed in a group of seven WNBF ex-combatants stated that that was their true intent and that they believed it to be possible, especially since most had already served in the ruling government's military under Amin. (Interview, group of WNBF ex-combatants, Arua, January 2010.)

[106] Hovil and Lomo 2004.

[107] While Kony had no position in a former government, soon after forming his group he invited Brigadier Odong Latek, a man with deep connections to the Obote government's military leadership, to be his primary military commander.

[108] Oris was involved with the UPDA, planning to launch a front of the UPDA in West Nile. Oris's Alur ethnic group is Luo-speaking, and thus he could comfortably communicate with people from the Acholi region. Like Odong Latek, who joined with Kony, Oris disagreed with the UPDA's decision to negotiate with the NRA, and decided to launch his own group in West Nile. From then on, while the West Nile and Acholi rebels were aware of one another, there was little coordination between them, save one joint mission in 1998. The groups had entirely distinct command structures, with one group answering to Oris and the other to Kony. Interview with former senior LRA commander, Gulu, November 2009, and interview with WNBF ex-combatants, Arua, January 2010.

[109] Interview with a professor in the Makerere University Department of Political Science, July 2008, Kampala; interview with former senior WNBF commander, November 2009.

a high degree of low-lying forest and jungle cover outside of populated areas. Both subregions lie on international borders with states that had lukewarm relations, at best, with the government in Kampala. The areas immediately over the borders – the southernmost regions of what is now the state of South Sudan (then part of Sudan), and the easternmost regions of DRC – are some of the most weakly governed territories in the world. Regarding these borders, the WNBF arguably had the more advantageous location for rebellion, since the area where it formed is much closer to, and has a much longer border with, weakly governed neighboring states (both DRC and Sudan). From the early stages, the WNBF had bases in Oraba, Sudan, also near the border area of DRC. This enabled them, at times to have large numbers of troops based safely out of the direct reach of Ugandan forces.[110]

However, the heterogeneity of West Nile, relative to the Acholi sub-region, is quite striking. According to ethnologue data, the Acholi sub-region has one language and four dialects, while West Nile – an area roughly 60 percent the size of Acholi – has nine languages and 23 dialects. Anthropologist Mark Leopold explains of West Nile, "The local languages vary so much that two 'Lugbara' villages more than a dozen miles apart are likely to speak mutually incomprehensible dialects. Most people therefore customarily speak to each other in a 'trading' language such as Kiswahili or English."[111] The multiplicity of dialects and languages likely indicates generations of insular relations in different pockets of West Nile. Many of my interviewees from West Nile indicated a strong awareness of the diversity of their region. For example, one local religious leader commented about West Nile: "Culturally, people here are in disarray." Another added, "Yes, here we are quite mixed up."[112]

Historical evidence suggests that West Nile has long been occupied by such diverse peoples. For example, the year after it became part of the British Empire, the colonial administrator charged with imposing government in West Nile commented, "The variety of tribes and languages does not tend ... to make Administration easy."[113] Even as far back as 1925, a Sudanese government officer who was in charge of West Nile remarked on the apparent fragmentation of kinship networks in this area:

[110] Group interview of WNBF ex-combatants, Arua town, Arua district, June 2008.
[111] Leopold 2005.
[112] Interview with West Nile religious leaders, Arua district, June 2008.
[113] Cited in Leopold (2005, 103) as Weatherhead, District Commissioner's Report for 1914–1915. RH mss Afr.s.586.

To the south of Wati (Mt. Eti) [which is toward the center of West Nile] . . . there are an immense number of little communities . . . The disorganization of this part of the country was so complete, that it was absolutely unparalleled by anything I have seen elsewhere or heard about . . . On pitching camp near a village, people would come out and stand in a group of about two hundred near a village and watch proceedings . . . On moving to a village only a mile or two away, one would have to go through the whole of this exasperating game again, *as there was seldom any communication between neighbouring villages* [emphasis added]. Each little group was perfectly isolated. (Stigland 1923, 4, quoted in Middleton 165, 9)[114]

As in the case of Bukedi, West Nile's diversity likely stems from migration patterns, since the area lies on a migration route of Nilotic and Sudanic tribes who came and settled in several different waves.[115] Anthropologist Mark Leopold suggests that West Nile's ethno-linguistic diversity may also be related to its varied interactions with numerous external forces: What is now known as West Nile changed imperial hands three times between 1894 and 1914. First, in the late 1800s, it was the personal property of King Leopold of Belgium. Then, during Europe's "scramble for Africa," Britain acquired it from Belgium in 1909, when it became part of Britain's Anglo-Egyptian condominium of Sudan. Finally, in 1913, as part of a territorial swap between components of the British Empire it became part of the Protectorate of Uganda.[116]

According to most accounts, the WNBF was (like the LRA) initially a volunteer army, made up mostly of former fighters from Amin's national military. Amin had reportedly filled the ranks of his army with people from the West Nile. Most of the WNBF's initial leadership core was from the Kakwa ethnic group, Amin's group. However, the Kakwa are quite

---

[114] Interestingly, it appears that the fragmentation of West Nile, and relative insularity of small localities there, may also extend to economic networks there. Anthropologist John Middleton, who lived in West Nile in the early 1950s, noted that ways of life there were highly economically localized. He said of West Nile: "Although there has always been a certain amount of traveling and trading across tribal boundaries, for special commodities, everyday traditional requirements can be satisfied locally within a small neighborhood. It is thus possible for a very small territorial group to exist economically with only very slight recourse to external trading." Middleton 1965.

[115] For a discussion of these migrations, and the droughts and wars that appear to have caused them, see Webster, Ogot, and Chretien 1992, 777–785. An interview with two leaders of the Lugbara-Madi Cultural Society in Arua municipality in November 2009 also underscored that different waves of migration contributed to the heterogeneity of the area.

[116] Leopold 2005, 11–12.

a small group, and beyond the initial top leadership core, the WNBF drew from a variety of ethnic groups based in West Nile.[117]

Former members of the WNBF indicated the importance of spreading news about their capabilities and intentions to the local population, stating, "[the WNBF] knows the importance of our people."[118] It was not possible to arrive at a precise account of how the WNBF initially spread information about their group, in part due to a variety of ongoing political sensitivities in Uganda regarding government amnesty packages for WNBF rebels.[119] While being interviewed as a group, former WNBF leaders insisted that they successfully shaped civilians' impressions of them from the start of their insurgency, and that civilians supported them from the very beginning. But when interviewed alone, the testimony of a former rebel leader there was surprisingly frank: "Support of the people is very important ... some people [initially] supported us, but others didn't."[120] Another former rebel interviewed alone said, when asked why the LRA was so successful compared to their rebellion: "Their Acholi brothers give them support."[121] A former LRA commander who had observed but not participated in the West Nile rebellion agreed that the WNBF failed due to lack of civilian support. He suggested that the opposite was true of the LRA in the Acholi region, saying: "They didn't have morale like we did in Acholi ... They had mixed clans and different languages."[122] A leader of another rebel group that was later based in West Nile, the NFA, commented that the WNBF appeared easy for the government to infiltrate.[123]

[117] Hovil and Lomo 2004; corroborated by WNBF ex-combatants group interview, July 2008, Arua. Of the roughly 2000 former WNBF fighters who received amnesty from the Government of Uganda and who reported their religion and ethnicity to the Amnesty Commission, 71% were Muslim, 19% were Catholic, and 9% were Protestant. In the same group with respect to ethnic affiliations, 59% were Lugbara, 12% Kakwa, 13% Alur, and 3% Madi.

[118] Group interview of former WNBF leaders, Arua town, Arua district, June 2008.

[119] I was able to meet with former WNBF leaders, but the information I was able to collect about the history of their group was scant, since their primary concern in meeting with me was to convince me to help them secure additional funds from the government of Uganda. Also, unlike other case study rebel groups, with the WNBF, I was unable to locate a former rebel leader who had kept fairly detailed personal records – or had detailed memories – of the initial stages of their group formation.

[120] Interview with former rebel leader, Kampala, November 2009.

[121] Interview with WNBF intelligence officer, Kampala, December 2009.

[122] Interview with former senior LRA commander, Gulu, November 2010.

[123] Interview with NFA leader, Kampala, March 2009.

Crucially, very different narratives consistently emerged from civilians and government intelligence officers where the WNBF rebels formed in contrast to those where the LRA formed. Civilians in West Nile almost uniformly recalled a rebellion that lacked the confidence of locals from the start. In one focus group, participants recalled that the WNBF had come near their community for one or two days looking for medicine, however, they were quickly driven away by soldiers, who were likely tipped off by locals about the rebels' presence.[124] A local leader said that the rebels tried hard to make a base in West Nile, but they consistently failed due to bad intelligence.[125] In another focus group, civilians recalled being gathered by rebels, and said that the rebels took great care to only gather small groups in isolated areas. Others in that focus group recalled numerous instances of rebels being "chased away" by the government, owing to civilians sharing information with the government.[126]

Several civilian accounts suggest that the limited nature of civilian support stemmed from beliefs that the rebels were not capable of succeeding, suggesting that WNBF was not successful at shaping perceptions there. For example, when I asked a focus group what happened when individuals there became aware of the WNBF, an individual replied amid several nods, "The WNBF was not supported here. They said they wanted to take over the government, but we knew they were not capable of it. They didn't have the manpower or the guns."[127] Doubts about their ability to succeed arose in another focus group in a different part of West Nile, as well.[128] Several other people suggested particular concern about the rebels' capabilities relative to the government. For example, when asked why the WNBF never had much success, one community leader replied, "Civilian support was lacking ... people here [in West Nile] saw that the government would be stronger."[129]

Perhaps most crucially, government intelligence officers in West Nile remarked repeatedly about the relative ease of collecting information in West Nile, and their comments about why this was the case are consistent

---

[124] Focus group in Aringa district, January 2010.
[125] Interview with local leader, Arua district, December 2009.
[126] Focus group in Koboko district, December 2009.
[127] Focus group in Alikwa town, Maracha county, Nyadri district, Wile Nile region, January 2010.
[128] Focus group in Drajina subcounty, Yumbe district, December 2009.
[129] Interview with local religious leaders, Aura town, Arua district, July 2008.

with the theoretical assertions about fragmented kinship networks in heterogeneous areas. For example, one government intelligence officer said, "People doubt rumors here in West Nile." Indeed, intelligence officers in West Nile felt that their job was relatively easy. One said: "People here cannot keep secrets. One does not need to buy intelligence here; people freely contributed information about rebel groups."[130] Another intelligence officer remarked that compared to the start of the LRA, at the start of the WNBF, "people [in West Nile] were more supportive of the government."[131] A former head of the central government's internal intelligence agency agreed: "To gain intelligence, you must be appreciated by the local population ... It is more difficult for rebels to mobilize in diverse areas, and easier for the government to gain information there ... People are more independent in such areas."[132]

Information leaks to the government eventually led to the WNBF's demise. As one former rebel explained, "We couldn't have a base on Ugandan territory because the government would soon know about it."[133] While the Ugandan government repeatedly flushed out nascent WNBF bases in Uganda, the group remained intact for almost a decade by retreating to bases in Sudan and DRC. According to a variety of sources, the WNBF reached at least 1,000 strong at its height,[134] and maybe many more: over 4,000 individuals have received amnesty from the Ugandan government for their participation in the WNBF.[135] The WNBF formally disbanded in 1998, after Ugandan forces pursued them across the border of Sudan, largely destroying WNBF bases there. In the meantime the WNBF caused a great deal of insecurity by making incursions into Ugandan territory in West Nile during that period. However, the violence

[130] Interview with government intelligence officer based in West Nile, Nyadri district, December 2009.
[131] Interview with intelligence officer, Kampala, March 2009.
[132] Interview with former senior official of internal intelligence agency, Bombo barracks, Luwero district, August 2009.
[133] Interview with former rebel leader, Kampala, November 2009.
[134] Interview with local leader, Yumbe district, June 2009, and interview with senior military officials, Bombo Barracks, Luwero district, February 2009. According to members of an organization of ex-combatants in Arua, over 7,000 individuals who claim to be former WNBF soldiers have "reported" seeking amnesty from the government.
[135] This figure is based on a database I collected from Uganda's Amnesty Commission. However, there is good reason to believe that the number of individuals receiving amnesty is higher than the actual number of soldiers since individuals receive a small resettlement "package" with at least $200 when they are granted amnesty. Former WNBF combatants I interviewed, however, insist that the Amnesty Commission has yet to grant amnesty to a number of individuals who were former soldiers.

committed by the WNBF was sporadic and small-scale; without a base on
Ugandan territory, the group could never become a viable threat. As many
observers and former leaders of other rebellions noted, given that West
Nile's location adjacent to DRC and Sudan makes it an ideal environment
for rebels, it is striking that the WNBF was not more successful. The other
two rebel groups that attempted to form in West Nile since 1986 – the
NFA and the UNRF II – similarly failed to become viable.

5.3 SUPPORT FROM A RELATED FIELD EXPERIMENT

The case study evidence is far from decisive but is consistent with several
features of the proposed causal mechanism about the spread of news and
beliefs through kinship networks. Beyond this evidence, a field experiment
I conducted with Jennifer Larson in Teso – the region where the UPA
formed – provides useful evidence in support of the proposition that
ethnic homogeneity facilitates the rapid spread of news via word-of-
mouth networks.[136]

Our research team seeded novel news in several randomly selected
households in two villages in Teso – one ethnically homogeneous, and
one heterogeneous.[137] While for obvious ethical reasons we did not seed
rumors about a coming rebellion, the news we seeded was novel: that in
three days, villagers could attend a nearby event where all adults could
receive a bar of soap in return for responding to a survey. Because of the
uncertainty surrounding the news and the difficulty of verifying it,
villagers appeared to perceive it as rather sensitive information to
share. Surveys conducted subsequently at the event and of every household in those villages examined who did and did not learn the news.
While this research design of closely examining two villages is, naturally,
constrained in its ability to support general claims, it allowed us to
collect sufficiently rich data on each village to shed light on the complex
process of information transmission in ethnically homogeneous versus
heterogeneous areas.

We found that everyone who learned the news did so via word-of-
mouth; not a single person learned about the news via telephone. Also, we
found that eight times more people in the homogeneous village learned the

---

[136] For more detail about the experiment's design and results, see Larson and Lewis 2017.
[137] While most villages in Teso are quite homogeneous, a small portion closer to another
      ethnic group's home area are somewhat mixed, with the minority Kumam reaching as
      much as one-third of the village population.

news than those in the heterogeneous village. The homogeneous village is located near the area of Teso where the UPA initially formed, and the ethnic demography changed little in the intervening years between 1988 and 2013. These findings therefore provide additional, suggestive support for a key component of the theory: that local networks in ethnically homogeneous settings can spread novel news much more effectively than those in ethnically mixed areas.

5.4 ALTERNATIVE EXPLANATIONS

There are many possible explanations for why only some rebel groups become viable; I have focused on attributes of local populations that I posit can help rebels keep secrets in the vulnerable initial stages. Because of the connections that I argue exist between this secrecy and information dissemination, trusted networks, and ethnic demography, this chapter has also advanced a specific argument about why and how ethnicity influences conflict onset that centers on how local ethnic homogeneity can shape incipient rebels' ability to spread their rumors.

I revisit two leading alternative explanations for ethnic homogeneity's association with rebel viability here: first, it could be that ethnic homogeneity coincided with rebel viability because it allowed for localized antigovernment grievances, born of the local ethnic groups' exclusion from central governmental power. Second, it could be the case that co-ethnics' advantages at in-group policing made ethnically homogeneous areas more felicitous for rebel group formation. Either could be a causal mechanism linking civilians in homogeneous areas' decision not to share information about rebels with the government. Neither is mutually exclusive with the causal mechanism I advanced here, but I probe the relative strength of the evidence for them here and find it limited.

A grievance-based approach would expect that *prior to the start of violence*, a much larger portion of the population in Teso and Acholi disdained the government than in Bukedi and West Nile. Entirely ruling out this explanation is difficult since it is impossible to determine individual preferences over two decades *ex post*, and surveys are not available for that period. Biases induced by the passage of time loom particularly large for conflict settings due to the complex and often interrelated relationship between preferences for rebellion and events that occur during conflicts. Due to such biases, regions where rebels succeed in becoming quite violent suffer more, often due in part to ham-fisted counterinsurgency responses, and that suffering becomes well documented. Indeed, that is the case for both Acholi and Teso; the NRM's responses to the LRA and UPA after the insurgencies were viable led to deeply unpopular, forced movements of villagers into camps, and in turn, strong antigovernment grievances. In contrast, such events naturally never occurred in regions where rebellions did not launch, or where they launched but failed early. Furthermore, these regions do not play an important role in Ugandan history since major violent conflict did not occur there; there has been much less study of political preferences in such regions. Observers of conflict can thus easily, retrospectively attribute the emergence of viable insurgencies in some areas to greater, or more widespread, antigovernment sentiment in those areas.

It is important to note that there is no shortage of retrospective accounts of the UPA and LRA rebellions that emphasize marginalization (at the hands of the government) experienced by the ethno-regions that these rebels claimed to represent. For example, one author of a book about the UPA explains in a section entitled "Why did it start?" that the UPA "was a movement of a desperate and frustrated people of Teso ... (the rebellion) was fought due to hatred and neglect ... "[138] Similarly, in northern Uganda, there is considerable evidence that NRA-allied fighters from central Uganda committed atrocities against Acholi civilians in the mid-1980s, in retaliation for Acholi atrocities during the Bush War of the early 1980s in central Uganda. These events stoked Acholi resentment, several analyses posit, generating distrust of the NRM government that fueled the LRA.[139]

However, scrutiny of the period in which these rebellions formed casts doubt on grievances' role in the *initial* phases of rebellion. As a first cut at assessing this relationship's relevance in Uganda for rebel groups' initial formation, in Chapter 4 I examined an objective measure of exclusion from 1988 (Table 4.2). A key finding was that no group in Uganda was greatly excluded from the central government's cabinet positions in 1988, at the outset (or within one year of formation) of the rebellions studied

[138] Otwal 2001, 40–41.
[139] Gersony, op cit and Otunnu, Ogenga. 2002. "Causes and Consequences of the War in Acholiland." In "Protracted Conflict, Elusive Peace: Initiatives to End the War in Northern Uganda," Accord, available at www.c-r.org/our-work/accord/northern-uganda/causes-dynamics.php. See also Branch 2013.

here. For example, the Iteso were 6 percent of Uganda's population (as of the 1991 census) but were 3.2 percent of the cabinet; the Acholi were 4.4 percent of the population but just 3.2 percent of the cabinet. Furthermore, Chapter 3 defended my characterization of the late 1980s as a time of great uncertainty in Uganda in terms of expectations of the fledgling NRM government. These findings are not consistent with widespread grievances in certain areas prior to the start of rebellion there.

Furthermore, turning back to the evidence from interviews and focus groups, in Teso, rebel and civilian accounts indicated almost unanimously that initially, people's private feelings about the UPA varied a great deal among individual villagers.[140] For example, conceding that numerous people in Teso did not initially support them, one of the initial UPA rebel leaders confirmed that the rebels sought to identify people who were not supportive of them.[141] He conceded that, at the start, many people would not have supported the idea of rebellion:

> If you will go … asking everybody here and there: "I'm going to start a rebellion, do you think we should do it?" then they would say no …
> It was wrong on one hand to act without the others [in the community] … But we could not go and consult everyone because of the [potential] leakage [to the government]. It was better for a few of us to handle the planning. … [T]hese people are going to be caught up in a war that they had never thought of … but for us, we said, ok, they never thought of it, [but] we are going to do it on their behalf. So, if things go bad, I will always say that we did it in good faith.

Moreover, when asked in individual interviews (with the author and a translator present), just a few out of over sixty villagers interviewed from Teso agreed that most people in their community had a strong distaste for the government prior to the initial start of violence in Teso.[142] According to another scholar's account, antigovernment grievances were far from high at the outset – after the NRM took over the government in January 1986, the Iteso were optimistic about their relationship with the

---

[140] Interview with civilian, Gweri subcounty, Soroti district, January 2011; interview with civilian, Gweri subcounty, Soroti district, January 2011.

[141] In another interview, another former UPA leader described the mixed preferences of the highly homogeneous civilian population near his initial rebel base as follows: "[Even in the initial stages,] some people [near to their initial base] didn't want the rebellion. We would ensure those people didn't get information … watch behavior of those who run to the soldiers."

[142] Many interviewees openly discussed distaste for the current government, so it does not appear that various plausible pro-government response biases were at work here.

new government and "when [the NRM] entered Teso [in late 1986], it was received with ululations and jubilation."[143]

Turning to the northern Ugandan paired cases, distinguishing prewar levels of antigovernment grievance is more complex because of the severity of the war that followed, and especially the government's counterinsurgency response, which led to intense antigovernment sentiment among the Acholi. While Acholis related to former fighters in Obote's military had suffered reprisal attacks after the Bush War, which some interviewees noted as a cause of early LRA support, most reported awareness that the attacks were mostly committed by a group that was organizationally distinct from the NRA. They were also aware that the group was composed of people from central Uganda, whereas the NRA was led predominantly by western Ugandans. Other scholars' accounts stress that there was a generally positive response to the NRM in Acholi in the late 1980s. For example, Tim Allen notes that villagers in Acholi "were seriously abused" by the military in counterinsurgency operations in the late 1980s, but also notes: "[V]isiting Gulu District in September 1989, I was struck by the presence of small NRA units in relatively remote locations to the west of Lamogi, as well as by the good relations they seemed to enjoy with the locals."[144]

At a minimum, there is good reason to believe that antigovernment sentiment among Acholis was not significantly more widespread than it was among West Nilers in the late 1980s – so this is unlikely to be driving the difference in viability outcomes in these cases (the LRA compared to the WNBF). While antigovernment – or at least skeptical – sentiment in Acholi was likely not negligible in the late 1980s, West Nilers had also previously suffered a great deal: In the aftermath of Amin's ouster in 1979, members of the new government's military chased Amin's former military men back to their home area of West Nile and committed grave atrocities against them and their communities. As a result, large numbers of civilians in West Nile poured out of Uganda, crossing primarily into Sudan, where they remained in refugee camps for much of the 1980s, for fear of danger back in Uganda. It was not until the late 1980s that those refugees dared to return to their homes.[145] Thus, West Nile was one of the, if not the most, economically desperate regions in Uganda in the late 1980s; likely much

---

[143] Epelu-Opio 2009, 41.   [144] Allen 1991, 375.

[145] See Dawin Dawa. "11,493 Ugandans return from Sudan." *The New Vision*, August 22, 1988. Dawa reports that over 11,000 refugees returned to West Nile in a UN convoy that month.

more so than Acholi. While West Nilers had little reason to blame these difficulties on the new NRM government, given that the new NRM government had almost no West Nilers in its upper ranks, there was also little reason for West Nilers to believe that it would assist them.

Interestingly, a rebel leader who later formed a different rebel group in West Nile (the NFA) argued that antigovernment sentiment there appeared strong; that even though the area was ethnically diverse, he felt motivation to rebel could still be widespread. He said of the population of West Nile, where the WNBF and the UNRF II also formed their groups, "They're mixed, but the majority are sympathetic to antigovernment [feelings] [sic]." In other words, this rebel leader did not equate ethnic homogeneity with preference homogeneity, and he perceived that there were sufficient grievances in West Nile to fuel a rebellion.

Looking to another subregion of northern Uganda, if antigovernment sentiment was a primary driver of how rebel groups became viable in homogeneous areas, then we should expect that a viable rebel group would have been likely to emerge in Lango – but, as described earlier in the chapter, it did not. Lango is located in northern Uganda to the east of Acholi and to the northwest of Teso, and is the home region of the then-recently ousted president Obote, who ruled Uganda from 1980 to 1985 (in addition to 1962 to 1971). Lango is also a highly homogeneous area. In the late 1980s, a rebel group called NOM formed there – but it was quickly defeated. Another rebel group, CAMP, formed there in the mid-1990s, but was again promptly defeated. If the extent or intensity of antigovernment resentment were the primary driver of rebel viability, then NOM would likely have become viable. But despite the prevalence of antigovernment feelings in Lango when these rebel groups formed, they did not become viable. As one local journalist who had been a fighter in NOM and had reported on CAMP observed, talking about long-standing suspicions of the NRM in Lango: "It's very easy for people [in the Lango region where NOM and CAMP formed] to want rebellion."[146] He explained that people shared information about rebels with the government due to a sense from early rumors that the leadership of the nascent rebel groups was not strong. While I did not conduct extensive fieldwork in this region, these impressions are consistent with the theory's

---

[146] Interview with local journalist who was a soldier for NOM, Lira municipality, March 2009.

contention that "favorable" networks underlying a homogeneous area can in fact work against rebels, enabling anti-rebel rumors to travel widely.

Finally, and crucially, it appears that in several cases, antigovernment narratives emerged *after* rebellions were well underway – likely as a result of rebels' efforts to shape these narratives.[147] For example, in Teso, observers commonly cite the devastating raids of the Iteso's cattle by the neighboring Karamojong ethnic group in the late 1980s as a reason why the Iteso people despised the NRM government and therefore supported rebels; they resented that the government did not exert greater effort to protect their cattle. However, upon closer scrutiny, it appears that the most severe cattle raids in Teso did not occur until several months *after* the UPA rebellion began; thus, those raids could not have generated widespread support for rebellion until after the rebels had become viable. In fact, one UPA rebel leader suggested that the rebels were aware that the cattle raiding could help their cause, and implied that some rebels may have been complicit in the raids – while spreading the word that the government had been involved.[148] Anthropological work also stresses the political uses of – and the scant concrete evidence – for the narrative that cattle raids in Teso were abetted by the NRM government.[149] While the raids were indeed devastating and unfortunate, most appear to have occurred after the start of the rebellion. Furthermore, there is little doubt that, at a minimum, narratives that stressed the injustice of the cattle raiding emerged during the initial stage of insurgency and served the interests of the rebels and other actors who were then mobilizing the Iteso civilian population.[150]

Interestingly, similar dynamics are reflected with respect to how cattle raiding influenced the rebellion in Acholi; today, many people cite the cattle raids – and the NRM's government being complicit in it – as a primary cause of the LRA rebellion. However, close analyses have suggested that the rebels were also complicit in these raids, and had formed prior to at least some of the raids that devastated Acholi stocks of cattle.[151]

---

[147] Several existing works find that wartime experiences importantly shape civilians' preferences regarding the warring factions. See, in particular, Kalyvas (2006), pages 111–114 on how civilian preferences arise out of the dynamics of violence in situations of internal war.

[148] Interview with UPA leader, Soroti, June 2009   [149] Buckley-Zistel 2008 101–104.

[150] Buckley-Zistel 2008; Jones 2008.   [151] Finnström 2008, 71.

In sum, levels of grievance in communities where rebels formed do not appear to be driving differences in viability in the two pairs of nascent rebel groups examined in this chapter. Furthermore, upon inspection, the grievances that are retrospectively associated with these conflicts' start appear to have, at least in part, emerged *out of* the early stages of the conflicts – which can help explain why it may appear upon cursory, retrospective examination that rebel viability is associated with grievances.

5.4.1 Intra-Ethnic Group Knowledge, Policing, and Punishment

Other seminal studies of ethnic politics emphasize co-ethnics' enhanced ability to obtain information about one another's behavior, and relatedly, an improved ability to punish one another for defection from the group. In particular, in their classic work about interethnic cooperation, Fearon and Laitin posit a co-ethnic advantage in detecting (and thus punishing) defectors.[152] While Fearon and Laitin focus on the emergence of cooperation between ethnic groups, the general logic can also be applied to understanding improved levels of cooperation among co-ethnics, particularly in overcoming free-rider problems.[153] Relatedly, Jason Lyall finds support for a co-ethnic advantage in identifying rebel sympathizers in Chechnya.[154] An application of these arguments in the context of rebel group initiation could be that in ethnically homogeneous areas, rebels who share the ethnic identity of the local population are better able to identify individuals who provide information to the government, and knowing this, individuals in such contexts are deterred from doing so.

For several reasons, this argument does not find much support in this chapter's case studies. First, if one accepts my contention from Chapter 4 that nascent rebels do not initially have the capacity to monitor and detect information leaks to the government, then it follows that rebels have a strong incentive, as they build their intelligence networks, to encourage individuals to convey their true, private preferences. Coercion and punishment would be counterproductive to that end. As described in Chapter 4, there is little evidence that rebels initially behaved in a coercive manner toward civilians. According to both rebels and civilians, rebels only rarely threatened or physically harmed civilians in the initial stages. On the contrary, almost all interviews – with civilians, government agents, and

[152] Fearon and Laitin 1996.
[153] Miguel and Gugerty 2005; Habyarimana et al. 2007; Habyarimana et al. 2011.
[154] Lyall 2010.

rebels – suggest strongly that rebels worked hard to maintain a "clean" image in the initial months.

One could argue that observing the absence of rebel coercion is consistent with a policing mechanism in homogeneous areas; coercion did not occur because would-be information leakers in homogeneous areas knew they would be discovered and punished. But this seems unlikely to have been the case given that not a single interview in Teso or Acholi surfaced civilian or rebel testimonies about concerns during the outset of the war about rebels or other civilians harming them if they did not go along with the rebellion. Especially in Teso, where the rebellion had ended well over a decade prior to my interviews, it seems unlikely that security or political concerns would have prevented civilians from freely sharing this consideration if it had been important to them.

Second, if this mechanism was operating, then rebels should have had trouble preventing information leaks in areas – even homogeneous ones – where the rebel leaders were not co-ethnics with the local population. However, two of the four rebel groups that succeeded in becoming viable met a great deal of success in areas where the local population, while homogeneous, did not share the ethnic identity of the rebel leaders. The ADF was led primarily by Muslims from Baganda and Basoga (central and eastern Uganda). According to an ADF leader, in part because Muslims do not dominate any area of Uganda, the ADF decided to establish its initial bases in an area of western Uganda inhabited predominantly by Bakonjo people. This area had several other appealing attributes for aspiring rebels: it was home to two prior, post-independence rebellions, and it is located in the foothills of the Rwenzori mountains on the border with DRC.[155] Yet even though the local Bakonjo people in this homogeneous area did not share an ethnic identity or religion with the rebel leaders, they initially did not pass information about the ADF to the government.[156] Similarly, the HSM, which formed in Acholi, experienced few information leaks as it moved through the homogeneous Lango and Teso areas on its march to capture Kampala. It was not until the HSM reached a highly

---

[155] When I asked a former ADF leader why the ADF selected that area for their rebellion, he emphasized the proximity to the Rwenzori mountains and the border with the DRC (Interview with former ADF leader, Kampala, January 2011).

[156] This is a case that instead points to the potential for prior ethnic grievances and/or a reservoir of prior rebel fighters to help rebel groups become viable; while I do not know of specific evidence showing this to be the case, the Bakonjo people's involvement in prior rebellions may indicate a high level of antigovernment grievance that may have helped the ADF.

heterogeneous area in eastern Uganda near Jinja that the government succeeded in gaining significant intelligence about them, and defeated them there.[157]

5.5 BEYOND UGANDA

The data needed to examine the correlates of rebel viability beyond Uganda are unavailable; acquiring the needed data on *all* rebel groups that formed, including groups that failed early, requires substantial time in numerous, remote localities of each country to gain highly local knowledge about conflict histories. Still, the best evidence we do have – accounts from contemporary, qualitative reporting in fragile states – suggests that the phenomenon of "small" rebel groups that never became substantial is widespread, especially in weak states, and such groups is omitted from major datasets. In prior chapters, I cited examples of rebel groups that other scholars identify as failing too early to be explicitly named and studied from Iraq, Sri Lanka, Kashmir, Latin America, and others.

Using the data on rebel group formation from central and eastern Africa I describe in Chapter 1 (and Appendix D), I find that over half of the eighty-three groups I identified committed violence for less than three years. I attempted to capture whether or not rebel groups became viable using the criteria I used for Uganda, along with ethnic demography data for the areas of group formation, but found that it was not possible to make reliable judgments with available sources. I return to the implications of this work for data collection efforts on conflict onset in Chapter 7.

Because the initial phases of insurgency leave only a faint trace in news reports and in the historical record, it is not possible to use standard datasets or cursory, retrospective measures to distinguish whether factors impel the *initial* onset of organized violence in weak states, or whether they instead exacerbate conflicts that have already begun. Evidence from Uganda that is highly unusual in its comprehensive coverage and detail supports the latter interpretation of how local ethnic dynamics influence the early stages of rebellion. While additional work will of course need to probe the external validity of these findings, they suggest that ethnic tensions that emerge *out of* the initial stages of violence can be just as important to generating subsequent organized violence as ethnic marginalization that existed *prior to* the start of violence – and that pre-existing

[157] Interview with senior military officer who served as a counterinsurgent against the HSM, Bombo Barracks, Luwero district, August 2008.

ethnic marginalization from central power is not a necessary condition for the emergence of what later becomes known as an ethnic rebellion.

Naturally, this evidence from Uganda does not eliminate the possibility that other mechanisms, including pre-existing ethnic grievances, can aid nascent rebels attempting to become viable. Rather, it demonstrates that prior, widely held grievances may not be necessary for the emergence of what later becomes known as an "ethnic rebellion." While resentment and motivation likely do play an important role in provoking certain types of political conflict – especially those that involve high-risk actions, such as rebelling against a strong regime or joining a rebellion that is underway, as others have documented[158] – they do not appear to have played a decisive role in the very initial stages of insurgency in Uganda. Instead, resentments largely emerged out of the initial phases of rebel-instigated violence.

5.6 DISCUSSION

While civilian support has long played a central role in theories of insurgency and counterinsurgency, and rumors commonly feature in accounts of war's start, this chapter has provided evidence for a new understanding of how both matter in the formative, initial stages of insurgent group formation. Civilians are important in these stages because they can provide information to the government, which can present an existential threat to incipient rebels. Therefore, the specific type of support rebels initially need from civilians is secrecy. Rumors seeded by rebels are critical because of how they influence civilians' perceptions of rebels' capabilities and intentions – and thus they influence each civilian's decision about whether or not to remain silent about them.

In addition to presenting detailed evidence from Uganda that is consistent with the theoretical account of civilian behavior posited in Chapter 2, this chapter contributes to a long-standing debate about whether and how ethnicity influences armed conflict. It suggests that kinship networks can, in effect, enable groups to coordinate their perceptions of a political environment. As a result, observing ethnic grievances alongside viable, successful rebel groups can be a natural result of the process that allowed the rebel groups to become viable in the first place.

For analysts and scholars who seek to understand the start of conflicts, this suggests a high risk of a selection problem: we may only "see" conflicts that became violent enough for ethnic grievances to be recorded –

---

[158] e.g. Petersen 2001; Wood 2003.

and we may lack evidence that allows us to see whether these grievances preceded conflict, or whether they instead resulted from it. In other words, if grievances in fact *emerge out of* the earliest stages of rebellion, if groups with the "right" networks coordinate grievances best – and if such groups are also the most likely to produce a viable challenger to the state – then one can easily, mistakenly conclude that because ethnic grievances appear so frequently among major rebellions in homogeneous areas, they must be the initial cause of rebellion. These findings underscore the need for great care in disentangling the relationship between ethnicity and conflict onset in future research. Doing so is not merely of academic concern, since having a clear picture of the processes underlying the start of organized violence is critical for devising policies that could end violent conflict before it has the chance to become a civil war.

6

The State

Intelligence is the decisive factor in planning guerilla operations ... [G]uerillas deny all information of themselves to their enemy, who is deprived of their eyes and their ears ... The enemy stands on a lighted stage; from the darkness around him, thousands of unseen eyes intently study his every move, his every gesture.

– Mao Zedong

Today [in Uganda] people appreciate stability ... the population acts as our intelligence. So now it's not so easy to start a rebellion. The population will end them.

– Senior Ugandan military officer (Interview with the author, Bombo Barracks, Luwero, February 2009)

While prior chapters focused on nascent rebels' and civilians' incentives and actions during the initial stages of insurgency, this chapter turns to the state's behavior. In doing so, it also seeks to further our understanding of how contemporary developing states come to monopolize the use of violence within their territory. Or, in the language of contemporary policy debates: How do weak states become stronger?

Building on the theory I presented in Chapter 2, I propose that a central initial challenge of contemporary state-building can be usefully conceptualized as one of *deterring new armed group formation, or expediently ending those that attempt to form* on a state's territory. A state plainly does not hold a monopoly on violence if non-state armed groups operate on its territory, and other core functions of statehood such as service provision tend to be predicated on stability. While the primary focus of research on state formation in Europe in the medieval and early modern period has been on *external* threats from foreign fighting forces, in contrast, *internal* armed groups tend to be a (if not *the*) primary source of instability for today's fragile states, particularly in Africa.[1]

As I described in Chapter 1, little existing work on state-building and conflict onset directly addresses the state's *informational* reach. Most existing work focuses instead on states' ability to repress or confront already-formed rebellions with military force. In contrast, the central argument of this chapter is that weak states can and do also act to prevent rebel groups from forming in the first place by developing the capacity to detect incipient rebel groups. Once this capacity is honed and widely known to civilians, the existence of this detection capacity can deter future groups from starting. This capacity to detect nascent rebels, I argue, comes primarily from information flows from the citizens to the state; in essence, whereas European states needed their citizens to provide *financing* (via taxes) for an army to protect their property from external threats, contemporary fragile states, particularly in Africa, need their citizens to provide *information* in order to protect them from internal threats. If correct, this suggests that research on state formation and civil conflict should consider states' informational penetration of their territory as a crucial aspect of contemporary state formation.

This chapter extends prior chapters' arguments about the importance of information in influencing rebel group formation. I show that by developing institutions through which the central government could learn about threats emanating from its territory, the post-1986 Ugandan state gradually gained an informational advantage relative to would-be insurgents. These institutions enabled the state to identify incipient insurrections and to "nip them in the bud"[2] before they gained substantial military capacity. Extensive evidence from interviews[3] with former rebel leaders, government intelligence officials, and civilians suggests that the state's ability to collect information about internal threats was an important component of prospective rebels' calculations of whether or not to organize violence – thus states that have the civil intelligence capacity to identify rebel group formation in its initial stages will be more likely to deter such groups from forming in the first place. Moreover, investing in

---

[1] Herbst 2000; Bates 2001; Bates 2008.

[2] This phrase was used by several former rebel and counterinsurgent interviewees who described how some rebel groups ended in the early stages.

[3] All interviews cited in this article were conducted by the author unless otherwise noted.

civil intelligence institutions allowed the Ugandan state to deter or end nascent rebellions before costly military intervention was necessary.

A focus on Uganda presents a rare opportunity to observe a transition from state fragility to relative stability. As described in Chapter 3, in the mid-1980s, Uganda was an archetypical failed state. Over the following two decades, Uganda faced sixteen insurgencies – but the incidence of new rebel groups forming in Uganda declined over those years, as did the likelihood that those groups that did form would become viable. Uganda has not experienced rebel group formation on its territory since 2005. While Uganda is not sufficiently capable of providing citizens with collective goods to meet most observers' standard of a "strong state," given Uganda's postcolonial history of violent political conflict, the fact that it has not had any armed group form on its territory for over a decade is striking.

Uganda also offers an opportunity to probe the functioning of domestic intelligence institutions – normally an exceedingly sensitive topic – due to an unusual relative openness about this subject among government officials and citizens in Uganda. This openness plays a role in the argument that follows, as would-be rebels can only be deterred if it is widely known that the state's civil intelligence apparatus is pervasive. Extensive interviews with former and current government intelligence agents throughout Uganda, as well as interviews with other government officials, civilians, and former rebels, reveal a great deal about Uganda's intelligence apparatus and perceptions of its effect. (These interviews are listed and discussed in Appendix B.)

Using such evidence, this chapter describes how the ruling NRM, after seizing control of the central government in January 1986, extended the state's civil intelligence institutions until they penetrated every region, and indeed every village of Uganda. Specifically, I describe three types of intelligence institutions developed in Uganda: the Local Council (LC) system, the political education system, and the former rebel reintegration system. While one often associates intelligence institutions with coercion in developing countries, as the discussion in subsequent sections indicates, the systems in Uganda are more subtle, relying on a mix of persuasion, political ideology, prestige, and financial incentives to induce civilians to serve as informers. To my knowledge, scholarship on Uganda has not previously described the intelligence functions of these institutions, or their role in preventing rebel group formation.

I then examine the extent to which this intelligence apparatus influenced the decisions of would-be and nascent rebels. I provide evidence that as these institutions became increasingly embedded in localities over time, more and more civilians became official or unofficial informants of the state. This substantially improved the state's ability to detect incipient threats, thereby making rebellion a less appealing option for potential rebel entrepreneurs. This evidence from Uganda suggests that – at least in the minds of these actors – because of these local intelligence institutions, the likelihood of a rebellion becoming viable decreased, and thus the option of launching violent rebellion in the first place became less attractive.

This chapter proceeds as follows. First, I chronicle how civil intelligence institutions[4] were installed and developed in Uganda, and present evidence from fieldwork in several regions of Uganda that demonstrates the relationship between these institutions and the deterrence and ending of nascent rebellion. Finally, I briefly consider a prominent alternative explanation about military capacity and conclude by probing the national-level conditions that allow this information-centric state-building strategy to be selected and successfully implemented.

6.1 BUILDING UGANDA'S DOMESTIC INTELLIGENCE INSTITUTIONS

Uganda's emergence as a stable country since the mid-2000s has been a bright spot in a region that is elsewhere still plagued by political violence, particularly in eastern DRC and South Sudan.[5] Uganda's progress in attaining stability and economic growth[6] has prompted international commendation, including Paul Collier's description of Uganda as "the main example of successful African post-conflict recovery."[7] On average, Uganda achieved a 6.4% annual GDP growth rate from 1986 to 2006 – compared to 2.4% in Brazil, 3.1% in the United States, and 6.1% in India over the same period. Uganda's stability has featured in scholarly work about the potential merits of rebel victory and "autonomous" recovery, since it was the NRA rebels who took over the central government in 1986

---

[4] I use the phrase "civil intelligence" and "domestic intelligence" interchangeably, and define them as an institution of the state designed to collect information about potential threats to the state emanating from the civilian population.

[5] Additionally, Uganda borders the regions of Kenya that suffered the most from post-election violence in late 2007 and 2008.

[6] This growth was consistent: beginning in 1987, Uganda's annual GDP growth did not dip below 3.4 percent. Data comes from the Economist Intelligence Unit.

[7] Collier 1999, 1.

who engineered this transition in Uganda, with minimal international intervention.[8]

Below, I describe three types of intelligence institutions developed in Uganda which, I argue, were fundamental to this transition: the LC system, the political education system, and the system of reintegrating former rebels. I then examine the extent to which this intelligence apparatus influenced the decisions of would-be and nascent rebels. It is noteworthy that each of these institutions' primary institutional function was something other than intelligence – for example, the LC system is Uganda's primary means of administering local governance, and the political education system is directed toward military recruitment. In the pages that follow, I highlight these institutions' role in intelligence.

6.1.1 The Local Council System

A cornerstone of the post-1986 Ugandan government is the extensive, five-tiered system of local administration that the NRM put in place throughout the country once they came to power. The NRM's LC system has been heralded by the World Bank and numerous scholars for its inclusive, democratic, and highly localized form of governance. However, almost entirely unappreciated in existing scholarship on Uganda is the *intelligence* function of these councils. Today, the lead governmental intelligence body is the Internal Security Organization (ISO), which deals with detecting all threats emanating from within Uganda.[9] ISO officials are represented at most levels of the LC system. The officials at lower (more local) levels generally report to those in the level above them, and information flows up the chain to the central ISO office in Kampala. Locally, each of these officials relies on a network of informants in their area of responsibility, some of whom are public about their informant role, and others of whom are not.

The NRM conceived of the LC system during the Bush War. After gaining control of the country in 1986, the NRM extended it throughout the entire country, much of which the NRM had not reached during the Bush War (particularly in northern and eastern Uganda). Upon arriving in

---

[8] Weinstein 2005; Toft 2010.

[9] The two other primary intelligence institutions in Uganda are the External Security Organization (ESO), which deals with threats from foreign territory, and the Chieftaincy of Military Intelligence (CMI), which handles military intelligence. In a counterinsurgency operation, typically ISO officials would work in collaboration with CMI officials.

these regions that had no prior experience with the new central government, the NRM dismantled the previous regime's local government structures and then set out to build local governance institutions largely from
scratch. To do so, they used the "Resistance Council" system that they
had developed in localities of central and western Uganda that they controlled during the Bush War.[10] The new Resistance Councils (RCs) – later
re-named Local Councils (LCs) – included the following nested administrative units, in descending order of size: districts, counties, subcounties,
parishes, and villages. From their inception, each level had
a democratically elected governing body, which operates alongside several
centrally appointed leaders and civil servants, particularly at the district
and subcounty levels.

This process of extending the RC system to northern and eastern
Uganda began in March 1986 when President Museveni appointed
Special District Administrators (SDAs, later renamed Resident District
Commissioners – RDCs) to lead each district. By January 1987, there was
an SDA stationed in every district of Uganda. Newspaper reporting about
these new administrators described their planned role: "(T)he main task of
the SDAs is to organize and mobilize their respective districts politically,
following the political lines of the National Resistance Movement … and
to ensure that the rights of citizens are protected."[11] The SDAs appointed
an ad hoc committee of three individuals: a Chairman, a Vice Chairman,
and a Defense Secretary, who would manage the area.

This committee's first task was to identify all individuals in the area
who had served in a military or intelligence capacity for the former regime,
screening them and offering them a position in the new national military if
they were found to be sufficiently skilled and loyal to the new regime.
Ascertaining whether citizens would be prone to taking subversive or
destabilizing actions was thus a fundamental role of these institutions
from the start. It continues to the present; as one RDC explained, "As
a head of security in a district … I work with everyday people in the

---

[10] The NRM's state-building project therefore arguably began prior to 1986 in the areas of
central and western Uganda that it controlled as a rebel group, prior to when it captured
the capital. For a discussion of NRM rebel governance in the early 1980s under the NRM,
see Kasfir 2005.

[11] "Museveni appoints SDAs," The Star, March 1, 1986. The districts included were
Kabarole, Kasese, Bundibugyo, Bushenyi, Mbarara, Rukungiri, Kabale, Rakai,
Masaka, Mubende, Mpigi, Luwero, Hoima, Mukono, Jinja, Kampala, Iganga, Kamuli,
Tororo, Mbale, Kumi, Soroti, Masindi, and Lira.

villages to make my work easy. I have contacts with the last man deep in the village."[12]

In late 1988, these committees were tasked with preparing their districts for local elections, to replace the ad hoc (unelected) committee and to fill numerous political posts in the new Resistance Councils and Committees. Local elections occurred throughout Uganda by 1989. The councils were comprised of all adults in an area, and the nine-person committees were elected by the councils. For example, each village council, which typically had 100–200 people, would elect a village committee which would include the following positions: Chairman, Vice Chairman, General Secretary, Treasurer, Secretary for Women, Secretary for Youth, Secretary for Displaced People and Production, Secretary of Information and Publicity, and Secretary of Defense.

A local paper said of the LCs that they "would enable the people to participate in the affairs that determine their own destiny."[13] President Museveni proudly introduced these local government structures during his swearing-in address on January 29, 1986, declaring:

In our liberated zones, the first thing we started with was the election of village Resistance Committees. My mother, for instance, cannot go to parliament; but she can, surely, become a member of a committee so that she, too, can make her views heard. We have, therefore, set up village, *muluka* [parish], *gombolola* [subcounty], and district committees . . .

From the beginning, the intelligence function of these councils was central to their operation and was public knowledge. Another excerpt from Museveni's swearing-in address made this intelligence function plain:

These committees we have set up in these zones have a lot of power. You cannot, for instance, join the army or the police without being cleared by the village committee . . .

Another important aspect of the committees is that they should serve as a citizens' intelligence system.

While Museveni's address did not explicitly mention that civilians should provide information to the LCs about potential armed rebel groups forming in their midst, the system's designers intended for them to adopt this role. Indeed, a chief architect of the LC system said of the reasons behind its inception during the Bush War: "We wanted a sure source of

---

[12] Jude Kagoro interview with RDC, northern Uganda, 2011. Found in Kagoro 2012, 9.
[13] "NRM Gov't Won't set up Intelligence Body." *Weekly Topic.* February 3, 1986.

intelligence about the enemy ... We needed allies from within ... We needed information on where and how many soldiers (the enemy) had."[14]

These systems were also put in place because NRM leadership had limited funding during and immediately after the Bush War, and they determined that this would be a cost-effective way to detect emerging threats. An official who helped to design this system explained about the days when these institutions were first conceptualized:

By 1982 ... in liberated areas [that the NRM controlled during the Bush War] the [former] government structures were dismantled, leaving a vacuum. There were no police; there was no law and order. We [the NRM] were less than 1,000 soldiers ... So we decided we should use the prominent (local) citizens to help us.[15]

Furthermore, at the end of the Bush War, the international community pressured the NRM to limit expansion of its military, urging it instead to invest in infrastructure. A senior ISO official expressed pride in the affordability of the country's intelligence system, saying, "If you look at our intelligence training budget, it is quite small (relative to the military budget) ... yet intelligence has become accepted in Uganda because it's structured at the local level."[16] Similarly, a former UPA rebel who is now active in local politics and intelligence said, "Research and intelligence is much cheaper than war."

Lead local intelligence officers appointed by ISO operate at two of the LC levels – the District Information Security Officer (DISO) at the district level and the Gombolola Information Security Officer (GISO) at the subcounty level. Much of the security activity of the state takes place at the village, subcounty, and district levels; each district and subcounty (and some villages) has an active "security committee" that meets on a regular basis to discuss crime and potential threats to the state. These committees at the district and subcounty levels include the centrally appointed representatives, plus top locally elected officials and police and military officials stationed in the area. The village Secretary of Defense – a position held in all villages – reports regularly to the subcounty village committee, which in turn reports regularly to the district security committee, who in turn report to the Internal Security Organization's central offices in Kampala. These institutions represent the primary channel through which the

[14] Interview with senior NRM official, Kampala, November 2009.
[15] Interview with senior NRM official, Kampala, November 2009.
[16] Former senior official in Uganda's civil intelligence agency (ISO), Bombo Barracks, Luwero district, August 2009.

central government stays systematically apprised of security threats in any village.

The identity of these local-level intelligence officials is not always a secret; they are often widely known by all citizens in the area. For example, one individual I met who held the official, public role of sub-county intelligence officer (GISO) was also a high school teacher and also a self-described "human rights activist."[17] In addition to these public, formal structures, a broad, clandestine network of informants also provides information to these ISO channels. These informants' identities are not typically public, although the citizenry is aware that this clandestine network exists. As one intelligence officer stated, "Even a senior security officer will not tell you definitively where security starts and where it ends, who is a security personnel and who is not ... In Uganda, everyone can be a security operative if he so wishes."[18] As one public intelligence official at the subcounty (GISO) level told me, when she gained her position in 1992, her first goal was to find "trusted people who give good information."[19] Another RDC stated: "When I am appointed RDC of a certain district, the first thing I do is to recruit trusted cadres. You cannot handle security without agents ... I have also given some small-scale military training to my agents, but on one-on-one bases, because I never want my agents to know each other."[20]

6.1.2 "Political Education": Mchaka Mchaka

Another channel through which the central government obtains information from civilians, and that has enabled it to extend its informational reach, is through training "cadres," who are "politically educated" by local government officials to be informants. This program, known as "Mchaka Mchaka," is primarily a civilian indoctrination program in "patriotism" and "civic education," but it also has a less prominent intelligence recruitment component. One Mchaka Mchaka instructor, who had been serving as an instructor since 1986, estimated that in 2011, 10 million people – or almost two-thirds of the population over age fifteen – had received at least one Mchaka Mchaka training course

---

[17] Interview with local intelligence official (GISO), Kasese district, July 2008.
[18] Jude Kagoro interview with intelligence officer, Kampala, January 2011. Found in Kagoro 2012, 9.
[19] Interview with local official, Busia district, Buteba subcounty, November 2009.
[20] Interview by Jude Kagoro in West Nile, January 2011 Kagoro 2012, 8.

since 1986.[21] Another instructor explained that the purpose of Mchaka Mchaka is "changing the attitude of the people" and the "awakening of Uganda through patriotism."[22] A former NRM intelligence officer explained that this "process of training is a socialization process that makes you loyal" to the NRM government.[23] An additional value of Mchaka Mchaka graduates for the NRM is that they provide information about nascent threats to local intelligence officials.

NRM leaders also conceived of this program during the Bush War. One NRM leader explained: "While in the struggle [during the Bush War], the NRM believed that fighting and political education must go hand in hand."[24] Since 1981, the NRM has undertaken extensive campaigns to train both soldiers and civilian cadres. Educating civilians about the need to protect the state, he explained, has been "part and parcel of our revolution." The first training after the Bush War took place in Mpigi in October 1987, when 430 people were trained as a local militia. One newspaper reported at that time: "The training of Local Defence Forces (LDFs) will be countrywide in order to relieve the army of the role of keeping internal peace." Those who were trained were directed to go back to their areas and "ensure security there."[25]

After seizing power in January 1986, the NRM required national Mchaka Mchaka courses for Uganda's rising elite; they were mandated for all secondary school graduates (men and women) who planned to enroll in a university. Before beginning their university courses, students would travel to one central location at the National Leadership Institute in Kyankwanzi for a three-month-long course. The course was comprised of three units: (1) "Politics and Education," in which students learned about Ugandan history and the NRM's 10 Point Programme; (2) "Military Science," which taught basic military skills, including how to load and fire a gun; and (3) "Parade Drills," which focused on physical fitness. The government would provide transportation to the training center from participants' home areas, meals, and a small stipend for all students who completed the course. Between 1986 and 1991, approximately 60,000 students from all over the country graduated from the course.

[21] Interview with Mchaka Mchaka instructor, Kampala, February 2011.
[22] Interview with Mchaka Mchaka instructor 2, Kampala, February 2011.
[23] Interview with a former Kampala-based NRM intelligence official, Kampala, July 2009.
[24] Interview with NRM leader who was one of the designers of the RC system, Kampala, July 2009.
[25] "Militias to disburden NRA." *The Star*, October 8, 1987.

After 1991, the courses were shortened to just one month and were decentralized, offered to all citizens on a voluntary basis at the district level. Courses were typically offered in each district three times per year, each time in a different subcounty, depending on the budgetary situation of the district and the discretion of the RDC, who is typically tasked with organizing the trainings. Citizens do not pay for the course, and are typically provided meals throughout its duration – a welcome contribution for many of the course participants, who are subsistence farmers. These trainings took place even in districts that suffered from insurgency; training centers would be heavily guarded and courses would serve as an opportunity for the government to persuade citizens not to join or support the rebels. Additionally, these trainings became required for all former rebels who had applied for amnesty from the government. All government officials have also been required to take the course since 1991; all civil servants and politicians, including the elected members of every nine-person village committee, are trained in Mchaka Mchaka. Opposition members of Parliament, government accountants, and the managing director of the government-owned newspaper *The New Vision* are among those who received the training. Some courses are taught in the public school system, including in primary schools. Today, the substance of the courses varies, but typically includes units on broad topics such as patriotism, the history of Uganda, economics, and practical fighting skills such as shooting. In one Mchaka Mchaka month-long course taught in February and March 2012, day-long training topics included those focused on development, such as "Social/Economic Progress of Uganda," "Personal and Financial Empowerment," and "Challenges of HIV/AIDS to Empowerment." Crucially for the argument I advance here, the courses also included several intelligence-focused topics with titles such as "Mobilization and Information Flow as a Life Blood of the Movement/Relevance of Local Government," "Who is the Enemy and Who is the Ally of the People of Uganda," and "Community Policing/The Role of the Citizen in Maintaining Security."

Furthermore, in addition to serving as political education for the citizens of Uganda, these courses serve as an important screening and recruitment device for the government intelligence (and military) forces. Among those who do not join the armed services, the majority of cadres return after Mchaka Mchaka to their prior, daily lives – but their behavior is monitored by other cadres and government security forces. Over time, senior officials classify them as either "Revolutionary Cadres," meaning that they are behaving well in their communities and supporting the government's activities, or "Reactionary Cadres," meaning that they appear to oppose the government or may commit criminal or otherwise unsavory behavior. Those who are deemed to be in the former groups are then invited back for follow-up training in subsequent years. As one instructor put it, "We look for those who have a heart for their country."[26]

Students can advance through a progression of Mchaka Mchaka courses, subject to the approval of instructors who are typically military officials. Advanced courses typically involve training in more advanced weaponry, and begin to informally groom a portion of the population to serve as a military reserve unit. John, a civilian living in West Nile, described his Mchaka Mchaka training quite positively, referring to it as "very exciting," remarking about the free food, the camaraderie, the jogging in companies, and the singing of patriotic songs. The training "makes you a complete person," he said. Indiscipline is not tolerated and results in caning, he said.[27]

After taking a more advanced Mchaka Mchaka course, cadres can ask their district security officials to be issued a government-owned gun to keep in their homes. Some are invited for follow-up trainings and target practice. One trainee I interviewed had a government-issued gun but said that he had only used the gun once: When there was "a commotion" in his village due to a suspected thief, he shot his gun into the air in order to alert the police. He was trained, he explained, to make it his first priority to inform officials if he suspected any "wrongdoing" in his community. He explained that he was also encouraged to maintain a consistent relationship with his subcounty's intelligence official (GISO), informing him about anything unusual he had seen in his community.

Certain graduates of these courses – presumably those deemed to be of high quality or trustworthiness – are invited to regular "reunions" where they are asked by their former instructors what they accomplished in their communities in the past year. Such activities allow the government to monitor these individuals over time, grooming them as intelligence providers to the government. Additionally, by inviting them to reunions in

[26] Interview with Mchaka Mchaka instructor, Kampala, February 2011.
[27] He also explained that he learned "interesting ideas" about Uganda at his trainings; for example, because the remains of the first humans in recorded history were found in neighboring Kenya, it is possible that lush, tropical Uganda was the actual site of the Garden of Eden.

localized groups, the government reinforces this network of individuals who monitor one another's activities.

Many of the most devoted cadres, who are promoted to formal, sometimes paid, public roles in the government's intelligence apparatus, are seen as leaders in their communities. Their position in society could be aptly termed an "information elite," meaning that they are known in their communities for being knowledgeable about the affairs of the community. Several are secondary school teachers, thus they are particularly knowledgeable about the community's youth. While such public intelligence officers did not, to my knowledge, know the identities of the covert officers, they were aware that covert officers likely existed in their communities.

Therefore, while Mchaka Mchaka serves many roles, training numerous civilians throughout the country in intelligence provision is a fundamental aim. Further, after graduating from the program, "cadres" come to understand that they are now part of a network that will be monitoring their behavior, and presumably their loyalty.

6.1.3 Reintegrated Rebels as Informants

Finally, although less penetrative at the local level than the LC system and Mchaka Mchaka, the reintegration of former rebels serves as an additional useful source of information for the Ugandan government. Over 22,000 individuals received amnesty from the Ugandan government for their actions in former rebellions; to obtain amnesty, in addition to renouncing violence, they have to formally register with the government. Many are also required to take Mchaka Mchaka courses to "rehabilitate" themselves and to be screened for their loyalty. Many would then be admitted into the national army or, in some cases, would begin serving as intelligence agents for the government in the regions where their rebel groups had operated – and in some cases were still operating.

One former rebel intelligence officer, who was captured by the government during the rebellion, recounted that a government agent told him: "You'll like this government once you understand it."[28] Today, he informally provides intelligence to the government; he volunteers information to the DISO and GISO if he learns of a potential threat. They summon him to their offices if they need information about the localities where he is well networked.

---

[28] Interview with UPA intelligence officer, Soroti district, January 26, 2011.

Numerous former rebel leaders also gained high-level roles in local government, and are able to draw on their networks of former rebel foot soldiers in order to keep apprised of potential threats emerging in their home areas. For example, a former NFA leader and a former ADF leader reported working currently to reach out on behalf of the Ugandan government to ADF "remnants" in DRC and encourage them to give up their arms and return to Uganda. In another example, after several leaders of the UPA surrendered, they joined the NRM and became local officials. One became the senior civil servant in his home area soon after surrendering to the government. After successfully convincing several of his former rebel colleagues to turn themselves over to the government, he was stationed in several districts throughout the 1990s in northern Uganda, western Uganda, and West Nile to continue similar counterinsurgency work. Later, in 2000, when the LRA entered his home region of Teso, the government sent him there to lead an effort to develop local militias to repel the LRA. It worked; the LRA never again returned to Teso. Currently, he is a Minister of State, and he said, "today, law and order keeps us safe ... it is easy to slide back into anarchy." Several other former rebels I interviewed explained that they "interact" regularly with government officials and share information about possible "negative elements" in their home areas.

6.2 DETERRING AND ENDING NASCENT REBELS

Up to this point, this chapter has described how over the course of the two decades after the NRM took power, the country experienced the development and expansion of a deeply penetrative domestic intelligence infrastructure. Alongside this expansion, the presence of rebel groups on Ugandan soil has diminished over the same period. In the late 1980s, rebel activity on Ugandan soil was rather common, peaking in 1988 when eight distinct groups operated in different areas of the country. But over time, the ubiquity of new rebel groups forming in Uganda declined. In this section I present evidence, largely from interviews with former rebels, as well as local intelligence and political officials, suggesting that the increasing penetration of intelligence institutions made rebellion less appealing because of an increasingly widespread perception that rebels would be caught early on.

Figure 3.2 in Chapter 3 showed that the incidence of new rebel group formation on Ugandan territory has declined substantially since 1986. The figure suggested a dramatic shift from the first five years that the

NRM held power (1986 to 1990), in which nine rebel groups formed in Uganda, to the period since 2006 in which no rebel groups have formed.[29] The gradual process of pacification that occurred in Uganda is also apparent from viewing the total number of rebel groups that committed violence in Uganda each year since 1986. Figure 6.1 shows an overall downward trend over time in the quantity of rebel groups operating in Uganda annually, with no groups operating there since 2006.

How did this process of pacification occur? Part of what changed was that, over time, more people in the country became part of, or at least were exposed to, the institutions described above. Beginning in the early 1990s, as part of a suite of comprehensive decentralization reforms, Uganda began breaking certain districts into two or more new ones, effectively "promoting" subdistrict units to the level of a district. From 1990 to 2000, the number of districts increased from thirty-four to fifty-six districts. Then, in the subsequent decade, the number of Ugandan districts continued growing dramatically, doubling from 56 to 112 districts by 2010. New districts were created throughout the country, affecting all

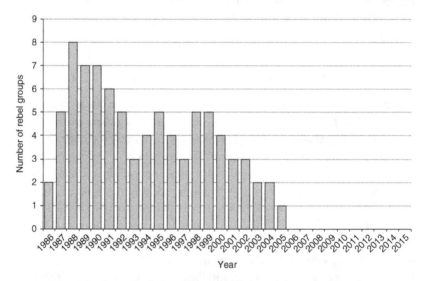

FIGURE 6.1 Number of rebel groups committing violence in Uganda per year (1986–2015)

[29] As of 2020, no rebel groups have formed on Ugandan territory since 2001.

regions of Uganda, and were generally quite popular where they were created, at least at the outset.[30] Among other decentralization reforms aimed at bringing the central government "closer to the people," this district creation generated numerous additional RDCs and DISOs in Uganda, and made the areas they are responsible for physically smaller, allowing them to more directly monitor security issues in a smaller area.[31] Through this process, the number of high-level intelligence officers in peripheral areas proliferated. Similarly, there has been a steady accretion of Mchaka Mchaka graduates throughout Uganda over this period, generating an expanding pool of pre-vetted, informal intelligence collectors for the central government.

Of course, the simple act of expanding the local density of intelligence collectors in rural Uganda did not ensure their success at deterring and ending rebellion. In fact, in some cases, local villagers initially shunned the new local administrative and intelligence officers.[32] In the late 1980s, in the areas where rebellions had started, people were uncertain that the LCs would remain in place, particularly because these officials became the targets of rebel groups.[33] One group of civilians reported that their village Chairman had slept in the bush for three years while rebels operated in their area, to avoid being attacked by rebels, which typically occurred at night.[34] In one area of northern Uganda, a community explained that when the NRM initially brought the LC system to their community and organized elections for local positions, people in the community "voted for people they hated, since they knew that the rebels would kill them."[35] Sometimes in such situations, LC officials hesitated to share information – or, at least, accurate information – with the central government, for fear of reprisals from rebels.[36] Because LCs would be rebels' targets, people in such areas feared interacting with LCs, especially in public. Thus, as one civilian told me, "people didn't 'report' to the LCs about the rebels, they whispered."[37] People apparently did not yet trust the intentions and the staying power of these new government intelligence institutions.

---

[30] Grossman and Lewis 2014.   [31] Lewis 2014, 24–25.

[32] Interview with local (village-level) official, Kasese, western Uganda, July 2008.

[33] Interview with civilian, Busia district, Dabani subcounty, November 2009; focus group with civilians, Soroti district, Gweri subcounty, December 2009.

[34] Focus group with civilians, Tororo district, Malaba Town Council, November 2009.

[35] Focus group in Pader District, Pajule subcounty, December 2009.

[36] Interview with local leader, Tororo district, Mella, November 2009.

[37] Interview with civilian, Busia district, Dabani subcounty, November 2009.

And yet, these LC officials are seen as trustworthy today in Uganda –
more even than traditional, tribal leaders, according to numerous
interviews.[38] How did citizens come to expect that these local intelligence
institutions would remain in place, and that they would be effective at
collecting information from the local population about emergent threats
to the incumbent government? Individual responses I received to questions about this process are somewhat opaque, but in the aggregate they
sketch a gradual process that involved the local officials' persistence and
sometimes use of selective benefits in order to win loyalty. When asked
about how intelligence networks took root and became effective, a local
official in western Uganda said: "It was a process ... you can educate
people to trust the government."[39]

What form did this "education" take? Most accounts stress the NRM's
focus on *persuasion*, rather than coercion. Some accounts stressed that the
moral rectitude of the NRM's cause meant that those who were educated
to understand their cause would voluntarily become NRM informants.
After initially being installed in the districts, the SDAs engaged in a public
outreach campaign aimed at convincing locals to trust the new government – and to share information with its representatives. One of the lead
NRM designers of these institutions said, "Our mission was to change the
attitude of the people towards intelligence. To have good intelligence, you
must be appreciated by the population ... We were very pro-people."[40]
Another of the system's original designers said that initially, "we needed
to convince the masses of our cause."[41]

One elder in northern Uganda explained that he had been the first
Secretary for Information in his village in 1987. He said that the local
council was very weak in those days, because the government found that it
was very difficult to communicate with civilians. In order to resolve this
problem, he had meetings every day with village defense secretaries to
discuss their progress in "reaching the people."[42] He explained that one of
the NRA's weaknesses in the area was that they had few Acholi as part of
their movement in 1986, so it took them time to win their loyalty. Some

---

[38] Focus group with civilians, Tororo district, Malaba Town Council, November 2009;
   local (village) official (for over twenty years), Soroti county; January 2011.
[39] Interview with local (village-level) official, Kasese, western Uganda, July 2008.
[40] Interview with former senior official of ISO, the lead domestic intelligence agency, Bombo
   Barracks, August 18, 2009.
[41] Interview with NRM leader who was one of the designers of the RC system, Kampala,
   July 2009.
[42] Interview with elder, Gulu town, Gulu district, northern Uganda, March 2009.

individuals mentioned that repeated meetings with local officials and with military intelligence agents who came to the area, helped and that it "changed their hearts" when they saw that former soldiers from their area who surrendered were not treated with brutality.[43]

Many other interviewees stressed that, over time, the government was able to use material incentives to induce people to provide information. In a community in northern Uganda, not far from where the LRA formed, members of a focus group explained that it was not until two years after the LCs were first elected that the community began to feel they could "trust" the government.[44] They explained that during that period, the local officials began to give civilians food (which had been originally provided by Oxfam) in order to gain their trust. "That was the turning point," one individual said as most others in the group nodded in agreement. She continued, "We hated them so much before that time."

Similarly, in one focus group of twelve people in eastern Uganda, a civilian described a process of government favoritism of those who provided information: "The community was divided. Some were supporters of the government, and others weren't ... Those who supported the government would gain benefits from the government. That's how the government gained the upper hand."[45] Indeed, according to one of the early leaders of this system, recruiting informers was not difficult because of the widespread unemployment in the country; providing information could earn the informer a small sum of money. The promise of such future benefits encouraged individuals to provide accurate information on a repeated basis. A former leader of the civil intelligence administration commented that informants are well paid, stating: "We take care of their needs ..."[46] Additionally, one local leader replied when asked why people are willing to give information to the government: "People here are poor, and are easily bought off."[47]

While it is difficult to directly link these changes to the reduction in rebel group formation over time, throughout the Ugandan government

[43] Focus group in Pajule subcounty, Pader district, December 2009.
[44] I do not take a position about whether these individuals "trust" the government in the usual, normatively positive sense. NRM officials and loyalists in Uganda often use this language, and I take it to mean – at least in the context of the above statements – that the government has found it easier over time to persuade civilians to serve as informants.
[45] Focus group with civilians, Tororo district, Mella town council, November 2009.
[46] Interview with former leader of Internal Security Organization, Bombo barracks, March 2009.
[47] Former local official in Bwera town, a community on the border of DRC in Kasese district, July 2008.

today – among individuals in military and civilian institutions and at central and local levels of government – there exists a strikingly common belief that Uganda's highly local civil intelligence structures protect the country from a resumption of violence. When asked why Uganda does not have new rebellions today, several government officials cited the intelligence system as the primary, if not the sole, reason. For example, when asked why the government had ended nascent rebellions with increasing frequency since 1986, an intelligence officer replied, "Because of government vigilance, up to the village level . . . today, rebels may attempt to form again, but they will not survive." He argued that "local leaders" are more important than the police in providing local security.[48] Similarly, a senior military officer explained, "People appreciate stability . . . the population acts as our intelligence. So now it's not so easy to start a rebellion. The population will end them."[49]

Local officials stationed across the country shared this assessment. For example, a local official in eastern Uganda said: "Rebellion can't happen here today. The LC system is too strong."[50] Similarly, a local official in western Uganda said: "The government is good at getting information from people through the LC system . . . in fighting rebels, the UPDF has to rely on informants."[51]

Strikingly, numerous former rebels also cited this intelligence system when I asked whether rebellion could occur today in Uganda. None mentioned the strength of the military, and in none of the cases did I prompt them to discuss intelligence or tell them that others had mentioned intelligence to me. For example, when asked if he could imagine a new rebel group forming in Uganda, a former senior NFA leader replied: "no, [starting a new rebel group] can't happen today. The government is too strong . . . it is too easy for them to pick information."[52] He said in a later interview, "Intelligence is somehow strong for the government today."[53] Similarly, when I asked a former FOBA rebel from eastern Uganda, who later joined the NRM government, about why there was no rebellion in Uganda in 2009, he replied simply: "Local people can be allies of the state," and explained that it would be too risky to try to rebel.

[48] Interview with intelligence official 1, Kampala, March 2009.
[49] Interview with senior military officer, Bombo Barracks, Luwero district, February 2009
[50] Interview with local official, Busia district, Buteba subcounty, November 2009.
[51] Former local official in Bwera town, a community on the border of DRC in Kasese district that experienced a great deal of violence as a result of the ADF rebellion.
[52] Interview with former NFA rebel, Kampala, April 2009.
[53] Interview with former NFA rebel leader, Kampala, May 2011.

Those who tried would likely be caught early, he said. Another former rebel in eastern Uganda explained that he had been part of the FOBA rebel group until the early 1990s, later surrendered, and then made a living providing intelligence to the military. When asked if there was a chance that rebellion could happen again in his district today, he said: "Today, there would be no support for rebellion ... The government has blinded people, and has recruited informers in every village. Out of every 10 people, three are loyal to the NRM government ... So everyone fears one another. To organize something today in Tororo is difficult."[54] Similarly, when asked why a group like the ADF has not formed in western Uganda in recent years, a former ADF rebel replied: "Intelligence for the government is somehow more strong today ... people would be reluctant to get involved."[55]

In addition to deterring new rebellions in recent years, the Ugandan intelligence institutions described earlier also played a critical role in ending rebellions that had already formed. For example, when describing the demise of the Holy Spirit Movement (HSM) rebels in 1988, anthropologist Heike Behrend described what happened when the HSM reached Busoga in eastern Uganda: "The Resistance Councils (RCs) and the Local Defence Units (LDUs) set up by the NRA denounced the Holy Spirit soldiers and betrayed their location with drums."[56] The HSM finally met its end there in Busoga. A senior military officer who had led the counterinsurgency against the HSM also heralded the RCs for providing the information about the HSM's location and plans to attack government forces in Busoga, which led to the group's demise.[57]

Similarly, in western Uganda, the Principal of Kichwamba Technical School, which had suffered an ADF rebel attack in which twenty-seven students were burned alive and roughly 200 abducted, said that the end of rebel activity in his area was the result of collaboration between "the people" and the local government.[58] Another community leader in that area commented on "good networking" between the community and the government, explaining that today "as soon as people see people they don't know in their communities, they report it to members of their [village or subcounty committees], or to their RDC ... people tend to

---

[54] Interview with former rebel foot soldier (now a farmer), Tororo district, Osukuru subcounty, June 2009.
[55] Interview with former ADF leader, Kampala, February 2011.   [56] Behrend 1999, 92.
[57] Interview with senior military official, Bombo Barracks, Luwero district, August 2009.
[58] Interview with Principal, Kichwamba, Kaborole district, western Uganda, July 2008.

fear the [military], so they prefer to report to local leaders, who bring the information to the military."[59] Mchaka Mchaka programs in the area "work to mobilize the people against insurgency," he explained, making it more likely that they will provide information to the government about nascent rebels. In the mountain community on the border of DRC where this man lived, most locals had received training, he said.[60]

Such success at ending rebellion was apparently more common as time passed; no rebel group that formed in Uganda after 1995 became viable.[61] For example, a rebel who attempted to launch a rebellion in 1996 in central Uganda, in a district adjacent to Kampala, said that a major problem he faced was "the difficulty in meeting with his fellow rebel commanders without the state security organs knowing … it is very easy for the government to get information from civilians."[62] He explained that he was caught because of a "double dealer," meaning that his group was infiltrated by a government spy. A covert intelligence agent who worked to end that rebellion told me that doing so was easy; he had several informants working for him in the villages near where this rebellion tried to establish their initial base.

6.3 AN ALTERNATIVE EXPLANATION

The dominant state-based, alternative explanation for (lack of) conflict onset is that states improve their *military* prowess at defeating rebels. It is thus worth considering the possibility that increases in Uganda's military effectiveness, rather than its domestic intelligence institutions, are responsible for the decline in insurgent group formation there since the mid-1980s. There are, however, three reasons to believe increases in Uganda's military effectiveness were not an important influence on insurgency onset there.

First, in order for national military effectiveness to matter, a national military must have an organized rebel fighting force to confront. However, this book has shown that nascent rebels in Uganda and beyond typically go through an incubation period before

---

[59] Interview with local NGO official, Kaborole district, July 2008.
[60] Interview with teacher who is also a local intelligence officer (GISO), Kasese district, July 2008.
[61] Only one group that formed in the 1990s – ADF, which formed in 1994 – managed to become viable.
[62] Interview with former UFDF leader, Mukono district, March 2009.

becoming viable groups, and during this period they are quite small, vulnerable, poorly armed groups. Even an extremely small, poorly trained military could militarily handle a dozen men with perhaps even fewer weapons. Clearly then, before rebel groups become viable, the central challenge for the state is identifying rebels' existence and locating them – an intelligence problem, not a military one. And, because fully fledged insurgencies are much more difficult to end than embryonic ones, states are better off using intelligence to end insurgencies before needing to confront them militarily.

Second, even when addressing rebel groups that have become viable, decades of counterinsurgency research suggests that military force cannot be effective without information to guide its use. Military force applied against the wrong targets can easily alienate civilian populations, increasing sympathies for insurgents.

Finally, while Uganda's military has grown and professionalized since the mid-1980s – and between 1987 and 1997, Uganda doubled its number of military personnel per capita – this military growth has not been extraordinary or overwhelming in comparison with neighboring states.[63] Uganda's military spending as a percentage of GDP in fact declined from 5.5 percent in 1988 to 2.2 percent in 2006, whereas in 2006, Kenya's was 1.7 percent and Rwanda's was 1.8 percent.[64] Furthermore, the Ugandan military does not have a substantial, visible presence in rural localities, whereas – as this chapter has shown – its domestic intelligence institutions do.

6.4 BEYOND UGANDA

What are the national-level conditions that lead governments of weak states to take this intelligence-centric path to stability? There are, of course, numerous plausible strategies that states can use to pacify their territory – in addition to honing their military capacity, states can persuade or repress their citizenry.[65] Central government surveillance of the

---

[63] Herbst 2004, 360.
[64] World Bank data from the Stockholm International Peace Research Institute (SIPRI) Military Expenditure Database.
[65] Davenport 2007; Pierskalla 2010; Sullivan 2015.

civilian population has been credited with success in deterring and stymying aspiring rebels in diverse contexts from post–World War II Japan[66] to British and French imperial administrations' "information order"[67] in the Middle East and North Africa,[68] and the "capillaries of empire" of the American colonial government in the Philippines.[69]

A likely reason that the NRM chose to pursue an information-centric pathway to managing internal threats in Uganda is simply that the other options, like repression, were too costly and difficult for a poorly institutionalized state. Uganda's dependency on foreign aid from the United States and Europe throughout the 1990s also would have made it difficult for the NRM to pursue a more overtly repressive approach; the aid was generally contingent on liberal political and economic reforms.[70] Additionally, their history as a rebel group gave them a head start in understanding both the importance of domestic intelligence institutions and experience in building them.

In particular, the NRM's five years of experience as a rebel group in the early 1980s gave it a deep appreciation for the importance of informational ties to villagers in order to control territory. As described above, the RC system it built during its rebellion formed the basis of the expanded domestic intelligence system that persists to this day. If successful in seizing control of a government, rebels often go on to build relatively enduring, stable states[71] – and sometimes even more democratic ones.[72]

Consistent with this interpretation, other African states led by former rebels appear to have similarly invested in building extensive domestic intelligence institutions that penetrate deep into the periphery. States such as Rwanda, Ethiopia, Eritrea, and Zimbabwe have also been led by former rebel groups, and have managed to be fairly successful at preventing armed rebellions from forming in their periphery. This focus on information control may also help to explain why revolutionary regimes are often the most enduring.[73] Indeed, similar to numerous other liberation movements around the globe, much of the language the NRM uses to describe its intelligence

---

[66] Fearon and Laitin 2014.

[67] In his use of the phrase "information order" Thomas is quoting Bayly 1999.

[68] Thomas 2008, 294.   [69] McCoy 2009, 20, 47.

[70] Uganda received gross inflows of foreign aid between $500 and $700 million annually in the early 1990s (Uganda, Ministry of Finance, Planning and Economic Development 1992).

[71] Toft 2010.   [72] Huang 2016.   [73] Levitsky and Way 2013.

apparatus – such as "cadre"[74] – indicates its revolutionary heritage, shared by the major post-independence leaders of Ethiopia, Mozambique, Zimbabwe, and Rwanda.[75] According to an NRM official who was an architect of the original RC system, it was modeled on the Tanzanian local government and cell-based intelligence system, which had replaced the failed Ujaama system. Many future African leaders who were drawn to socialism, including Museveni, studied this system while at Dar es Salaam University in the late 1960s.[76] Recent research argues that ideology can influence victorious rebel groups' trajectory once they govern.[77]

Future work should more systematically assess these patterns, although this will require overcoming the extraordinary challenge of developing a reliable, cross-national measure of domestic surveillance capacity. As a plausibility check on these arguments, I use a common, albeit highly coarse measure of state capacity (GDP per capita, 1997 to 2015 average), to examine the national-level (cross-sectional) relationship between state capacity and rebel group formation from 1997 to 2015. This analysis makes use of the new, fine-grained data on rebel group formation in eastern and central Africa that I describe in Chapter 1 and Appendix D, which uses a threshold of just one anti-state violent attack, or evidence of planning for such an attack, for inclusion. I added data on rebel group formation for southern African states for this analysis, using the same inclusion and coding rules as for the eastern and central African data, to allow for greater variation in state capacity. In addition to showing the expected negative relationship between state capacity and rebel group formation, the scatterplot in Figure 6.2 also shows that among the poorer states, several of those that have managed to avoid having numerous rebellions form on their territory are those noted above that had post-independence leaders with revolutionary pasts.

[74] As Selznick 1979, 18–19 explains: "'Cadre' is a key word in communist parlance … [Cadres] constitute the precious and indispensable vanguard of the revolution."

[75] While Rwandan President Paul Kagame is not typically associated with a socialist ideology, he served as an intelligence officer for the NRM during the rebellion, and as Museveni's first Chief of Military Intelligence. As part of his training for these positions, he spent nine months in Cuba.

[76] During this time, Museveni and John Garang, later leader of the SPLA, visited liberated zones in northern Mozambique and met Samora Machel, future leader of FRELIMO (Reno 2011, 129).

[77] Thaler 2018.

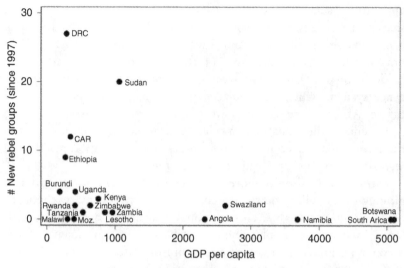

FIGURE 6.2 Rebel groups formation and state capacity (GDP per capita)

6.5 DISCUSSION

This chapter has shown that Uganda developed domestic intelligence institutions that penetrate deep into its localities and that involve both public and covert participation of a substantial number of citizens. The development of these institutions since 1986, and their gradual process of becoming widespread and deeply rooted in localities, coincided with a decline in new rebel group formation in Uganda. While it is difficult (if not impossible) to obtain the ideal data to test the causal influence of these intelligence institutions on the formation and viability of rebel groups, and to rule out the relevance of other plausible explanations for the decline of rebellion in Uganda, the interview evidence presented here suggests a strong relationship between them. At the very least, relevant actors in several regions of Uganda today – former rebels, government officials, and civilians – perceive that the existence of these intelligence networks makes it likely that the government would receive information that would end incipient rebels before they could get off the ground. Without fully considering information flows between citizens and the state, theories of state-building and conflict onset risk overlooking an important feature of how states may become more stable, and one way in which states' relationships with their citizens can fundamentally change as states strengthen.

This chapter has also noted that such intelligence institutions are advantageous for weak states seeking to deter and defeat nascent rebellions because doing so is cost-effective relative to military confrontation. I have defended this claim on theoretical grounds, and provided supporting evidence in the narrative that followed about Uganda. Of course, highly penetrative and capable civil intelligence institutions are not without substantial, potential problems; these institutions can be abused for political ends and have impeded freedom of speech and development of strong opposition parties in Uganda.[78] I return to this theme in the next, concluding chapter.

[78] Kagoro 2012.

PART III

IMPLICATIONS

7

Implications for Scholarship and Policy

We cannot fully understand why civil wars start, or craft informed policy about how they may be best detected or prevented, without detailed knowledge of how the armed challengers that typically instigate civil wars initially form. This book has taken a step in that direction, using new evidence from Uganda and surrounding states.

In seeking to shed light on the earliest stages of rebel group formation in weak states, this book has presented considerable evidence that rebels typically start as small, poorly endowed, clandestine groups – at least in weak state contexts in eastern and central Africa. Under these conditions, nascent rebels' primary challenge is to prevent local civilians from sharing information with the government about rebels' location and identity. During this fragile, formative period, rebels therefore need to convince local civilians to give them the benefit of the doubt – even as they begin committing sporadic, small-scale violence in the community. These arguments – which are at the core of this book's conceptualization of insurgencies' start – are contrary to characterizations of rebellion "erupting" out of social movements, full of pre-mobilized believers in a cause.

Several arguments presented in this book follow from these foundations, and offer a new perspective about how to think about conflict onset in weak states. I briefly recap them here, and then turn to implications for scholarship and policy.

As rebel groups form clandestinely, they carefully vet new recruits to ensure that they keep their identities, plans, and locations secret. It would be unwise for the vulnerable group to welcome vast waves of new recruits, given the risks of information leaks. These dynamics also have implications for nascent rebels' early uses of violence. It is prudent for them to use

only sporadic violence with the aim of testing their operational environment and shaping positive local narratives about themselves, and negative
ones about the government. I showed that incipient rebel groups often use
only infrequent, small-scale violence against the state, and rarely use
violence against civilians. Due to a desire for secrecy, they may whisper
locally about their rebellion, while not making public, attention-seeking
pronouncements about their existence as an armed group. As a result,
these secretive and sometimes slow-moving stages of rebellion often stay
out of the national and international news for months or longer.

Rebels know that local narratives shaped during these earliest stages of
rebellion greatly influence local villagers' decisions about whether or not
to inform on them. Rebels' marked vulnerability in this early stage also
means that just a few informants can end them. Rebels therefore try to
shape narratives proactively by seeding rumors in the communities where
they are forming.

Civilians make decisions about whether to provide information to the
government based largely on rumors about rebels that they receive from
other civilians they trust – mainly their kin. Therefore, the structure of
civilian kinship networks, which transmit rumors about rebels, often
seeded by the rebels themselves, importantly influences incipient rebels'
chances of becoming viable. Specifically, I find that the kinship network
structures that underlie ethnically homogeneous areas are more easily co-
opted by rebels, allowing them to persuade civilians not to leak information about the rebels to the government. I revisit the implications of these
arguments about ethnicity later in this chapter.

Among other insights, these arguments point to the importance of
a particular type of state capacity in deterring and ending attempted
rebellion: the state's domestic intelligence apparatus. Where the state
has strong local information networks already in place, rebel groups will
be defeated early – or deterred from attempting rebellion in the first place.

I turn now to the scholarly and policy implications of these arguments,
and conclude by discussing how processes of rebel group formation may
differ in stronger state contexts.

7.1 IMPROVING DATA ON THE START OF ORGANIZED VIOLENCE

Several lessons from this book underscore how deeply the challenges of
observing armed conflicts' start have affected existing knowledge about
conflict onset. As discussed in Chapter 1, of all quantitative articles

about civil conflict onset published in ten major political science journals since 2003, almost 80 percent rely on at least one of what Samuel Bazzi and Christopher Blattman call the "four major datasets" on internal warfare.[1] The datasets have thus been an extraordinarily valuable public good for researchers, allowing for a rapid expansion of knowledge about empirical patterns of conflict. However, none of these datasets aim to identify the start of new rebel groups – in part because of the inherent challenges of observing clandestine behavior. Instead, they capture medium- or large-scale violence – at least 25,100, or 1,000 battle-related deaths recorded in newspapers in a calendar year – and thus intentionally omit groups that failed early.[2] Especially because – as this book has shown – nascent rebels need to keep secrets, and often commit only sporadic, small-scale violence for which they often do not publicly claim credit, months or even years may pass before incipient rebels cause twenty-five battle-related deaths that are both reported in news media and attributed to the rebel group. In sum, the datasets underpinning a vast swath of findings on conflict can tell us little about the very initial stages of organized armed conflict onset, when rebel groups first form and begin committing violence against the state.

This book has shown that this problem has also led to numerous omissions of early-failed rebel groups from standard conflict datasets. These omissions are most likely in rural areas of weak states, the context in which rebel groups are most likely to form but where information quality is lowest. These findings support those who have conveyed concern about conflict data quality and the risk of false negatives,[3] and underscore the promise of new conflict event data initiatives that integrate more local sources. The dataset on rebel group formation in central and eastern Africa used throughout this book, especially in Chapter 3, relied a great deal on the Armed Conflict Location and Event Data (ACLED) dataset in order to identify initial rebel group formation (see Appendix D). Doing so, alongside extensive secondary research, allowed my research team to identify over three times as many instances of rebel group formation in central and eastern Africa as are found in the UCDP/PRIO list of

---

[1] Blattman and Bazzi 2014, 8.
[2] For example, COW, Fearon and Laitin (2003), and Sambanis (2004b) all use fairly large battle-death thresholds (respectively 1,000 over one year, 100 over one year, and 1,000 over three years) to determine the start of the civil war. See Sambanis (2004) for an extensive discussion of conflict datasets' coding rules and extensive critical analysis of how sensitive various findings are to those rules.
[3] Salehyan 2015.

armed conflict actors. Future work on conflicts' start, including those with rebel groups as the unit of analysis, would therefore do well to consider using ACLED's events and listed actors as a starting point.

Yet while conflict event datasets are enormously valuable, they are not a panacea in capturing conflict initiation in highly remote areas since they tend to rely on media coverage. For example, for the period August 2009 to December 31, 2010, the ACLED dataset identifies twenty-seven conflict-related events in a region of South Kivu, a remote area of eastern DRC. In contrast, during the same period, using "crowd-seeding" – providing cell phones to community members and training them in reporting via text – community members from just eighteen villages in this region identified 1,439 conflict-related events.[4] Supplementing event datasets with multiple local sources of evidence – such as interviews and surveys generated in partnership with local researchers,[5] new technologies,[6] and local-language news sources – may hold the greatest promise in generating accurate knowledge about the microfoundations of conflict onset in remote areas.

These data limitations have implications for policy, especially efforts to detect and prevent conflict, such as those that attempt to provide early warning of impending armed conflict. Findings from this book suggest that ambiguous acts of violence – even those appearing to be criminal, rather than political – may indicate that would-be rebels are "testing the waters" for rebellion. Tracking such acts may offer a useful way of identifying communities that are at risk of rebellion. Highly local knowledge can also help to distinguish political versus nonpolitical violence in such cases, but will not be trivial for outsiders to access. Machine learning techniques hold promise for violent conflict prediction, but to date have had limited success even in data-rich environments.[7] More optimistically, in-depth, *retrospective* studies of the early stages of rebellion in a variety of contexts – and especially rural areas of post-conflict states – appear to be a promising avenue for scholars hoping to build empirically informed theories about the origins of armed conflict, and for policymakers hoping to better understand the start of armed conflicts.

[4] Van der Windt and Humphreys 2015. [5] See, for example, Sanchez de la Sierra 2020.
[6] See Van der Windt and Humphreys 2015 on the promise of "crowd seeding" to learn about conflict events from knowledgeable citizens in conflict regions who are trained to report about them via mobile phone; see also DeFoe and Lyall for an analysis of the promises and pitfalls of ICT for the study (and practice) of organized violence.
[7] Bazzi et al. 2019.

7.2 DISENTANGLING ETHNICITY'S ROLE

For a wide variety of questions about the dynamics, duration, and termination of conflict, the data problems delineated earlier – poorly measuring the start of armed conflict, and omitting early-failed groups – are unproblematic. However, for studies that aim to understand causes of the *emergence* of non-state violence, excluding low levels of conflict induces a selection problem. One of the resulting issues is that studies can mistakenly conclude that factors drive the *emergence of* violence, when in fact those factors are causally relevant after, and possibly *driven by,* the initial stages of violence.[8]

This risk is high for the study of ethnicity's role in armed conflict onset. Numerous works show that the salience of ethnic identity and narratives about ethnic marginalization are responsive to political dynamics in general[9] and violent conflict in particular.[10] Understanding the influence of ethnicity on conflict start, and vice versa, thus requires close analysis.

This book's findings suggest why the data problems described earlier may exacerbate confusion about ethnicity's role. If it is true that rebel groups that form in ethnically homogeneous areas are more likely to become viable – as I have shown in Chapter 5 to be the case in Uganda – then those rebel groups are substantially more likely to be captured in existing conflict datasets than groups that form in ethnically heterogeneous areas. Those that become viable may be more likely to have their narratives about the conflict enshrined in national histories – including narratives about ethnic grievances causing the initial rebel group formation. Indeed, all of the post-1986 Ugandan groups that formed in ethnically homogeneous areas and became viable are in the UCDP/PRIO Armed Conflict Dataset, while only two out of the eight groups that formed in heterogeneous areas are in the dataset.

To illustrate the importance of the this issue more concretely, I turn to contrasting my approach and findings with those of Cederman, Wimmer, and Min's (2010) highly influential analysis of ethnic group mobilization and rebellion.[11] Cederman, Wimmer, and Min (2010) – hereafter CWM – posit "a direct relationship between the degree of state power [held by an ethnic group] and the likelihood that an armed rebellion will be instigated

---

[8] This section draws on Lewis 2017.   [9] Kasfir 1979; Bates 1983; Posner 2005.
[10] Brubaker 2002; Gagnon 2004; Valentino 2004; Kalyvas 2008a; Fujii 2009; Christia 2012.
[11] According to Google Scholar, as of October 2019, Cederman, Wimmer, and Min (2010) had been cited over 1,000 times.

in the name of that group."[12] CWM ambitiously seek to include "all
politically relevant ethnic groups" in a given country each year in their
now widely used global Ethnic Power Relations dataset. Their unit of
observation is the ethnic group-year. They also coded the "status" of each
politically relevant ethnic group to capture how well each group was (or
was not) represented in the central government. For their core analyses,
they collapse these categories into a dichotomous variable that indicates
whether the group is excluded (if the group is "powerless" or "discriminated" against) or not excluded (if the group is "irrelevant" or part of the
governing coalition). This measure is a great improvement over past data
and is a remarkably rich data source, useful for examining a wide range of
issues.

   However, because it is based on country experts' retrospective, subjective measures of which ethnic groups were "politically relevant," it is –
as CWM note – fraught with issues of historical interpretation and judgment. CWM describe their primary criterion for political relevance as
follows: "We ... assume that ethnic categories become politically relevant
as soon as there is a minimal degree of political mobilization or intentional
political discrimination along ethnic lines."[13] Yet, as the findings of this
book and many other works on ethnic conflict indicate, conflict heightens
ethnic salience *after* violence has begun. Thus, especially because of common challenges to measuring the rebellion's start, it is easy to mistakenly
identify "politically relevant groups" post hoc as those that were mobil-
ized *because of* conflict's start, not prior to it.[14] Omissions of early-failed
groups worsen these problems – especially given this book's finding that
kinship networks that help nascent rebels become viable can also allow
those rebels to coordinate and amplify a sense of ethnic grievance. Because
of these issues, CWM's coding strategy is prone to including ethnic groups
that rebelled (especially those with enduring rebellions), while omitting
ethnic groups (even aggrieved or otherwise politically salient ones) that

---

[12] Cederman, Wimmer, and Min (2010, 9). The same authors conducted a country-level
   analysis and draw similar conclusions in Wimmer, Cederman, and Min 2009. I focus on
   the 2010 piece since it uses subnational data, thus presenting a more precise test of their
   theory.
[13] Wimmer, Cederman, and Min 2009, Online Appendix, 2.
[14] In other words, these coding rules are susceptible to the problem about which Laitin
   (2000, 142) warns: "[T]he clear identification of ethnic groups as entities is often the
   result of their mobilization ... But if ethnic mobilization becomes the criterion for ethnic
   groupness, there is a problem, as the value of the independent variable becomes dependent on the value of the dependent variable."

did not rebel. It is also prone to inferring prior grievances where they were not, in fact, present.

The portion of CWM's dataset on conflict in Uganda from 1986 through 2005 is consistent with their core hypothesis about ethnic exclusion leading to rebellion. Their data show that two northern groups (the Iteso and the Acholi/Langi[15]) were discriminated against, while three southern groups were part of the central government either as a junior or a senior partner in the governing coalition. According to their data, just one "ethnic rebellion" formed during this period (the LRA), and it occurred in the name of the Acholi and Langi groups. This data is thus consistent with CWM's argument about ethnic exclusion and rebellion, since none of the three groups that are coded as being a partner (junior or senior) in the central government rebelled. In other words, if their dataset had only included Uganda since 1986, CWM's coding strategy would have led them to findings consistent with the findings that they produced using their global dataset. They find broad, highly statistically significant support for this argument using their entire dataset of over 22,000 group-year observations, leading them to conclude that they "are able to establish an unequivocal relationship between the degree of [an ethnic group's] access to state power and the likelihood of armed rebellion."[16]

However, reconsidering this analysis with the finer-grained evidence from Uganda presented in this book indicates a different picture of ethnicity's role in conflict onset there. CWM's approach overlooks several cases of rebellion identified in this book. Moreover, census data from Uganda suggests that CWM also excluded several ethnic groups from their analysis that were arguably politically relevant, and could have – and sometimes did – served as the basis for an initial core of aspiring rebel leaders.

This issue can be seen more clearly by contrasting Figure 7.1 with Figure 7.2, in which I simplify exclusion as a dichotomous variable, taking negative values for "status" as excluded and positive values as not excluded. To build my measure of exclusion, I use the data displayed in Chapter 4, Figure 4.2, which uses a measure of whether

---

[15] They attribute this rebellion to the "Langi/Acholi." The LRA started in the Acholi region and later spread to Lango (the area where the Langi people live). Consistent with the Ugandan census, analyses in this book code the Acholi and Langi as distinct groups; each lives in a distinct area of northern Uganda, and they are recognized by locals to be distinct groups with a history of rivalry. Their languages are generally mutually intelligible.

[16] Cederman, Wimmer, and Min 2010, 30.

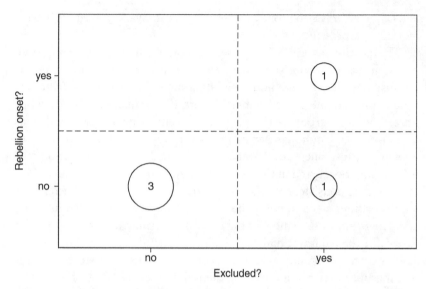

FIGURE 7.1 Ethnic exclusion and rebellion onset: Cederman, Wimmer, and Min's (2010) Uganda data (post-1986)
The unit of analysis is the ethnic group. Circles are proportional in size to the number of ethnic groups in the quadrant.

an ethnic group's representation in the cabinet is larger or smaller than its population share in the country. This coding takes a generous approach to defining exclusion, since a group that is even just one percentage point underrepresented would be considered "excluded." For example, it codes the Acholi as excluded since they were 4.4 percent of the Ugandan population and held 3.4 percent of cabinet positions, and it coded the Iteso as excluded since they were 6 percent of the population and held 3.2 percent of cabinet seats. Recall from Chapter 5 that I used extensive evidence from interviews with rebels and civilians in Teso and Acholi to argue that prior ethnic grievances were not decisive factors in the initial stages of rebellion there, even though today they are often remembered as ethnic rebellions.

Contrasting Figures 7.1 and 7.2 reveals that coding ethnicity's role in rebellion with fine-grained evidence indicates a much more ambiguous relationship between ethnic exclusion and the initiation of rebellion than one would conclude using CWM's data. Part of the difference between these figures is that I included many more small-scale rebellions than CWM, who relied on UCDP/PRIO's Armed

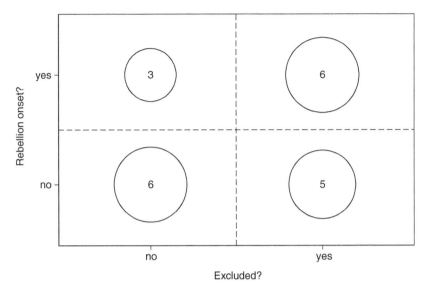

FIGURE 7.2 Ethnic exclusion and rebellion onset: improved Uganda data (post-1986)
The unit of analysis is the ethnic group. Circles are proportional in size to the number of ethnic groups in the quadrant. All ethnic groups included in the 1991 Uganda census, with greater than 1 percent of the population, are included. Exclusion data comes from Lindemann (2011), as presented in Table 4.2. Rebel group data is from multiple sources; see Appendices A and B.

Conflict Data;[17] another is that I include many more ethnic groups as a potential basis for rebellion.[18]

Relying on data from Uganda, this analysis of course does not refute the general proposition that ethnic exclusion or grievances can influence the likelihood of armed conflict. Mechanisms of ethnic grievance on one hand, and of ethnic coordination based on underlying kinship network

[17] UCDP/PRIO counts six rebellions in Uganda during this period; CWM drops all but one (the LRA), presumably because they do not count the others as a rebellion by an ethnic group. This highlights how measurement will differ greatly based on one's conceptual foundations of early-stage rebellion: Since I presume that rebels start with a small group, and thus any rebel group could become an ethnic one, I include all instances of rebel group formation in Uganda, and associate them with ethnicity based on the ethnic identity of the leadership.

[18] I follow Fearon (2003) in including all groups with at least one percent of the country's population. While this size may sound small, recall that the Acholi – from which the Lord's Resistance Army emerged – are 4.4 percent of Uganda's population, according to the 1991 Uganda census.

structure, on the other, are not mutually exclusive. Further, it seems likely that widespread, antigovernment grievances – where they do exist – would only help nascent rebels. However, this book finds strong evidence for the ethnic coordination mechanism in Uganda, even in the absence of strong prior grievances. It also shows that ethnicity's role in coordinating perceptions of the rebels and the government can lead to an amplified sense of unified, ethnic grievance, which in turn generates inferential pitfalls for scholars. To mitigate these problems, scholars should scrutinize ethnicity's role in the initial stages of armed conflict. Measuring pre-conflict ethnic salience with objective measures, and measuring the *start* of rebel group violence with care, can go a long way toward this end. As discussed earlier, creative data collection strategies that privilege local sources are also promising for getting a close look at these processes.

The importance of getting the details right about whether and how ethnicity generates armed conflict is not merely of academic concern. For example, *The U.S. Army and Marine Counterinsurgency Manual* reads: "Many insurgencies begin because groups within a society believe that they have been denied political rights."[19] The moral imperative to advocate for political rights of excluded groups is clear, and naturally many people who participate in insurgencies are those who have been treated unjustly by their governments. However, this book joins those who have argued that denial of rights is unlikely to be a key factor distinguishing places and times most vulnerable to new insurgent groups' formation from those that are less so. Instead, evidence presented in this book shows that in weak state contexts, aspiring rebels can use violence and rumor during the early stages of the insurgency to influence ethnic narratives. By the time a rebellion has persisted long enough for civilians to develop informed views, armed groups have often developed strong intelligence and coercive capacity – which substantially limits the paths through which civilians can help end the rebellion without putting themselves in grave danger.

7.3 STATE-BUILDING AND DOMESTIC INTELLIGENCE

This book's findings point to a straightforward implication about how states can detect and end rebellions in the early stages: through strengthening domestic intelligence capacity in their outlying territories. In Chapters 2 and 6, respectively, I presented theory and evidence that a

---

[19] Petraeus 2006, 75.

state's presence in its periphery matters not because of the military or other advantage it confers to states, but because of the *intelligence* advantage it allows for. If it becomes common knowledge that the state has *informationally* penetrated its rural territories, then rebels will typically not even bother to try to form. Interview evidence from former rebel leaders in Uganda confirmed this insight; when asked why rebel groups no longer form in Uganda, they almost uniformly pointed to the increased and substantial informational strength of the state in rural areas.

This argument is not a controversial one, but this book clarifies how important and effective a state's informational penetration of its localities can be in deterring rebel group formation – even in states that are relatively weak in more conventional dimensions of state capacity like local service delivery. In particular, the book's findings about how Uganda transitioned from having numerous rebel groups form on its territory to having none form there for over a decade – by building a civil intelligence apparatus that penetrated villages throughout the country – also has implications for scholars and policymakers.

With notable exceptions indicated in previous chapters, most theories of state-building and conflict onset have not focused on this dimension of state capacity. The findings of this book indicate that this oversight, while understandable given data collection challenges, should be reconsidered. For example, examining why some African states invest in this dimension of state capacity, while others do not, remains a largely open question. Subnational measures of state surveillance capacity would be extraordinarily difficult to obtain for most states; a country-level measure of each state's informational penetration of its rural areas is more plausible, but would require great investment in culling highly local, and potentially sensitive, knowledge for each country-period.

Practitioners in this area – especially counterinsurgents and peace-keepers engaged in state-building – are often already aware of the relevance of domestic intelligence institutions. For example, recognition of the importance of intelligence from civilians about incipient security threats has likely, in part, driven an increase in training police as part of international peace operations.[20] The US security posture in Africa over the past decade is also consistent with this understanding. A cornerstone of US military activity in Africa for over a decade has been building African partner militaries' capacity to prevent and manage insurgencies. These efforts are predicated on the notion that such groups could threaten US national

---

[20] Caparini 2018.

security interests if they metastasize into transnational groups, as Boko Haram and Al-Shabaab did. In addition to training African militaries, a key feature of these partnerships is providing technical assistance that allows for improved monitoring of outlying territories.[21]

Of course, complex ethical issues are unavoidable for third parties weighing whether and how to support African states in building their domestic intelligence capacity. Domestic intelligence institutions designed to detect internal security threats can be easily used also to repress or co-opt budding, non-violent political opposition; this is exceedingly difficult for third parties to monitor. This possibility is particularly worrisome in contemporary eastern and central Africa where, with the exception of Ethiopia, political space for nonviolent opposition has been steadily shrinking since the mid-2000s.[22]

7.4 BEYOND WEAK STATES: VARIETIES OF REBELLION

This final section revisits the primary scope condition of this book: It has sought to explain rebel group formation *in weak states*. To reiterate from earlier, a key conceptual foundation of the book's theory is that where a state is weak – and thus its presence is minimal – barriers to entry for new rebel groups are low, and thus rebel groups are often quite small and weak when they begin. They lack the organizational, material, and motivational endowments that paradigmatic, long-lasting rebel groups like the LRA, the FARC, and the Tamil Tigers have at their peak. As noted earlier, most theoretical arguments in the book follow from that contention.

What does this imply about rebellion's start in strong state contexts? Barriers to entry for new rebel groups will be much higher; people contemplating rebellion know that they can be discovered and crushed quickly. As a result, usually only those that can marshal substantial coercive capacity quickly will dare to form. One obvious implication is that rebel group formation should be rarer in stronger states. While such a pattern would surprise few, this book has shown that rebel group formation is likely much more common in weak states than previously accounted for, putting this pattern into sharper focus.

These arguments also suggest that the *processes* of rebel group formation should be quite different in a stronger state context, which can help explain some of the differences between this book's findings and those from prior works. First, it suggests that when rebel groups do form in

---

[21] Demmers and Gould 2018.   [22] Cheeseman and Smith 2019.

stronger states, they will be more likely to draw on strong prior organizational or material foundations that will allow them to muster strong capacity quickly. The sources of readily marshaled capacity are potentially numerous, but plausible ones are soldiers and organizational systems from prior rebellions or armies, or systems and skills learned from previous, nonviolent organizations of tightly knit, devoted members. Nonviolent protests, if they allow highly motivated people to identify one another and build organizations that could be later repurposed for violent ends, could serve a similar function. Recall from Chapter 2 that this book's theory did not emphasize the importance of prewar material, organizational, or motivational endowments – including ethnic or other ideological grievances – in the early stages of rebel group formation. I noted that several recent studies do posit the importance of these factors to the early stages of resistance or rebel violence – but that those studies focused on stronger states, such as Colombia, Nazi Germany, Arab Spring countries, and even parts of contemporary South Asia. The arguments in this paragraph potentially account for the difference between such findings and those of this book; in stronger states, material, organizational, and motivational endowments may matter more to initial rebel group formation.

Second, these arguments suggest that when rebellion occurs in stronger states, violence can escalate much more quickly. Armed groups may not dare to form unless they can quickly assemble organizations that can survive violent confrontations with the state; therefore, the modal group that does form will meet those criteria, and violence will quickly ensue. This may lead to the quick "eruption" of violence that is commonly assumed as characterizing the start of civil war – an assumption with which this book has taken issue. It may be the case that a sudden outbreak of violence is more common when civil wars start in stronger state environments – and that the selection biases that this book identifies are less severe there.

This book has not directly assessed evidence for these contentions, opting instead to focus on understanding variation among rebel groups forming *within* weak states. In doing so, it joins a rich, recent literature on the meso- and microfoundations of political violence. However, this discussion suggests that mid-range theorizing that aims to explain the varied pathways through which internal armed conflict begins, conditional on distinct macro-level factors, may be a fruitful path for future research. Among other benefits, such theorizing has the potential to synthesize the wealth of recent meso- and micro-level findings that have emerged in the conflict literature. Doing so promises to shed light on distinct patterns of conflict processes in the varied contexts from which organized political violence emerges.

APPENDIX A

Identifying Ugandan Rebel Groups

Table 3.1 in Chapter 3 lists the sixteen rebel groups I identified as forming in Uganda since January 1986. To be counted as crossing the threshold of forming a rebel group, each had to have developed an organization with, at a minimum, a discernable command and control structure that aimed to violently challenge the Ugandan state and to have committed – or planned to commit – at least one act of violence against a state target. I did not count as distinct groups those that splintered from an original group, unless the majority of the splinter group's leadership, soldiers, and area of operation were different from that of the original group. Conversely, while some groups did contain fighters from former rebel groups, I counted them as distinct groups if they had distinct leadership and the majority of their soldiers were not from a single, prior group. Each rebel group was thus a distinct organization. No two groups were based in the same district at the same time, and while some of the groups occasionally communicated with one another and considered coordinating arms shipments or attacks, actual acts of coordination or of violence against one another were extremely rare.

To identify these groups, I first developed an inclusive list of potential rebel groups using a Uganda Amnesty Commission database of all former rebels who had received amnesty from the government (which included the rebel group affiliation of each former rebel), a complete set of all Ugandan English-language articles I collected about armed conflict from January 1986 through 2002 (most of which were available only in hard copy in Uganda's libraries),[1] and meetings and correspondence with

---

[1] No groups formed in Uganda after 2002.

leaders of Uganda's intelligence services, who worked with their staff to arrive at a list of all Ugandan rebel groups since 1986.[2] I then eliminated several groups either because I determined that they ended prior to 1986, or because I could not find credible evidence, based on the above sources, that these groups committed or planned to commit a single act of violence on Ugandan territory. By "credible evidence," I mean that a group had to appear in the Amnesty Commission list or in newspaper reporting, and its existence and plans for violence had to be confirmed by at least two qualified sources of two different "types" (e.g. at least one government source and one former rebel or one qualified local journalist). For example, I confirmed the existence of the CAMP rebellion – an early-failed group involved in the deaths of just a handful of people in the Lango region in the mid-1990s – by finding it in both the Amnesty Commission database and newspaper articles, and by confirming its existence and handful of violent attacks with several well-respected local journalists based in Lango as well as local government officials.

In most cases, such as that of CAMP, it was straightforward to identify whether an organized, violent group had indeed existed. Two groups warrant additional discussion because of the murkier evidence available when deciding whether to include them on the final list of Ugandan rebel organizations: Severino Lukoya's (unnamed) group in the Acholi region, which I did not include, and the People's Redemption Army (PRA) from western Uganda, which I did include. The analyses presented in the book are not highly sensitive to the inclusion or exclusion of either group.

Regarding Lukoya's group, the primary evidence in favor of its inclusion is that it features in historical and anthropological accounts of this period in northern Uganda, especially in Henke Behrend's excellent *Alice Lakwena and the Holy Spirits*. However, a careful reading of Behrend's account suggests that it was a splinter group from Lakwena's HSM, composed almost entirely of her former soldiers in the immediate aftermath of her fleeing to exile in Kenya, and thus does not meet this study's criteria for inclusion. Furthermore, I could not find clear evidence that Lukoya's group committed violence. According to Behrend, Lukoya "declared that his mission was not so much to fight as to spread the

---

[2] The two Ugandan institutions responsible for internal intelligence are the Chieftaincy of Military Intelligence, a military agency, and the Internal Security Organization, a civilian agency. In arriving at this list, I met with the head of Uganda's Chieftaincy of Military Intelligence as well as several Internal Security Organization officials.

message of the spirits and to heal."[3] While Behrend explains that Lukoya had a military department and that his group "reportedly" attempted to capture Kitgum in March 1988,[4] his source for this event is an unpublished manuscript, and I was unable to identify a single violent event described in a Ugandan newspaper attributed to Lukoya's group.[5] The impression that Lukoya's group did not commit violence against the state was also generally reflected in several interviews and focus groups I conducted in the Kitgum/Pader area.[6] Finally, no individuals from the group were reported in data from Uganda's Amnesty Commission as having received amnesty from the government.

Regarding the PRA, this group was the only rebel group whose existence poses political sensitivities in the present, since there have been unsubstantiated reports that opposition politician Kizza Besigye once had links with the group. Several individuals, including purported former PRA leader Samson Mande, have denied that the group existed. However, according to data from Uganda's Amnesty Commission, sixty-six former PRA members received amnesty. While apparently no record exists indicating that group committed violence, several sources inside and outside the government indicated that an organized group formed in eastern Democratic Republic of Congo (DRC) with attempted bases just over the border in western Uganda and plans to attack state targets near there.[7] Furthermore, more recent reports from non-government-aligned media in Uganda have suggested the (prior)

---

[3] Behrend 1999, 175.   [4] Behrend 1999, 176.

[5] Robert Gersony writes that Lukoya's group was composed of former members of the HSM, and is "remembered for" attacks on Kitgum town – but could not confirm details and also notes the "obscure memories of [his] interviewees" about this group (Gersony 1997, 29).

[6] For example, one man at a focus group of eight people in Pajule subcounty in Pader district in December 2009 explained that Lukoya "mostly prayed and did not engage the government. [Lukoya] was trying to convert people into his religion and to revive the Holy Spirit Movement of his daughter." One person present thought that maybe he had once fought in Kitgum but did not know the details, and no one else at the focus group, nor any of my other interviewees in Pader or Kitgum, could confirm this fighting. I conducted five focus groups of between six and twenty-three people in the Acholi region; two in Gulu, two in Pader, and one in Kitgum, and interviewed several local officials as well as former members of the LRA, UPDA, and HSM.

[7] Author interview with former NFA leader, Kampala, January 2010; author interview with former UPA leader, Soroti, July 2008; author interview with senior military leader, Kampala, June 2008; author interview with former intelligence officer, Kampala, June 2008; author interview with former local official, Kasese district (western Uganda), July 2008.

existence of the PRA as a group that did indeed form and planned attacks against Uganda.[8]

To gain broader evidence about rebel group formation, I conducted over 170 interviews with former rebel commanders, intelligence officers and foot soldiers, local government officials who operated where rebels launched, Members of Parliament, military leaders, intelligence officers, and conflict experts such as Ugandan academics and NGO leaders. To learn further detail about civilians' experiences and beliefs, in addition to the information gained from the interviews described above, I conducted sixty-eight semi-structured individual interviews with civilians in Teso and fourteen focus groups with civilians in four, in-depth case study areas that were affected by the early stages of conflict: the Acholi, Bukedi, Teso, and West Nile regions.[9] Most of these interviews were conducted in private with only the author and the interviewee present; an exception occurred when the interviewee did not speak English, thus a translator was also present. Use of translators was common for interviews with rural villagers but not for any other type of interviewee.

---

[8] Edris Kiggundu, "Uganda: 'PRA' Existed – Ex-Operative." *The Observer*, April 15, 2015.

[9] In Teso, I conducted focus groups in Soroti and Kumi. In Bukedi, I conducted focus groups in Tororo and Busia. In West Nile, I conducted focus groups in Nyadri, Koboko, and Yumbe. In Acholi, I conducted focus groups in Gulu, Pader, and Kitgum.

APPENDIX B

List of Interviews and Focus Groups

This appendix describes and lists the interviews I conducted for this project. I do not list the countless informal conversations with knowledgeable Ugandans that also deeply informed this work. This fieldwork occurred during more than fourteen months I spent in Uganda (in twenty districts[1]) between August 2007 and February 2011. The project was conducted under Harvard University IRB Protocol F16950-104 and with permission from the Uganda National Council for Science and Technology. Locations and dates of the interviews are listed below; a map showing the location of these interviews can be found in Chapter 1 (Figure 1.3).

The interviews were semi-structured and conversational. With the exception of focus groups and individual interviews with civilians, all interviews were conducted in English without the aid of a translator. All interviews, except those with rural villagers, took place in offices or public places such as hotel lobbies or restaurants, typically in a quiet corner where I could ensure that individuals nearby could not overhear our conversation. Due to the potential sensitivity of the topics raised and my desire to put the interviewees at ease, I did not record the interviews, except in rare cases in which I had developed a relationship with an interviewee and they agreed to be taped. Interviewees were all guaranteed anonymity, and are therefore referenced in the dissertation by type – for example, "senior military official" or "local government

---

[1] The districts in which I conducted interviews, based on 2009 district boundaries, are: Amuria, Arua, Busia, Gulu, Kabarole, Kampala, Kasese, Kitgum, Koboko, Kumi, Lira, Luwero, Masindi, Mbale, Mukono, Nyadri, Pader, Soroti, Tororo, and Yumbe.

official in [name] county." In all cases, these titles refer to the individual's current position unless otherwise indicated (e.g. "former local official," which connotes that the individual was a local official during the period that the applicable rebel group formed).

Anonymity for people I interviewed helped me ensure that they could speak to me openly; while the political climate in Uganda today allows for generally open discussion on past events, neither the interviewees nor I could know for certain if information linking them to past violence, or opinions about violence, could someday be used against them. Keeping senior officials and former rebel leaders anonymous was a more difficult decision, since doing so precludes historians or other interested parties from using this information to understand what particular actors in these conflicts stated about these past events. While some senior officials and rebel leaders I interviewed expressed willingness for me to use their names, I informed them prior to the interview that I would not do so. My aim was to guard against a tendency for interviewees to view me as a conduit for their transmitting their legacy to an international audience – and thus perhaps to exaggerate their authority, their prescience, or the extent of their success. While such biases are to some extent inevitable in retrospective interviewing of leaders, I sought to minimize them as much as possible by informing interviewees at the outset that I would not use their names in my writing.

Regarding my information collection from rural villagers, I conducted both focus groups and individual interviews in my four case study regions (Teso, Bukedi, West Nile, and Acholi). I conducted both individual interviews and focus groups because they served different purposes: focus groups were more effective for arriving at a basic sketch of the history of the conflict in a community, since participants could interact and refresh one another's memory about key events and locations, whereas for more sensitive questions, such as those that elicited stories about whether and why a villager initially believed that the rebels would (or would not) eventually capture the state, an individual interview setting was more effective.

Focus group participants were recruited by a local (village- or subcounty-level) official with the aim of gathering a broad range of individuals, in terms of sex, political beliefs, and age – although I specified that I only wanted participants over age thirty-eight, so that they would have been at least fifteen years old in 1986. I also only recruited focus group participants who lived in the community in the late 1980s. Based on my interactions with the local officials who recruited participants and in the course of the focus groups themselves, I found no reason to believe that participants stifled their opinions due to the presence of the local officials. Local officials were always elected officials who were from the local area – they were not central government appointees – and often voluntarily enjoined the participants to "speak freely." In only two of my focus groups, my translator and I perceived that some participants might have been uncomfortable or not eager to share their views. I did not include evidence from these focus groups in the dissertation.

At the focus groups, after introducing the study, I began by asking each person their age and occupation when the rebel group formed. I then asked a series of questions about precisely when their community learned about the existence of a rebel group, where the rebel group was based, whether and how rebel leaders interacted with the community, perceptions about the government that existed at the time, and a battery of questions about how the rebellion unfolded and how people responded. The focus groups lasted between forty-five and ninety minutes.

The individual interviews with villagers took place in the homestead of the interviewee, typically in the area outside of the interviewee's dwelling, on the interviewee's family property. I began the interview with an introduction to myself and to the study's goals, and then a semi-structured set of questions that allowed for collection of information that was comparable across interviews – for example, about from whom he initially learned about the rebels, and the extent to which he had perceived the rebels to be strong and capable during those early days. Based on responses to these questions, I asked more detailed questions about his experiences with the group and knowledge about how it began. I directed these questions first toward basic information about the rebel group(s) – for example, who their leaders were, and what the interviewee understood their goals to be – and then turned toward his experiences and beliefs (at the time) about the rebels, as well as his knowledge of the specific behaviors of the rebels, government actors, and civilians during the initial phases of conflict. The unstructured portion of the interviews that followed afforded an opportunity to ask more sensitive questions or complex questions about sequences of events. It also allowed me to more deeply probe responses that were interesting or unexpected.

I identified villagers to interview with the aid of village-level local officials and with the aim of obtaining a broad range of perspectives on the events that occurred in the area. They thus do not represent a random sample of individuals who lived near nascent rebel bases, but I have no reason to believe that they are biased in any particular direction. My process for identifying them was as follows. With the assistance of former rebel leaders, I first identified where initial rebel bases were located. I then sought out (with the assistance of a village official – a different one for each study area) interviewees from several villages surrounding the area. I informed my village official guide that I wanted to speak with people with a broad range of perspectives and ages, and I wanted to speak with both men and women. I have no reason to believe that the village officials directed me to any specific people; it appeared clear to me that people we approached were surprised to see a foreigner and therefore had not been prepared for this encounter by any official in advance of our meeting. On occasion, the official would suggest that we stop at a particular homestead, and I would decline, suggesting that we instead walk in a different direction. The officials did not seem fazed when I did so, which gave me additional confidence that I was not being led to a particular planned set of homes.

We then traveled to homesteads – clusters of huts where a family lives – surrounding the former rebel base area. The village officials played an important role because I was seeking out information about events that occurred over twenty-three years prior, and thus I needed assistance to identify people old enough to remember these events, and who were living in the area during these events. The village officials did not attend the interviews; the only people present at the individual interviews with villagers were the interviewee, a translator who spoke the local language (which varied depending on the location), and I. These interviews lasted between forty minutes and one and a half hours.

LIST OF INTERVIEWS

Listed by Interviewee Type, in Order of Meeting Date

- Description of interviewee(s); location; date(s)

Former Rebels

- Group of five former WNBF leaders and soldiers; Arua; June 2008
- Former UPA leader 1; Soroti and Amuria; July 2008, June 2009, July 2009

- Former UPA intelligence officer 1; Soroti and Amuria; July 2008, June 2009, January 2011
- Former UPA leader 2; Soroti; July 2008, July 2009, January 2011
- Former UPA leader 3; Soroti; July 2008
- Former UPA soldier 1; Soroti; July 2008
- Former UPA soldier 2; Soroti; July 2008
- Former NFA leader; Kampala; February 2009, March 2009, April 2009, October 2009, January 2010
- Former FOBA leader 1; Kampala; February 2009
- Former LRA soldier 1; Gulu; March 2009
- Former UPDA soldier 1; Gulu; March 2009
- Former LRA soldier 2; Gulu; March 2009
- Former NOM soldier; Lira municipality; March 2009
- Former UFDF leader; Mukono; March 2009
- Former FOBA leader 2; Tororo municipality; June 2009
- Former UPA leader 4; Amuria; June 2009
- Former UPA leader 5 (also current local intelligence officer); Soroti municipality; June 2009
- Former FOBA soldier 1; Tororo municipality; June 2009, July 2009
- Former local official; Busia (Samia-Bugwe); June 2009
- Informal local leader (elder); Busia (Samia-Bugwe); June 2009
- Former UPA leader 6; Amuria; July 2009
- Former UPA leader 7; Amuria; July 2009
- Group of three former FOBA fighters; Tororo county; July 2009
- Former FOBA soldier 2; Tororo county; July 2009
- Former FOBA leader 3; Tororo municipality; July 2009
- Former FOBA leader 4; Busia Town Council; July 2009
- Former UNRF II leader 1; Kampala; November 2009
- Former UNRF II leader 2; Kampala; November 2009
- Former WNBF leader 1; Arua; November 2009
- Former UNRF II leader 3; Aringa county (Yumbe district); November 2009
- Former UNRF II leader 4; Aringa county (Yumbe district); November 2009
- Former UNRF II leader 5; Aringa county (Yumbe district); November 2009
- Former LRA leader 1; Gulu municipality; November 2009
- Former UPDA leader; Gulu municipality; November 2009
- Former FOBA soldier 3; Tororo; November 2009
- Former WNBF leader 2; Kampala; December 2009

- Former HSM leader; Kitgum Town Council; December 2009
- Former LRA leader 2; Gulu municipality; December 2009
- Former ADF leader; Kampala; January 2011, February 2011
- Former UPA soldier 3; Soroti; February 2011
- Former UPA intelligence officer 2; Soroti; February 2011

Ugandan Officials – Military (Uganda People's Defense Force) and Domestic Intelligence

- Former intelligence officer 1; Kampala; September 2007, June 2008
- Senior military official[2] 1; Kampala; June 2008
- Senior intelligence officer; Kampala; June 2008
- Senior military official 2; Kampala; June 2008
- Local (subcounty) intelligence official; Kasese district; July 2008
- Senior military official 3; Luwero (Bombo barracks); July 2008, August 2009
- Senior military official 4; Luwero (Bombo barracks); February 2009
- Intelligence officer 1; Kampala; March 2009
- Intelligence officer 2; Kampala; March 2009
- Senior military official 5; Masindi; March 2009
- Senior military official 6; Gulu; March 2009
- Intelligence officer 3; Kampala; March 2009
- Intelligence officer 4; Kampala; April 2009
- Intelligence officer 5; Kampala; April 2009
- Intelligence officer 6; Kampala; April 2009
- Senior military official 7; Luwero (Bombo barracks); August 2009
- Former intelligence official in Tororo; Kampala; August 2009
- Intelligence officer 7; Kampala; October 2009
- Local intelligence officer; Terego county; December 2009
- Local intelligence officer; Nyadri county; December 2009
- Local intelligence officer; Koboko county; December 2009
- Military official and Mchaka Mchaka instructor 1; Kampala; February 2011
- Military official and Mchaka Mchaka instructor 2; Kampala; February 2011

---

[2] "Senior military official" refers to any member of the Uganda People's Defense Force ranked Lieutenant Colonel or above.

Ugandan Officials and Politicians – Civilian

- Deputy Speaker; Gulu municipality, Gulu district; August 2007
- Senior official at Amnesty Commission 1; Arua municipality, Arua district; June 2008
- Director, Uganda Amnesty Commission; Kampala; July 2008
- Local (village) official; Kaborole District; July 2008
- Senior official at Amnesty Commission 2; Kampala; July 2008
- Senior official at Amnesty Commission 3; Kampala; July 2008, July 2009
- Member of Parliament 1; Kampala; March 2009
- Member of Parliament 2; Kampala; March 2009
- Official, Ministry of Foreign Affairs; Kampala; March 2009
- Official, Ministry of Local Government Finance Commission; March 2009
- Former local (district) official in Tororo; Kampala; March 2009
- NRM senior official who designed the RC system; Kampala; March 2009, February 2011
- Senior official at Amnesty Commission 4; Mbale municipality; July 2009
- Local (municipality) official; Tororo municipality; July 2009
- Former local (district) official; Tororo municipality; July 2009
- Local (district) official; Tororo municipality; July 2009
- Local (district) official; Busia (Samia-Bugwe); July 2009
- Local (district) official 1; Busia Town Council; July 2009, November 2009
- Local (subcounty) official; Busia; July 2009
- Former local (district) leader in Tororo; Kampala; August 2009
- Local opposition politician; Busia Town Council; July 2009
- Local (district) leader; Arua; November 2009
- Mchaka Mchaka graduate; Arua; November 2009, December 2009
- Local (district) official 2; Busia Town Council; November 2009
- Local (parish) official; Samia-Bugwe (Busia); November 2009
- Local (subcounty) official; Tororo; November 2009
- Local (subcounty) official 1; Omoro county (Gulu district); December 2009
- Local (subcounty) official 2; Omoro county (Gulu district); December 2009
- Local (district) official; Agago county (Pader district); December 2009

- Local (district) official; Kitgum Town Council; December 2009
- Former local (village) official; Soroti county; January 2011

Ugandan Experts, Researchers, NGO Officials, and Other Local Leaders

- Lecturer in Human Rights; Makerere University, Kampala; August 2007
- Professor 1, Department of Political Science, Makerere University; Kampala; August 2007, July 2008
- Professor 2, Department of Political Science, Makerere University; Kampala; August 2007
- Journalist 1, *The Monitor*; Kampala; August 2007
- Researcher 1, Kaborole Research Center; Fort Portal municipality; August 2007, July 2008
- Researcher 2, Kaborole Research Center; Fort Portal municipality; July 2008
- Researcher 1, Refugee Law Project; Kampala; June 2008
- Researcher 2, Refugee Law Project; Kampala; June 2008, March 2009
- Group of three leaders of the Arua Justice Peace and Human Rights Commission; Arua municipality; June 2008
- Opposition politician; Fort Portal municipality; July 2008
- Local (district) official; Kumi; November 2009
- Principal, Kichwamba Technical School; Burahya county; July 2008
- NGO officials, AMNET-R; Kasese Town Council; July 2008
- NGO official, ARUCEDE; Kasese Town Council; July 2008
- Former local (subcounty) official; Bukonjo county; July 2008
- Independent researcher; Kampala; July 2008, March 2009, July 2009
- Opposition politician; Soroti municipality; July 2008
- Managing Director, *The New Vision*; Kampala; July 2008
- Anglican religious leader; Kumi; July 2008
- NGO official, CARE International; Kampala; February 2009
- NGO official, ACODE; Kampala; March 2009
- Director, Human Rights Focus; Gulu municipality; March 2009
- Local contractor with USAID; Gulu municipality; March 2009
- Local journalist, *Mega Radio*; Gulu municipality; March 2009
- Local freelance journalist; Gulu municipality; March 2009
- Wife of former CAMP leader; Lira municipality; March 2009
- Journalist, *Radio Rhino*; Lira municipality; March 2009

- Journalist, *the BBC*; Tororo municipality; March 2009
- Leader of Tororo Civil Society Network; Tororo municipality, June 2009
- Local opposition politician; Tororo municipality, June 2009
- NRM party official; Tororo municipality; July 2009, November 2009, February 2011
- Local historian; Busia Town Council; July 2009
- Two leaders, Lugbara-Madi Cultural Society; November 2009
- Local historian; Arua; November 2009
- Former teacher; Kisoko/Budama county; November 2009
- Local informal leader (elder); Kisoko/Budama county; November 2009
- Local informal leader 1 (elder); Kasilo county; November 2009
- Local informal leader 2 (female elder); Kasilo county; November 2009
- Local informal leader 3 (female elder); Kasilo county; November 2009
- Local NGO leader; Aringa county (Yumbe district); November 2009

Other – US and International Organization Officials

- Former US Defense Attaché to Uganda 1; Arlington, Virginia; July 2007, January 2008
- USAID official; Kampala; August 2007, September 2007, June 2008, July 2008, March 2009, August 2009
- UNHCR official, Kampala, August 2007
- World Bank official, Kampala, August 2007
- USAID official, Gulu, August 2007
- Former US Defense Attaché to Uganda 2, Kampala, September 2007
- Country Director, International Republican Institute; Kampala; June 2008, March 2009

Ugandan Civilians

- Group interview of three survivors of FOBA attack, Samia-Bugwe county; November 2009
- Survivor of UPA attack 1; Ngora county; November 2009
- Survivor of UPA attack 2; Ngora county; November 2009
- Survivor of UPA attack 3; Ngora county; November 2009
- Survivor of WNBF attack; Koboko county; November 2009
- Individual interviews with thirty-four civilians in Soroti county in villages close to the UPA's initial base (Alere, Omugenya, Angopet, Opucet villages), January 2011

- Individual interviews with thirty-four civilians in Tororo and Samia-Bugwe counties in villages close to FOBA's two initial bases (Kinjil village near Mella; Namuwo, Mbatu, and Silangirine villages near Busitema); January 2011

LIST OF FOCUS GROUPS

Teso Subregion

- Soroti district; Gweri subcounty; December 2009 (twelve people)
- Kumi district; Kumi Town Council; December 2009 (seven people)

Bukedi Subregion

- Tororo district; Malaba Town Council; November 2009 (fourteen people)
- Tororo district; Mella subcounty; November 2009 (twelve people)

Acholi Subregion

- Gulu district; Lakwana subcounty; December 2009 (thirteen people)
- Gulu district; Lalongi subcounty; December 2009 (six people)
- Pader district; Pajule subcounty 1; December 2009 (eight people)
- Kitgum district, Mucwini subcounty; December 2009 (twenty-three people)
- Pader district, Laceekocot subcounty; December 2009 (six people)

West Nile Subregion

- Yumbe district, Drajina subcounty; December 2009 (seventeen people)
- Yumbe district, Romogi subcounty; December 2009 (nine people)
- Koboko district; Koboko Town Council; December 2009 (fifteen people)
- Koboko district; Koboko Town Council; December 2009 (twenty people)
- Maracha district; Nyadri town; December 2009 (seven people)

APPENDIX C

Supplementary Statistical Analyses

The following two sections supply additional information about the statistical analyses conducted in Chapters 4 and 5 respectively. The first section displays summary statistics for and shows correlations among variables used to examine rebel launch in Chapter 4; the second section shows results of the statistical analyses described in Chapter 5 and examines the potential sensitivity of the results about rebel viability in Chapter 5 to certain measurements, influential observations, and model specifications.

MATERIALS SUPPLEMENTING CHAPTER 4

Summary Statistics and Correlation Matrix for Rebel Launch Analysis

What follows summarizes information about the correlation between variables used in the logistic regression analyses in Chapter 4 that examine the correlates of rebel group formation at the county level. A correlation matrix of all variables used in the analysis, shown in Table C.1, shows the bivariate relationships among each pair of variables. The only highly correlated variables (greater than 0.7) are those that are not used in the same model because they proxy for the same concept; for example, the two measures of exclusion are highly correlated.

TABLE C.I *Summary statistics, variables for rebel launch analysis*

	Variable	Mean	SD	Range	Description	Data source
DV	*launch*	0.10	0.30	{0, 1}	"1" if a rebel group committed the first attack in that county, otherwise "0"	Interviews with rebels, government, and civilians; newspaper articles
Ethnic demography	*ELF*	0.38	0.25	(.01, .88)	Probability that two randomly selected people are from different ethnic groups	Uganda census (1991)
	largest ethnic group size	.74	.20	(0.22, 0.99)	Portion of the county's total population comprised by largest ethnic group (logged)	Uganda census (1991)
Exclusion	*cabinet representation*	2.32	7.49	(−2.9, 16)	Weighted average of ethnic groups' cabinet share minus Uganda population share	Lindemann (2011)
	cabinet rep 2	0.82	0.74	(0.0002, 1.99)	Same as earlier, except ethnic representation scores are trichotomous: difference between eth cabinet share and pop share score is "0" if difference is < -1, "1" if > -1 and < 1, "2" if > 1	Lindemann (2011)

(continued)

TABLE C.1 (continued)

	Variable	Mean	SD	Range	Description	Data source
Terrain	elevation (km)	1,731	815	(912, 4,858)	Difference between highest and lowest point (km)	USGS
	forest	24.75	25.86	(0, 95.23)	Percentage of area covered by non-agricultural vegetation	UN FAO (2002)
	population density (log)	4.55	1.38	(0.07, 9.23)	Number of people per square kilometer (logged)	Uganda census (1991)
Borders	distance to border (m) (log)	10.87	0.89	(8.84, 12.13)	Distance in meters from centroid of county to closest international border (logged)[1]	Measured using GIS
	contiguous with border	0.21	0.41	{0, 1}	Whether or not county is on international border	n/a
Development	poverty line	63.46	13.94	(26.1, 93.1)	Percentage of people living below the poverty line in 1992	Uganda Bureau of Statistics (2003)
	poverty gap	23.38	9.72	(3, 49.4)	Among those living below poverty line, average consumption (% below poverty line) in 1992	Uganda Bureau of Statistics (2003)
	literacy	50.68	15.02	(0.003, 88.39)	% literate in 1991	Uganda Bureau of Statistics (2003)

(continued)

State				
distance to capital (m) (log)	12.04	1.07	(1, 12.89)	Distance in meters from centroid of county(ies) to capital city (logged)	Calculated using GIS
prior NRM institutions	0.33	0.47	{0, 1}	Whether or not a county had been under NRM's control and had NRM local institutions prior to January 1986	Interview with senior NRM official; newspaper articles

Note: Unit of analysis is the county (all 163 counties in Uganda).
[1] I only count land borders as international borders; I do not count the shores of Lake Victoria or Lake Albert or Lake Edward as an international border, since bodies of water are not generally sanctuaries for rebels.

TABLE C.2 Correlation matrix, variables for rebel launch analysis

	ELF	elev	forest	pop. dens	dist to Int'l brdr	cont brdr	dist to K'la	Prior NRM	liter	pov line	pov gap	excl	excl2
ELF	1.00												
elev	-0.21	1.00											
forest	-0.06	0.41	1.00										
pop. dnsty	0.20	-0.11	0.44	1.00									
dist to brdr	0.11	-0.52	-0.26	-0.15	1.00								
contg brdr	-0.20	0.34	0.20	-0.09	-0.66	1.00							
dist to K'la	-0.26	0.26	0.23	-0.21	-0.41	0.26	1.00						
prior NRM	0.34	-0.03	0.07	0.09	0.18	-0.18	-0.22	1.00					
litrcy	0.25	-0.23	-0.38	0.34	0.24	-0.27	-0.40	0.28	1.00				
pov. line	-0.42	0.09	0.26	-0.49	-0.03	0.24	0.40	-0.40	-0.57	1.00			
pov. gap	-0.38	0.11	0.33	-0.48	-0.02	0.19	0.34	-0.40	-0.57	0.96	1.00		
excl	0.40	-0.18	-0.12	0.03	0.24	-0.17	-0.50	0.42	0.47	-0.40	-0.41	1.00	
excl2	0.37	0.12	-0.03	0.11	-0.19	0.02	-0.23	0.30	0.39	-0.40	-0.46	0.74	1.00

Unit of analysis is the county (all 163 counties in Uganda).

Correlates of Rebel Viability: Variables, Measurement, and Core Results

In constructing variables to capture potential correlates of rebel viability, I used the following data and measurements: To capture variation in terrain that may facilitate rebel viability, I first generated a variable *elevation* that measures (in kilometers) the difference between highest and lowest points in an area where a rebel group initially operated, using data compiled by the US Geological Survey.[2] I also constructed a measure of *forest cover*, measuring the percentage of each county that has natural (non-agricultural) vegetation, such as trees and shrubs, using data from the UN Food and Agriculture Organization (FAO)'s Africover project.[3] I constructed these variables for each county using ArcGIS. As an additional terrain-related proxy, I also compiled a logged *population density* variable using the complete 1991 census, measuring the number of people per square kilometer. To examine the importance of access to borders with states that may shelter or sponsor rebel groups, I measured the distance (as a straight line) from the centroid of the county to the closest international border (in kilometers), using ArcGIS, generating the variable *border*. I also code a second measure of border that is a binary variable for whether or not an area is on an international border; because the results do not substantively or statistically differ much when using that latter measure, I do not show the results here. To measure the extent of local *poverty* in a given area, I used literacy rate measures from the 1991 census and a county-level, 1992 measure of the percentage of a county's population living below the poverty line, obtained from the Ugandan Bureau of Statistics based on their household survey data (Emwanu et al. 2003). I measured *exclusion* using the same data and procedure from Chapter 4, using Stefan Lindemann's data for the ethnic composition of Uganda's cabinet in 1988. First, I developed an exclusion score for each ethnic group by subtracting the ethnic group's share of Uganda's total population from its share of the cabinet.[4] I then developed exclusion scores for each area where a rebel group operated according to a weighted average based on the ethnic composition of each area. Negative scores indicate "under-

---

[2] See Digital Elevation Models available at http://srtm.usgs.gov/index.php, accessed August 23, 2010.

[3] Africover uses satellite remote sensing to generate land cover maps. This data is available at www.africover.org/aggregation.htm, accessed August 24, 2011.

[4] Lindemann 2011, 397–400.

representation" in the cabinet – meaning that on average, the ethnic groups in a given area are underrepresented – and positive scores indicate "over-representation." To measure state strength, I generated a binary variable state, indicating whether the NRM controlled the territory as a rebel group during the Bush War. I also include distance to the capital as a second measure of state strength. Recall from Chapter 5 that unit of analysis is the rebel group, with spatial variables measured in county/ies where a rebel group initially operated. Summary statistics are shown in Table C.3.

Because of the small number of observations,[5] I run primarily trivariate linear probability models, with ELF and one of the control variables in each regression.[6] The results of the regression analyses are displayed in Table C.4.

TABLE C.3 *Summary statistics, variables for rebel viability analysis*

Variable	Mean	SD	Range	Description	Data source
viability (DV)	0.25	0.45	{0, 1}	Takes value "1" if viable, "0" if not viable	Interviews with rebels, government, and civilians; Ugandan newspaper articles
ELF	0.40	0.25	(.02, .76)	Probability that two randomly selected people are from different ethnic groups	Uganda census (1991)

(continued)

---

[5] In addition to having limited degrees of freedom, the fundamental problem of having a small number of observations – less than twenty-nine observations – is that the analysis cannot rely on the central limit theorem to provide assurance that the sampling distribution of the coefficients is normal. Thus, it is not possible to know whether the standard errors are accurate.

[6] I note, however, that ELF is also significant in several analyses using three covariates. For example, in a regression with ELF, poverty line, and elevation as covariates, ELF retains significance at the 95% level. In another example, in a regression with ELF, state strength, and distance to the border as covariates, ELF is significant at the 90% level.

TABLE C.3 *(continued)*

Variable	Mean	SD	Range	Description	Data source
largest ethnic group size	0.70	0.21	(0.33, 0.99)	Portion of Uganda's total population comprised by largest ethnic group	Uganda census (1991)
exclusion	1.37	5.15	(-2.72, 12.61)	Weighted average of ethnic groups' cabinet share minus Uganda population share	Lindemann (2011)
elevation (km)	1900	1113	(1015, 1196)	Difference between highest, lowest points (m)	USGS
forest	26.59	17.03	(1.24, 64.23)	Percentage of area comprised of non-agricultural vegetation	UN FAO (2002)
population density (log)	4.40	0.64	(2.95, 5.23)	Number of people per square kilometer (log)	Uganda census (1991)
distance to border (m) (log)	10.72	1.11	(9.14, 12)	Distance in meters from centroid of country(ies) to closest international border (log)	Calculated using GIS
contiguous with border	0.5	0.52	{0, 1}	Is county on international border	n/a
poverty line	66.2	12.7	(43.4, 91.4)	Percentage of people living below poverty line in 1992	Uganda Bureau of Statistics (2003)

(continued)

TABLE C.3 *(continued)*

Variable	Mean	SD	Range	Description	Data source
poverty gap	25.6	8.34	(13.7, 47.43)	Among those living below poverty line, average consumption (% below poverty line) in 1992	Uganda Bureau of Statistics (2003)
literacy	48.7	9.5	(29.6, 66.8)	Percentage of people who are literate	Uganda Bureau of Statistics (2003)
Distance to capital (m) (log)	12.18	0.84	(10.04, 12.86)	Distance in m from centroid of county(ies) to Kampala (log)	Uganda Bureau of Statistics (2003)
state strength	1.25	1.29	{0, 1}	Was area under NRM control prior to January 1986	Interview with senior NRM officials, newspaper articles

Note: Unit of analysis is the rebel group. Geographic variables correspond to the county(ies) where rebel groups initially operated.

TABLE C.4 *Correlates of rebel viability in Uganda*

	1	2	3	4	5	6	7	8	9
ELF	-.873†	-.898†	-.899†	-.826†	-.870†	-.873†	-.894†	-.806†	-.716
	(.418)	(.489)	(.445)	(.447)	(.429)	(.436)	(.440)	(.451)	(.431)
elevation		.000							
		(.000)							
forest			-.002						
			(.007)						
pop. density				-.066					
				(.198)					
distance to border					.003				
					(0.88)				
literacy						.000			
						(.005)			
poverty line							-.001		
							(.008)		
state strength								-.083	
								(.121)	
exclusion									-.013
									(.010)
N	16	16	16	16	16	16	16	16	16

DV for all models is a dichotomous measure of rebel viability. All models estimated using OLS with robust standard errors. Results are not substantively changed when using alternative measures of ethnic demography, poverty, or state capacity. Alternative measures are shown in the table of summary statistics earlier.
† $p < 0.10$, * $p < 0.05$, ** $p < 0.01$

Correlations among Covariates

Table C.5 summarizes the pair-wise correlation between each of the variables used in regression analyses in Table C.4.

TABLE C.5 *Correlation matrix, variables for rebel viability analysis*

	ELF	elev	forest	pop. dens.	dist to brdr	state	liter	pov line	excl
ELF	1.00								
elev	−0.27	1.00							
forest	−0.21	0.46	1.00						
pop. density	0.27	0.07	−0.45	1.00					
dist. to border	−0.25	−0.59	−0.26	−0.25	1.00				
state	0.05	0.03	0.21	0.48	−0.20	1.00			
literacy	−0.04	−0.32	−0.48	0.44	0.47	0.13	1.00		
poverty line	−0.38	−0.07	0.40	−0.80	0.00	−0.20	−0.47	1.00	
excl.	0.57	−0.30	−0.09	0.24	0.31	0.20	0.45	−0.62	1.00

Unit of analysis is the rebel group; variables are measured in the area where rebels initially operated.

Alternative Measure of Ethnic Homogeneity

Because of its mathematical construction, the measure of ethnic demography I use, the ELF score, may overlook certain politically consequential differences between various ethnic demographic compositions.[7] For example, consider two hypothetical areas, the first with two groups of equal size and the second with three groups that respectively constitute two-thirds, one-sixth, and one-sixth of the area's population.[8] For both areas, the ELF score (calculated with the Herfindahl Index formula[9]) would be 0.5. However, the intergroup political dynamics in these respective areas would likely be different – for example, only in the latter area is there a clear majority group that could dominate politics by virtue of their numbers.

---

[7] Posner 2004, 851.   [8] I borrow this instructive example from Posner (2004).
[9] Recall that the ELF score is based on the Herfindahl Index, and its substantive interpretation is the probability that two randomly sampled individuals from the area's population would be from different ethnic groups.

A straightforward measure of local ethnic homogeneity that captures such differences is the share of an area's total population that is comprised of that area's largest ethnic group. For the analyses presented in Chapter 5, using this alternative measure does not meaningfully change the results. In fact, this alternative measure is almost perfectly (negatively) correlated with ELF.[10] Therefore, it is not surprising that the same descriptive pattern holds: only groups that formed in areas above this variable's mean value for the sixteen cases became viable.

Further, the regression results presented in Table C.4, change little (and are in fact substantively and statistically slightly stronger) when estimating the models instead with this alternative measure of ethnic demography. Substantively, model 1 finds that a 10 percentage point increase in the largest ethnic group's share of the area's population is associated with a 10.5 percentage point increase in the probability of a nascent rebel group in that area becoming viable. Further, six of the models are significant at the 5% level, whereas most using the ELF measure were significant only at the 10% level.

Leave-One-Out Estimation

The fact that these analyses are based on only sixteen observations raises concerns that an outlier could drive the results. To examine the results' sensitivity to individual observations, I re-estimate the model of Table C.4 that controls for literacy sixteen times, leaving out one of the observations (one rebel group) each time.[11] Table C.6 shows the results of this exercise. The first row re-reports the results from Table C.4, and each additional row shows the coefficients and *p*-values that result when each rebel group is dropped from the dataset. The mean of the resulting sixteen coefficients on ELF is −0.88, and the coefficient is significant at the 10% level in fourteen of the models. The LRA and the ADF are the most influential datapoints; when they are removed from the dataset, the coefficient on ELF is significant at the 13 and 16 % levels, respectively. Since the ADF and LRA were high-profile rebel

---

[10] The correlation coefficient is −0.98.

[11] I note that this technique is related to, but distinct from, the nonparametric estimation technique known as the "jackknife." Jackknifing entails using the difference between the original parameter estimates (estimated using the whole dataset) and new parameter estimates (estimated using the data with a dropped observation) to estimate the parameter of interest. Here, I simply show the results of each estimate when I re-run the model sixteen times, each with a different observation removed.

TABLE C.6 *Results of leave-one-out estimation*

Regressors: Omitted rebel group:	ELF	literacy	n
None (baseline)	−0.87	0.00	16
	(0.07)	(0.97)	
FOBA	−.90	0.00	15
	(0.08)	(0.86)	
UPA	−.76	0.00	15
	(0.10)	(0.76)	
NOM	−0.96	0.00	15
	(0.07)	(0.92)	
NALU	−0.88	0.00	15
	(0.07)	(0.79)	
ADF	−0.67	0.00	15
	(0.16)	(0.84)	
PRA	−0.87	0.00	15
	(0.07)	(0.76)	
UPDA	−1.07	0.00	15
	(0.05)	(0.37)	
HSM	−0.78	0.00	15
	(0.09)	(0.68)	
LRA	−0.72	0.00	15
	(0.13)	(0.84)	
CAMP	−1.19	0.00	15
	(0.02)	(0.98)	
WNBF	−0.89	0.00	15
	(0.08)	(0.97)	
UNRF II	−0.86	0.00	15
	(0.07)	(0.94)	
NFA	−0.86	0.00	15
	(0.07)	(0.87)	
NDA	−0.85	0.00	15
	(0.08)	(0.79)	
UDA	−0.85	0.00	15
	(0.09)	(0.91)	
UFDF	−0.89	0.00	15
	(0.08)	(0.98)	

All models are estimated using a linear probability model, with a binary dependent variable indicating whether the rebel group became viable. P-values are reported in parentheses below coefficient estimates. The results presented in the first row, in which no rebel groups are omitted, are those presented in Table C.4, model 6.

groups, the information I collected about these groups was high quality; it would be more concerning if rebel groups with probable higher measurement error (such as PRA or NDA) were highly influential.

Logistic Regression

Another potential issue with the model I used to generate the core results of Table C.4 is that it is linear and continuous, allowing for predicted values below 0 and above 1 (and in between), whereas my dependent variable is binary. I also ran the same models using a standard logit model. The results are shown in Table C.7. These results are similar to those in the linear probability model shown in Table C.4.

TABLE C.7 *Logit results: Correlates of rebel viability in Uganda*

	1	2	3	4	5	6	7	8	9
ELF	-6.27* (3.11)	-6.39† (3.44)	-6.39† (3.99)	-5.99† (3.15)	-6.24* (3.11)	-6.67† (3.74)	-6.49† (3.43)	-7.17* (3.34)	-3.30 (4.07)
elevation		0.00 (0.01)							
forest			-.017 (.038)						
pop. density				-0.39 (1.23)					
distance to border					0.03 (0.56)				
literacy						0.03 (0.07)			
poverty line							-0.01 (0.05)		
state strength								-1.51 (1.61)	
exclusion									-0.47 (0.56)
N	16	16	16	16	16	16	16	16	16

DV for all models is a dichotomous measure of rebel viability.
All models estimated using logistic regression with robust standard errors, reported in parentheses.
† $p < 0.10$, * $p < 0.05$, ** $p < 0.01$.

Bootstrapping

I also employ bootstrapping, a nonparametric approach to modeling the relationship between ethnic demography and rebel viability. Doing so addresses the concern that because the sample size is so small for the earlier analyses, the typical assumption of parametric regression that the error is normally distributed is tenuous. Bootstrapping does not make this assumption, and instead entails using iterated sampling with replacement from the original dataset in order to generate several pseudo-replication datasets. Doing so allows for estimation of the empirical average of the coefficient over all bootstrapped samples. The bootstrap standard errors are the standard deviation of the distribution of the re-estimated means of the bootstrapped samples.

The results of this exercise are also broadly consistent with that which I reported in Table C.4. Further, I show the results when including both ELF and literacy in the model, including the bootstrapped observed coefficient, standard errors, and confidence intervals. The results are not substantively different and, similar to the linear modeling results, ELF is significant while the coefficient on literacy is not. When running the models with other "control" variables (other than literacy), none of the normal-based 95% confidence intervals for ELF cross zero.

TABLE C.8 *Results using the bootstrap method*

	Observed coefficient (SE)	95% Confidence interval (type)	
ELF	−0.87	(−1.59, −0.16)	(Normal)
	(0.37)	(−1.74, −0.35)	(Percentile)
		(−1.67, −0.29)	(Bias corrected)
		(−1.60, −0.21)	(Bias corrected and accelerated)
literacy	0.00	(−0.02, 0.02)	(Normal)
	(0.01)	(−0.01, 0.02)	(Percentile)
		(−0.01, 0.02)	(Bias corrected)
		(−0.01, 0.02)	(Bias corrected and accelerated)

DV is a dichotomous measure of rebel viability.
Estimated using bootstrapping with 1,000 replications of sixteen draws with replacement.

APPENDIX D

Dataset on Rebel Group Formation in Central and Eastern Africa

CODING PROCESS

The dataset aims to include as close as possible to all non-state armed groups that formed in central and eastern Africa from January 1, 1997 to December 31, 2015, which had political goals and made concrete plans to violently challenge the authority of the state – even those that failed soon after launching their group. The states included are: Burundi, Central African Republic, Democratic Republic of Congo, Ethiopia, Kenya, Malawi, Mozambique, Rwanda, Sudan, South Sudan, Tanzania, and Zambia. For an additional analysis in Chapter 6, I also identified instances of rebel group formation since 1997 for several southern African countries: Angola, Botswana, Lesotho, Madagascar, Namibia, South Africa, Swaziland, and Zimbabwe.

To do so, the research team started with a list of potential rebel groups using all actors (actor1 and actor2) listed in the ACLED data for these countries that remained after we removed all events with irrelevant ACLED "interaction types" (e.g. military interactions with foreign militaries or civilians such as protesters or rioters.). We then eliminated all groups that were not rebel groups, ethnic militia, or a political militia. Such eliminated actors were, for example, "civilians," "protesters," or "rioters" in ACLED[1]

---

[1] ACLED uses the actor "civilians" to denote victims of violent acts and "protestors" for actors who are "by definition non-violent" (ACLED Codebook p. 7). While ACLED uses "rioters" to denote perpetrators of violence, the term is for actors who engage in "violent demonstrations or spontaneous acts of disorganized violence" (Codebook p. 6).

or "unidentified" actors.[2] In addition to using ACLED to generate our initial list of actors, we also made an effort to include additional groups identified in secondary sources and newspaper articles.

We then used publicly available news media, government, NGO, and United Nations reports, first with the aim of excluding armed groups that we determined to have formed prior to January 1, 1997, and to determine whether groups met our inclusion criteria, which are described in the next section. If actors met our inclusion criteria, we included them in the dataset and used the same sources to code variables for each group. For DRC, Ethiopia, and Kenya, we also consulted scholars with relevant country and subject expertise.

Determining which rebel groups met our inclusion criteria was not a trivial task. When analyzing information from secondary sources, we remained attentive to evidence of bias in reporting or the existence of contradictory accounts. In the case of several sources contradicting each other, we documented these issues and our ultimate coding decisions in an extensive Record of Analysis document, which is available upon request from the author along with the data and codebook.

We also coded a series of variables on the organizational basis of a group (or lack thereof), its start date and patterns of initial violence, and other characteristics. In several cases, information was unclear or conflicting. For instance, some news sources listed the founding date of central African Republic rebel group Convention des Patriotes pour la Justice et la Paix (CPJP) as October 2008, while other sources listed it as January 2009. We listed the former as the founding date because the information from sources identifying October as the founding date was more detailed, implying greater knowledge of the group. Additionally, according to their own press releases, CPJP originally operated clandestinely but went public in January 2009, perhaps explaining why some sources incorrectly identify January as the founding date.

---

[2] We originally investigated each event involving an unidentified actor for evidence of rebel group activity, e.g. many attackers that appeared to be coordinated, or multiple attacks occurring close together from a temporal standpoint. While we believe ACLED's "unidentified armed group" actors likely include additional rebel groups, our investigation of these ACLED events was extremely resource-intensive and rarely generated sufficient information to code a rebel group. As such, we ceased investigating unidentified actors except when it appeared based on contextual information that further investigation of an incident involving an unidentified actor might add to our understanding of named actors.

INCLUSION CRITERIA

We aimed to include all non-state armed groups that formed since January 1, 1997,[3] that had political goals, and made concrete plans to violently challenge the authority of the state. Our specific criteria were as follows:

- "Armed group" means a group of people (at least three) that aims to build an organization (has an organizational structure, meaning people with designated leadership roles) and makes concrete plans to commit violence – for example, discussing specific targets, strategies, and/or tactics.
- "Non-state" means the majority of the people in the nascent group should be outside of the state (i.e. not employed by the state) during the time of rebel group formation – the period of planning and initial one to three attacks. If a rebel group emerges from within the state (a coup or mutiny), in order to count for this dataset, they need to abandon their position in the state and form a separate organization. Examples of evidence of forming an organization separate from the state include (a) having leadership that is not from high levels of the central government, (b) physically retreating away from the capital, or (c) physically leaving the barracks and/or the capital city in order to regroup.
- "Formed since January 1, 1997" means the first act of violence (attack) occurred (or there were plans for it to occur) on or after January 1, 1997.
  - In the case of a group disbanding and then re-emerging, we tried to identify: Was the majority of the leadership and majority of the membership in the reincarnated group new people? If so, we consider it a new group. If this is not possible to discern, or if the reincarnation occurs more than five years after the prior group had died out, we consider it a new group.
  - In the case of a rebel group crossing borders, we do not count this as a new group when it enters a new country.
- "Political goals" includes taking over the government, secession, controlling territory, or advancing a particular policy position (local or national). Sometimes groups do not initially publicly articulate political goals; we do not exclude them in all of those cases but rather infer political goals if there are political targets of violence.

---

[3] The end date for formation of groups we capture is December 31, 2015, because ACLED ended on this date at the time we began our coding.

- "Violence challenging the authority of the state" means intentionally killing (or planning to kill) government officials or other agents of the state.
  - Traditional leaders (chiefs) do not count as government officials, unless they have authority from the government to provide public goods (including security) to citizens.
  - If only one person is killed, there must be evidence that this was not a random murder but rather was part of a strategy to use political violence on an ongoing basis by a group.
  - Rebels that fight peacekeeping/occupying forces (e.g. the United States in Iraq in 2005, Ethiopia in Somalia in 2007) count in cases where the state is absent and these forces are standing in for the central state.
  - Rebels that fight other rebels count only in cases in which the "other rebels" have clear control over territory such that they are the de facto state in that territory.
  - Judgment may be needed in determining whether an attack was intended to kill people; for example, if a bomb goes off during work hours at a place where agents of the state work (e.g. a police station) but no one was killed, it would be reasonable to infer that the intent was to kill agents of the state.
  - Violence intended to alter the outcome of an election does not count for the purposes of this dataset.
- In cases where group formations are rumored, but difficult to verify, we try to confirm the existence of a rebel group (as defined earlier) with multiple sources.
- In cases where two or more rebel groups merge into a new group, we do not count the new group as a separate group. We record only the original formation of the groups that later merged. However, where several groups merge to form a new group and the majority of the original groups did not meet our criteria for rebel groups, we include both the new group and any original groups that did meet our criteria. For example, suppose there is Group A, which meets our criteria for a rebel group, and Groups B and C, which do not meet our criteria for a rebel group. Groups A, B, and C merge to form Group D. Group D also meets our criteria for a rebel group. We include both Groups A and D. (We do not include groups that are mergers of former splinter groups (where at least half of the groups are splinters).
- For cases in which a splinter group breaks away from a parent group or in which a parent group splinters into several smaller groups, we

count only the formation of the original group; we do not count the splinters as new groups. One exception is if the "mother" group has become part of the government – a splinter off of this group counts as a new rebel group. We define a splinter group using the following criterion: Did most leaders (who actively command/control) and most members come from the same pre-existing group? Consideration of membership is based on original membership, that is, a splinter group is still disqualified if it immediately begins recruiting and this recruitment tilts the balance in favor of new members within the first year. This is also true when a mother group *creates* a franchise (subgroup) and *maintains control* of the subgroup; we do not count this as a new group. If it either does not create the group or does not maintain control, then we do count it as a new group. Here, note that the mother group is a non-state actor. If a foreign government creates a rebel group, we count this as a new group.

References

Allen, Tim. 1991. Understanding Alice: Uganda's Holy Spirit Movement in Context. *Africa* 61 (3): 370–397.

Amnesty International. 1989. *Uganda: The Human Rights Record, 1986–1989*. London: Amnesty International Publications. www.amnesty.org/download/Documents/AFR590011989ENGLISH.PDF

Arjona, Ana. 2017. *Rebelocracy: Social Order in the Colombian Civil War*. New York: Cambridge University Press.

Arjona, Ana and Stathis N. Kalyvas. 2009. Rebelling against Rebellion: Comparing Insurgent and Counterinsurgent Recruitment. Centre for Research on Inequality, Human Security and Ethnicity.

Arjona, Ana, Nelson Kasfir, and Zachariah Mampilly, eds. 2015. *Rebel Governance in Civil War*. Cambridge, New York, Melbourne, Delhi, and Singapore: Cambridge University Press.

Atalas, Vivi, Abhijit Banerjee, Arun G. Chandrasekhar, Rema Hanna, and Benjamin A. Olken. 2015. Network Structure and the Aggregation of Information: Theory and Evidence from Indonesia. Technical Report, National Bureau of Economic Research. www.nber.org/papers/w18351

Atkinson, Ronald. 1999. *The Roots of Ethnicity: The Origins of the Acholi of Uganda before 1800*. Philadelphia: University of Pennsylvania Press.

Balcells, Laia. 2017. *Rivalry and Revenge: The Politics of Violence during Civil War*. Cambridge, New York, Melbourne, Delhi and Singapore: Cambridge University Press.

Balcells, Laia. 2010. Rivalry and Revenge: Violence against Civilians in Conventional Civil Wars. *International Studies Quarterly* 54 (2): 291–313.

Banerjee, Abhijit, Arun G. Chandrasekhar, Esther Duflo, and Matthew O. Jackson. 2013. The Diffusion of Microfinance. *Science* 341 (6144). DOI:10.1126/science.1236498

Barnes, Nicholas. 2017. Criminal Politics: An Integrated Approach to the Study of Organized Crime, Politics, and Violence. *Perspectives on Politics* 15 (4): 967–987.

Barr, Abigail. 2004. Kinship, Familiarity and Trust: An Experimental Investigation. In *Foundations of Human Sociality: Economic Experiments and Ethnographic Evidence from Fifteen Small-Scale Societies*, edited by Joseph Heinrich, Robert Boyd, Samuel Bowles, Colin Camerer, Ernst Fehr, and Herbert Gintis. Oxford: Oxford University Press, 305–334.

Bates, Robert H. 2008. *When Things Fell Apart: State Failure in Late-Century Africa*. New York: Cambridge University Press.

Bates, Robert H. 2001. *Prosperity and Violence: The Political Economy of Development*. 2nd ed. New York: W.W. Norton & Co.

Bates, Robert H. 1983. Modernization, Ethnic Competition, and the Rationality of Politics in Contemporary Africa. In *State versus Ethnic Claims: African Policy Dilemmas*, edited by Donald Rothchild and Victor A. Olunsorola. Boulder, CO: Westview Press, 152–171.

Bates, Robert H. 1981. *Markets and States in Tropical Africa: The Political Basis of Agricultural Policies*. Berkeley, CA: University of California Press.

Bates, Robert H., Avner Grief, and Smita Singh. 2002. Organizing Violence. *Journal of Conflict Resolution* 46 (5): 599–628.

Bayly, C. A. 1999. *Empire and Information: Intelligence Gathering and Social Communication in India, 1780–1870*. Cambridge; New York: Cambridge University Press.

Bazzi, Samuel, Robert A. Blair, Christopher Blattman, Oeindrila Dube, Matthew Gudgeon, and Richard Merton Peck. 2019. The Promise and Pitfalls of Conflict Prediction: Evidence from Colombia and Indonesia. NBER Working Paper No. 25980. www.nber.org/papers/w25980

Behrend, Heike. 1999. *Alice Lakwena and the Holy Spirits: War in Northern Uganda, 1985–97*. Oxford; Kampala; Nairobi; Athens: J. Currey; Fountain Publishers; EAEP; Ohio University Press.

Berhe, Aregawi. 2004. The Origins of the Tigray People's Liberation Front. *African Affairs* 103 (413): 569–592.

Berman, Eli and Aila M. Matanock. 2013. The Empiricists' Insurgency. *Annual Review of Political Science* 18 (1): 443–464.

Berman, Eli, Joseph H. Felter, Jacob N. Shapiro, and Vestal McIntyre. 2018. *Small Wars, Big Data: The Information Revolution in Modern Conflict*. 1st ed. Princeton, NJ: Princeton University Press.

Berman, Nicholas and Mathieu Couttenier. 2015. External Shocks, Internal Shots: The Geography of Civil Conflicts. *Review of Economics and Statistics* 97 (4):758–776.

Bhavnani, Ravi, Michael G. Findley, and James H. Kuklinski. 2009. Rumor Dynamics in Ethnic Violence. *Journal of Politics* 71 (3): 876–892.

Biziouras, Nikolaos. 2012. The Formation, Institutionalization and Consolidation of the LTTE: Religious Practices, Intra-Tamil Divisions and a Violent Nationalist Ideology. *Politics, Religion & Ideology* 13 (4): 547–559.

Blattman, Chris and Jeannie Annan. 2016. Can Employment Reduce Lawlessness and Rebellion? A Field Experiment with High-risk Men in a Fragile State. *American Political Science Review* 110 (1): 1–17.

Blattman, Chris and Samuel Bazzi. 2014. Economic Shocks and Conflict: The Evidence from Commodity Prices. *American Economic Journal: Macroeconomics* 6 (4): 1–38.

Blattman, Chris and Bernd Beber. 2013. The Logic of Child Soldiering and Coercion. *International Organization* 67 (1): 65–104.

Blattman, Chris and Edward Miguel. 2010. Civil War. *Journal of Economic Literature* 48 (1): 3–57.

Blaxland, Joel. 2018. Insurgents, Incubation, and Survival: How Prewar Preparation Facilitates Lengthy Intrastate Conflicts. Ph.D. Dissertation. Temple University.

Boas, Morten and Kevin C. Dunn, eds. 2007. *African Guerrillas: Raging against the Machine*. Boulder, CO: Lynne Rienner.

Boone, Catherine. 2003. *Political Topographies of the African State: Territorial Authority and Institutional Choice*. Cambridge: Cambridge University Press.

Bose, Sumantra. 2007. JKLF and JKHM: Jammu and Kashmir Liberation Front and Jammu and Kashmir Hizb-ul Mujahideen. In *Terror, Insurgency, and the State*, edited by John Tirman, Marianne Heiberg, and Brendan O'Leary. Philadelphia: University of Pennsylvania Press.

Braithwaite, Jessica Maves and Kathleen Cunningham. 2020. When Organizations Rebel: Introducing the Foundations of Rebel Group Emergence (FORGE) Dataset. *International Studies Quarterly* 64(1): 183–193. doi.org/10.1093/isq/sqz085

Branch, Adam. 2013. *Displacing Human Rights: War and Intervention in Northern Uganda*. New York: Oxford University Press.

Branch, Adam and Zachariah Cherian Mampilly. 2015. *Africa Uprising: Political Protest and Political Change*. African Arguments. London: Zed Books.

Bratton, Michael. 1989. Beyond the State: Civil Society and Associational Life in Africa. *World Politics* 41 (3): 407–430.

Brubaker, Roger. 2002. Ethnicity without Groups. *Archives européennes de sociologie* 43 (2): 163–189.

Brubaker, Rogers and David D. Laitin. 1998. Ethnic and Nationalist Violence. *Annual Review of Sociology* 24 (1): 423–452.

Buckley-Zistel, Susanne. 2008. *Conflict Transformation and Social Change in Uganda: Remembering after Violence*. Rethinking Peace and Conflict Studies. Basingstoke; New York: Palgrave Macmillan.

Bueno de Mesquita, Ethan. 2010. Regime Change and Revolutionary Entrepreneurs. *American Political Science Review* 104 (3): 446–466.

Buhaug, Havard and Jan Ketil Rod. 2006. Local Determinants of African Civil Wars, 1970–2001. *Political Geography* 25 (3): 315–335.

Buhaug, Havard, Lars-Erik Cederman, and Jan Ketil Rod. 2008. Disaggregating Ethno-Nationalist Civil Wars: A Dyadic Test of Exclusion Theory. *International Organization* 62 (3): 531–551.

Burke, Fred G. 1964. *Local Government and Politics in Uganda*. Syracuse, NY: Syracuse University Press.

Butcher, Charles and Isak Svensson. 2016. Manufacturing Dissent: Modernization and the Onset of Major Nonviolent Resistance Campaigns. *Journal of Conflict Resolution* 60 (2): 311–339.

Byman, Daniel. 2007. Understanding Proto-Insurgencies. RAND Corporation Occasional Papers, OP-178. Santa Monica, CA: RAND Corporation. www .rand.org/content/dam/rand/pubs/occasional_papers/2007/RAND_OP178.pdf

Byrnes, Rita M., ed. 1990. *Uganda: A Country Study.* Washington, DC: Government Printing Office for the Library of Congress.

Caparini, Marina. 2018. UN Police and Conflict Prevention. SIPRI Discussion Paper. Stockholm International Peace Research Institute. www.sipri.org/publi cations/2018/un-police-and-conflict-prevention

Cederman, Lars-Erik, Kristian Skrede Gleditsch, and Halvard Buhaug. 2013. *Inequality, Grievances, and Civil War.* Cambridge Studies in Contentious Politics. New York: Cambridge University Press.

Cederman, Lars-Erik, Nils Weidmann, and Nils Petter Gleditsch. 2011. Horizontal Inequalities and the Ethno-Nationalist War: A Global Comparison. *American Political Science Review* 105 (3): 478–495.

Cederman, Andreas Wimmer and Brian Min. 2010. Why Do Ethnic Groups Rebel? New Data and Analysis. *World Politics* 62 (1): 87–119.

Chandra, Kanchan. 2004. *Why Ethnic Parties Succeed: Patronage and Ethnic Head Counts in India.* Cambridge: Cambridge University Press.

Cheeseman, Nic and Jeffrey Smith. 2019. The Retreat of African Democracy. *Foreign Affairs.* www.foreignaffairs.com/articles/africa/2019-01-17/retreat-african-democracy.

Chenoweth, Erica and Maria J. Stephan. 2013. *Why Civil Resistance Works: The Strategic Logic of Nonviolent Conflict.* Paperback ed. Columbia Studies in Terrorism and Irregular Warfare. New York: Columbia University Press.

Christia, Fotini. 2012. *Alliance Formation in Civil Wars.* New York: Cambridge University Press.

Cohen, Dara Kay. 2016. *Rape during Civil War.* Ithaca, NY: Cornell University Press.

Collier, Paul. 2000. Rebellion as a Quasi-Criminal Activity. *Journal of Conflict Resolution* 44 (6): 839–553.

Collier, Paul. 1999. The Challenge of Ugandan Reconstruction, 1986–98. The World Bank. http://documents.worldbank.org/curated/en/408991468760804 971/pdf/28136.pdf

Collier, Paul and Anke Hoeffler. 2004. Greed and Grievance in Civil War. *Oxford Economic Papers* 56 (4): 563–595.

Condra, Luke N. and Austin L. Wright. 2019. Civilians, Control, and Collaboration during Civil Conflict. *International Studies Quarterly* 53(4): 897–907.

Cunningham, David. 2010. Blocking Resolution: How External States Can Prolong Civil Wars. *Journal of Peace Research* 47 (2): 115–127.

Cunningham, David. 2006. Veto Players and Civil War Duration. *American Journal of Political Science* 50 (4): 875–892.

Cunningham, David E., Kristian Skrede Gleditsch, Belén González, Dragana Vidović, and Peter B. White. 2017. Words and Deeds: From Incompatibilities to Outcomes in Anti-government Disputes. *Journal of Peace Research* 54 (4): 468–483.

Cunningham, Kathleen. 2013. Understanding Strategic Choice: the Determinants of Civil War and Nonviolent Campaign in Self-Determination Disputes. *Journal of Peace Research* 50 (3): 291–304.

Cunningham, Kathleen Gallagher and Katherine Sawyer. 2019. Conflict Negotiations and Rebel Leader Selection. *Journal of Peace Research* 56 (5): 619–634.

Dagne, Ted. 2010. Uganda: Current Conditions and the Crisis in North Uganda. Congressional Research Service. www.fas.org/sgp/crs/row/RL33701.pdf.

Darden, Keith and Harris Mylonas. 2012. The Promethean Dilemma: Third-Party State-Building in Occupied Territories. *Ethnopolitics* 11 (1): 109–112.

Davenport, Christian. 2007. State Repression and Political Order. *Annual Review of Political Science* 10: 1–23.

Day, Christopher. 2019. *The Fates of African Rebels: Victory, Defeat, and the Politics of Civil War.* Boulder, CO: Lynne Rienner.

Day, Christopher R. 2011. The Fates of Rebels: Insurgencies in Uganda. *Comparative Politics* 43 (4): 439–458.

Della Porta, Donatella. 2013. *Clandestine Political Violence.* New York: Cambridge University Press.

Demmers, Jolle and Lauren Gould. 2018. An Assemblage Approach to Liquid Warfare: AFRICOM and the "Hunt" for Joseph Kony. *Security Dialogue* 49 (5): 364–381.

Do, Quy-Toan and Lakshmi Iyer. 2010. Geography, Poverty and Conflict in Nepal. *Journal of Peace Research* 47 (6): 735–748.

Dube, Oeindrila and Juan Vargas. 2013 Commodity Price Shocks and Civil Conflict: Evidence from Colombia. *Review of Economic Studies* 80(4): 1384–1421.

Eck, Kristine. 2009. From Armed Conflict to War: Ethnic Mobilization and Conflict Intensification. *International Studies Quarterly* 53 (2): 369–388.

Emwanu, Thomas, Paul Okiira Okwi, Johannes G. Hoogeveen, and Patti Kristjanson. 2003. *Where Are the Poor? Mapping Patterns of Well-Being in Uganda: 1992 and 1999.* Nairobi, Kenya: The Regal Press Kenya.

Epelu-Opio, Justin. 2009. *Teso War, 1986–1992: Causes and Consequences.* Kampala: Fountain Publishers.

Esteban, Joan, Laura Mayoral, and Debraj Raj. 2012. Ethnicity and Conflict: Theory and Facts. *Science* 336 (6083): 858–865.

Evans-Pritchard, E. E. 1951. *Kinship and Marriage among the Nuer.* Oxford: Clarendon Press.

Evans-Pritchard, E. E. 1940. *The Nuer: A Description of the Modes of Livelihood and Political Institutions of a Nilotic People.* Oxford: Clarendon Press.

Fafchamps, Marcel and Bart Minten. 1999. Relationships and Traders in Madagascar. *Journal of Development Studies* 35 (6): 1–35.

Fearon, James and David Laitin. 2014. Civil War Non-onsets: The Case of Japan. *Journal of Civilization Studies* 1 (1): 67–90.

Fearon, James and David Laitin. 2003. Ethnicity, Insurgency and Civil War. *American Political Science Review* 97 (1): 75–90.

Fearon, James and David Laitin. 1996. Explaining Interethnic Cooperation. *American Political Science Review* 90 (4): 715–735.

Finkel, Evgeny. 2017. *Ordinary Jews: Choice and Survival during the Holocaust.* Princeton, NJ; Oxford: Princeton University Press.

Finkel, Evgeny. 2015. The Phoenix Effect of State Repression: Jewish Resistance during the Holocaust. *American Political Science Review* 109 (2): 339–353.

Finnström, Sverker. 2008. *Living with Bad Surroundings: War, History, and Everyday Moments in Northern Uganda.* Durham: Duke University Press.

Fujii, Lee Ann. 2009. *Killing Neighbors: Webs of Violence in Rwanda.* Ithaca, NY: Cornell University Press.

Gagnon, V. P. 2004. *The Myth of Ethnic War: Serbia and Croatia in the 1990s.* Ithaca, NY: Cornell University Press.

Gates, Scott. 2002. Recruitment and Allegiance: The Microfoundations of Rebellion. *Journal of Conflict Resolution* 46 (1): 111–130.

Geddes, Barbara. 1996. *Politician's Dilemma: Building State Capacity in Latin America.* 1st pbk. ed. Berkeley, CA: University of California Press.

Gennaioli, Nicola and Ilia Rainer. 2007. The Modern Impact of Precolonial Centralization in Africa. *Journal of Economic Growth* 12: 185–234.

George, Alexander L and Andrew Bennett. 2005. *Case Studies and Theory Development in the Social Sciences.* Cambridge, MA: MIT Press.

Gersony, Robert. 2003. Sowing the Wind . . . History and Dynamics of the Maoist Revolt in Nepal's Rapti Hills. Report Submitted to Mercy Corps International.

Gersony, Robert. 1997. The Anguish of Northern Uganda: Results of a Field-Based Assessment of the Civil Conflicts in Northern Uganda. US Embassy and USAID Mission, Kampala, Uganda.

Gleditsch, Nils Petter, Peter Wallensteen, Mikael Eriksson, Margareta Sollenberg, and Håvard Strand. 2002. Armed Conflict 1946–2001: A New Dataset. *Journal of Peace Research* 39 (5): 615–637.

Goldstone, Jack A., Robert H. Bates, David L. Epstein, Ted Robert Gurr, Michael B. Lustik, Monty G. Marshall, Jay Ulfelder, and Mark Woodward. 2010. A Global Model for Forecasting Political Instability. *American Journal of Political Science* 54 (1): 190–208.

Goodwin, Jeff. 2001. *No Other Way Out: States and Revolutionary Movements, 1945–1991.* Cambridge: Cambridge University Press.

Greenhill, Kelly M. and Ben Oppenheim. 2017. Rumor Has It: The Adoption of Unverified Information in Conflict Zones. *International Studies Quarterly* 61 (3): 660–676.

Grossman, Guy and Janet I. Lewis. 2014. Administrative Unit Proliferation. *American Political Science Review* 108 (1): 196–207.

Grossman, H. I. 1991. A General Equilibrium Model of Insurrections. *American Economic Review* 81 (4): 912–921.

Gubler, Joshua R., and Joel Sawat Selway. 2012. Horizontal Inequality, Crosscutting Cleavages, and Civil War. *Journal of Conflict Resolution* 56 (2): 206–232.

Gurr, Ted Robert. 1970. *Why Men Rebel.* Princeton, NJ: Princeton University Press.

Gyimah-Boadi, Emmanuel. 1997. Civil Society in Africa. In *Consolidating the Third Wave Democracies*, edited by Larry Diamond, Marc F. Plattner, Yun-han Chu, and Hung-mao Tien. Baltimore, MD: Johns Hopkins University Press.

Habyarimana, James, Macartan Humphreys, Daniel N. Posner, and Jeremy M. Weinstein. 2011. *Coethnicity: Diversity and the Dilemmas of Collective Action*. New York: Russell Sage.

Habyarimana, James, Macartan Humphreys, Daniel N. Posner, and Jeremy M. Weinstein. 2007. Why Does Ethnic Diversity Undermine Public Goods Provision? *American Political Science Review* 101 (4): 709–725.

Haim, Dotan. 2019. Civilian Social Networks and Credible Counterinsurgency. Working Paper. http://dotanhaim.com/wp-content/uploads/2019/08/Haim_CivilianNetworks.pdf

Hardin, Russell. 1995. *One for All: The Logic of Group Conflict*. Princeton, NJ: Princeton University Press.

Harris, J. A. 2012. "Stain Removal": Measuring the Effects of Violence on Local Ethnic Demography in Kenya. Working Paper, Harvard University,

Harvey, Neil. 1998. *The Chiapas Rebellion: The Struggle for Land and Democracy*. Durham: Duke University Press.

Hegre, Havard, Gudrun Østby, and Clionadh Raleigh. 2009. Poverty and Civil War Effects: A Disaggregated Study of Liberia. *Journal of Conflict Resolution* 53 (4): 598–623.

Hegre, Havard, and Nicholas Sambanis. 2006. Sensitivity Analysis of the Empirical Results on Civil War Onset. *Journal of Conflict Resolution* 50 (4): 508–535.

Herbst, Jeffrey. 2004. African Militaries and Rebellion: The Political Economy of Threat and Combat Effectiveness. *Journal of Peace Research* 41 (3): 357–369.

Herbst, Jeffrey. 2000. *States and Power in Africa: Comparative Lessons in Authority and Control*. Princeton, NJ: Princeton University Press.

Hirshleifer, Jack. 1994. The Dark Side of the Force: Western Economic Association International 1993 Presidential Address. *Economic Inquiry* 32 (1): 1–10.

Hoover Green, Amelia. 2018. *The Commander's Dilemma: Violence and Restraint in Wartime*. Ithaca, NY: Cornell University Press.

Horowitz, Donald. 2000. *Ethnic Groups in Conflict*. Berkeley, CA; London: University of California Press.

Hovil, Lucy and Zachary Lomo. 2004. Behind the Violence: Causes, Consequences and the Search for Solutions to the War in Northern Uganda. *Refugee Law Project* Working Paper No. 11. https://reliefweb.int/report/uganda/refugee-law-project-working-paper-no-11-behind-violence-causes-consequences-and-search

Hovil, Lucy and Eric Werker. 2005. Portrait of a Failed Rebellion. *Rationality and Society* 17 (1): 5–34.

Huang, Reyko. 2016. *The Wartime Origins of Democratization: Civil War, Rebel Governance, and Political Regimes*. Problems of international politics. New York: Cambridge University Press.

Hug, Simon. 2003. Selection Bias in Comparative Research: The Case of Incomplete Datasets. *Political Analysis* 11: 255–274.

Human Security Report Project. 2010. *Human Security Report 2009/2010: The Causes of Peace and the Shrinking Costs of War*. New York: Oxford University Press.

Humphreys, Macartan. 2005. Natural Resources, Conflict, and Conflict Resolution: Uncovering the Mechanisms. *Journal of Conflict Resolution* 49 (4): 508–537.

Ichino, Nahomi, and Noah Nathan. 2013. Crossing the Line: Local Ethnic Geography and Voting in Ghana. *American Political Science Review* 107 (2): 344–361.

Jenkins, J. Craig. 1983. Resource Mobilization Theory and the Study of Social Movements. *Annual Review of Sociology* 9: 527–553.

Jha, Saumitra, and Steven Wilkinson. 2012. Does Combat Experience Foster Organizational Skill? Evidence from Ethnic Cleansing during the Partition of South Asia. *American Political Science Review* 106 (4): 883–907.

Jones, Ben. 2008. *Beyond the State in Rural Uganda.* Edinburgh: Edinburgh University Press.

Kagoro, Jude. 2012. Security Counterweights: A Power-Maximizing Sociopolitical Strategy in Uganda. *Africa Peace and Conflict Journal* 5 (1): 1–13.

Kalyvas, Stathis N. 2008a. Ethnic Defection in Civil War. *Comparative Political Studies* 41 (8): 1043–1068.

Kalyvas, Stathis N. 2008b. Promises and Pitfalls of an Emerging Research Program: The Microdynamics of Civil War. In *Order, Conflict, and Violence*, edited by Tarek Masoud and Stathis N. Kalyvas. New York: Cambridge University Press, 397–421.

Kalyvas, Stathis N. 2006. *The Logic of Violence in Civil War.* Cambridge and New York: Cambridge University Press.

Kalyvas, Stathis N. 1999. Wanton and Senseless? The Logic of Massacres in Algeria. *Rationality and Society* 11 (3): 243–285.

Kalyvas, Stathis N. and Laia Balcells. 2010. International System and Technologies of Rebellion: How the End of the Cold War Shaped Internal Conflict. *American Political Science Review* 104 (3): 415–429.

Kaplan, Oliver. 2018. *Resisting War: How Communities Protect Themselves.* Reprint ed. Cambridge, United Kingdom; New York, NY: Cambridge University Press.

Karugire, Samwiri. 1980. *A Political History of Uganda.* Nairobi; New Hampshire: Heinemann Educational Books.

Karugire, Samwiri. 1996. *Roots of Instability in Uganda.* 2nd ed. Kampala Uganda: Fountain Publishers.

Kasara, Kimuli. 2013. Separate and Suspicious: Local Social and Political Context and Ethnic Tolerance in Kenya. *Journal of Politics* 75 (4): 921–936.

Kasfir, Nelson. 1998. Civil Society, the State and Democracy in Africa. *Commonwealth & Comparative Politics* 36 (2): 123–149.

Kasfir, Nelson. 1979. Explaining Ethnic Political Participation. *World Politics* 31 (3): 365–388.

Kasfir, Nelson. 2005. Guerillas and Civilian Participation: The National Resistance Army in Uganda, 1981–1986. *Journal of Modern African Studies* 43 (2): 271–296.

Kasozi, A. 1994. *The Social Origins of Violence in Uganda, 1964–1985.* Montreal; Buffalo: McGill-Queen's University Press.

Kilcullen, David. 2010. *Counterinsurgency*. Oxford; New York: Oxford University Press.

King, Charles. 2007. Scots to Chechens. *Harvard International Review* 28(2): 68–72.

Kiyaga-Nsubuga, John. 2004. Uganda: The Politics of Consolidation under Museveni's Regime, 1996–2003. In *Durable Peace: Challenges for Peacebuilding in Africa*, edited by Taisier M. Ali and Robert O. Matthews. Toronto: University of Toronto Press.

Kizza, Immaculate N. 1999. *Africa's Indigenous Institutions in Nation Building: Uganda*. Lewiston, NY: Edwin Mellen Press.

Lacina, Bethany. 2006. Explaining the Severity of Civil Wars. *Journal of Conflict Resolution* 50 (2): 276–289.

Laitin, David. 2004. Ethnic Unmixing and Civil War. *Security Studies* 13 (4): 350–365.

Laitin, David. 2000. What is a Language Community? *American Journal of Political Science* 44 (1): 142–155.

Larson, Jennifer M. and Janet I. Lewis. 2017. Ethnic Networks. *American Journal of Political Science* 61 (2): 350–364.

Larson, Jennifer M. and Janet I. Lewis. 2018. Rumors, Kinship Networks, and Rebel Group Formation. *International Organization*: 72(4):871–903. doi-org.proxygw.wrlc.org/10.1017/S0020818318000243

Lawrence, Adria. 2010. Triggering Nationalist Violence: Competition and Conflict in Uprisings against Colonial Rule. *International Security* 35 (2): 88–122.

Lee, Melissa and Nan Zhang. 2017. Legibility and the Informational Foundations of State Capacity. *Journal of Politics* 79 (1): 118–132.

Leites, Nathan. 1970. *Rebellion and Authority: An Analytic Essay on Insurgent Conflicts*. Markham Series in Public Policy Analysis. Chicago: Markham Pub. Co.

Leopold, Mark. 2005. *Inside West Nile: Violence, History and Representation on an African Frontier*. Oxford; Sante Fe N.M.; Kampala: J. Currey; School of American Research Press; Fountain Publishers.

Lessing, Benjamin and Graham Denyer Willis. 2019. Legitimacy in Criminal Governance: Managing a Drug Empire from Behind Bars. *American Political Science Review* 113 (2): 584–606.

Leventoğlu, Bahar and Nils W. Metternich. 2018. Born Weak, Growing Strong: Anti-Government Protests as a Signal of Rebel Strength in the Context of Civil Wars. *American Journal of Political Science* 62 (3): 581–596.

Levitsky, Steven and Lucan Way. 2013. The Durability of Revolutionary Regimes. *Journal of Democracy* 24 (3): 5–17.

Lewis, Janet I. 2017. How Does Ethnic Rebellion Start? *Comparative Political Studies* 50 (10): 1420–1450.

Lewis, Janet I. 2014. When Decentralization Leads to Recentralization: Subnational State Transformation in Uganda. *Regional and Federal Studies* 24 (5): 571–588.

Lewis, Paul M. (ed.). 2009. *Ethnologue: Languages of the World*. 16th ed. Dallas, Texas: SIL International. www.ethnologue.com/

Lichbach, Mark. 1998. *The Rebel's Dilemma*. "First paperback ed. 1998."– Verso title page. Ann Arbor: University of Michigan Press.

Lijphart, Arend. 1971. Comparative Politics and the Comparative Method. *American Political Science Review* 65 (3): 682–693.

Lindemann, Stefan. 2011. Just Another Change of the Guard? Broad-Based Politics and Civil War in Museveni's Uganda. *African Affairs* 110 (440): 387–416.

Lugard, Frederick D. 1898. The Kingdom of Uganda. In *Africa: Its Partition and Its Future*, edited by Harry Thurston Peck. New York: Dodd, Mead and Company, 187–197.

Lujala, Paivi. 2010. The Spoils of Nature: Armed Civil Conflict and Rebel Access to Natural Resources. *Journal of Peace Research* 47 (1): 15–28.

Lyall, Jason. 2010. Are Coethnics More Effective Counterinsurgents? Evidence from the Second Chechen War. *American Political Science Review* 104 (1): 1–20.

Lyall, Jason. 2020. *Divided Armies: Inequality and Battlefield Performance in Modern War*. Princeton, NJ: Princeton University Press.

Malone, Iris. 2019. Uncertainty and Civil War Onset. Working Paper.

Mamdani, Mahmood. 1996. *Citizen and Subject: Contemporary Africa and the Legacy of Late Colonialism*. Princeton, NJ: Princeton University Press.

Mao, Zedong. 1978. *On Guerrilla Warfare*. Garden City, NY: Anchor Press.

McAdam, Doug. 2001. *Dynamics of Contention*. Cambridge Studies in Contentious Politics. Cambridge; New York: Cambridge University Press.

McAdam, Doug, John D. McCarthy, and Mayer N. Zald. 1988. Social Movements. In *Handbook of Sociology*, edited by Neil J. Smelser. Newbury Park, CA: Sage, 695–738.

McCauley, John F. 2017. *The Logic of Ethnic and Political Conflict in Africa*. Cambridge; New York; Melbourne; Delhi; Singapore: Cambridge University Press.

McCarthy, John D. and Mayer N. Zald. 1977. Resource Mobilization and Social Movements: A Partial Theory. *The American Journal of Sociology* 82 (6): 1212–1241.

McCoy, Alfred W. 2009. *Policing America's Empire: The United States, the Philippines, and the Rise of the Surveillance State*. Madison, WI: University of Wisconsin Press.

McDoom, Omar Shahabudin. 2014. Antisocial Capital: A Profile of Rwandan Genocide Perpetrators' Social Networks. *Journal of Conflict Resolution* 58 (5): 865–893.

McLauchlin, Theodore. 2015. Explaining the Origins of Military Rebellion. Working Paper Presented at the Annual Meeting of the International Studies Association.

Michalopoulos, Stelios. 2012. The Origins of Ethnolinguistic Diversity. *American Economic Review* 102 (4): 1508-1539.

Michalopoulos, Stelios and Elias Papaioannou. 2012. Pre-Colonial Ethnic Institutions and Contemporary African Development. NBER Working Paper No. 18224. nber.org/papers/w18224

Middleton, John. 1965. *The Lugbara of Uganda*. Holt: Rinehart & Winston.

Miguel, Edward and Mary Kay Gugerty. 2005. Ethnic Diversity, Social Sanctions, and Public Goods in Kenya. *Journal of Public Economics* 89 (11–12): 2325–2368.

Ministry of Planning and Economic Development. 1987. Rehabilitation and Development Plan, 1987/88 – 1990/91, Volume 1. Republic of Uganda.

Mueller, John. 2000. The Banality of "Ethnic War." *International Security* 25 (1): 42–70.

Mukherjee, Shivaji. 2014. Why Are the Longest Insurgencies Low Violence? Politician Motivations, Sons of the Soil, and Civil War Duration. *Civil Wars* 16 (2): 172–207.

Museveni, Yoweri. 1997. *Sowing the Mustard Seed: The Struggle for Freedom and Democracy in Uganda*. London: Macmillan.

Narayan Swamy, M. R. 2003. *Tigers of Lanka*. Colombo: Vijitha Yapa.

National Consortium for the Study of Terrorism and Responses to Terrorism (START). 2012. Global Terrorism Database. www.start.umd.edu/gtd

O'Donnell, Guillermo. 1993. On the State, Democratization, and Some Conceptual Problems: A Latin American View with some Glances at Post-Communist Countries. *World Development* 21 (8): 1355–1369.

Olson, Mancur. 1993. Dictatorship, Democracy, and Development. *American Political Science Review* 87 (3): 567–576.

Østby, Gudrun. 2008. Polarization, Horizontal Inequalities and Violent Civil Conflict. *Journal of Peace Research* 45 (2): 143–162.

Otwal, Jonah Emong. 2001. *The War in Teso, 1987–1992: How, Where and Why It Started*. Soroti, Uganda: Ateso Language Association.

Parkinson, Sarah E. and Sherry Zaks. 2018. Militant and Rebel Organization(s). *Comparative Politics* 50 (2): 271–293.

Parkinson, Sarah Elizabeth. 2013. Organizing Rebellion: Rethinking High-Risk Mobilization and Social Networks in War. *American Political Science Review* 107 (3): 418–432.

Pearlman, Wendy. 2011. *Violence, Nonviolence, and the Palestinian National Movement*. 1st ed. Cambridge; New York: Cambridge University Press.

Petersen, Roger. 2001. *Resistance and Rebellion: Lessons from Eastern Europe*. Cambridge; New York: Cambridge University Press.

Petraeus, David. 2006. *The U.S. Army and Marines Counterinsurgency Manual*. Chicago and London: The University of Chicago Press.

Pierskalla, Jan Henryk. 2010. Protest, Deterrence, and Escalation: The Strategic Calculus of Government Repression. *Journal of Conflict Resolution* 54 (1): 117–145.

Ponnambalam, Satchi. 1983. *Sri Lanka: National Conflict and the Tamil Liberation Struggle*. Thornton Heath, Surrey: Totowa, NJ: Tamil Information Centre.

Popkin, Samuel. 1979. *The Rational Peasant: The Political Economy of Rural Society in Vietnam*. Berkeley, CA: University of California Press.

Posner, Daniel N. 2005. *Institutions and Ethnic Politics in Africa*. Cambridge; New York: Cambridge University Press.

Posner, Daniel N. 2004. Measuring Ethnic Fractionalization in Africa. *American Journal of Political Science* 48 (4): 849–863.

Przeworski, Adam and Henry Teune. 1982. *The Logic of Comparative Social Inquiry*. Malabar, FL: R.E. Krieger Pub. Co.

Raleigh, Clionadh, Andrew Linke, Havard Hegre, and Joakim Karlsen. 2010. Introducing ACLED-Armed Location and Event Data. *Journal of Peace Research* 47 (5): 1–10.

Ravallion, M. 1994. *Poverty Comparisons*. Switzerland: Hardwood Academic Publishers.

Reno, William. 2011. *Warfare in Independent Africa*. Cambridge; New York: Cambridge University Press.

Robinson, Amanda. 2016. Nationalism and Ethnic-Based Trust: Evidence from an African Border Region. *Comparative Political Studies* 49 (14): 1819–1854.

Robinson, Amanda Lea. 2017. Ethnic Diversity, Segregation and Ethnocentric Trust in Africa. *British Journal of Political Science* 50(1): 1–23. doi-org.proxygw.wrlc.org/10.1017/S0007123417000540

Roessler, Philip G. 2016. *Ethnic Politics and State Power in Africa: The Logic of the Coup-Civil War Trap*. Cambridge New York: Cambridge University Press.

Ross, Michael. 2004. How Do Natural Resources Influence Civil War? Evidence from Thirteen Cases. *International Organization* 58: 35–67.

Salehyan, Idean. 2015. Best Practices in the Collection of Conflict Data. *Journal of Peace Research* 52 (1): 105–109.

Salehyan, Idean. 2009. *Rebels without Borders: Transnational Insurgencies in World Politics*. Ithaca, NY: Cornell University Press.

Samaranayaka, Gamini. 2008. *Political Violence in Sri Lanka, 1971–1987*. New Delhi: Gyan Pub. House.

Sambanis, Nicholas. 2004a. Using Case Studies to Expand Economic Models of Civil War. *Perspectives on Politics* 2 (2): 259–279.

Sambanis, Nicholas. 2004b. What is a Civil War? Conceptual and Empirical Complexities of an Operational Definition. *Journal of Conflict Resolution* 48 (6): 814–858.

Sanchez de la Sierra, Raul. 2020. On the Origin of States: Stationary Bandits and Taxation in Eastern Congo. *Journal of Political Economy* 128(1). doi.org/10.1086/703989

Sanín, Francisco Gutiérrez and Elisabeth Jean Wood. 2014. Ideology in Civil War: Instrumental Adoption and Beyond. *Journal of Peace Research* 51 (2): 213–226.

Sarkees, Meredith Reid and Frank Wayman. 2010. *Resort to War: 1816–2007*. Los Angeles; London; New Delhi; Singapore; Washington DC: CQ Press.

Scott, James C. 2008. *Seeing Like a State: How Certain Schemes to Improve the Human Condition Have Failed*. Nachdr. Yale agrarian studies. New Haven, CT: Yale University Press.

Selznick, Philip. 1952. *The Organizational Weapon: A Study of Bolshevik Strategy and Tactics*. New York: McGraw Hill.

Seymour, Lee J. M. 2014. Why Factions Switch Sides in Civil Wars: Rivalry, Patronage, and Realignment in Sudan. *International Security* 39 (2): 92–131.

Shesterinina, Anastasia. 2016. Collective Threat Framing and Mobilization in Civil War. *American Political Science Review* 110 (3): 411–427.

Skarbek, David. 2011. Governance and Prison Gangs. *American Political Science Review* 105 (4): 702–716.

Soifer, Hillel David. 2016. *State Building in Latin America.* New York: Cambridge University Press.

Soifer, Hillel David. 2019. Units of Analysis in Subnational Research. In *Inside Countries: Subnational Research in Comparative Politics,* edited by Agustina Giraudy, Eduardo Moncada, and Richard Snyder. Cambridge, New York, Melbourne, and New Delhi: Cambridge University Press, 92–112.

Staniland, Paul. 2010. *Explaining Cohesion, Fragmentation, and Control in Insurgent Groups.* MIT: Dissertation.

Staniland, Paul. 2014. *Networks of Rebellion: Explaining Insurgent Cohesion and Collapse.* Cornell Studies in Security Affairs. Ithaca, NY: Cornell University Press.

Staniland, Paul. 2012a. Organizing Insurgency: Networks, Resources, and Rebellion in South Asia. *International Security* 37 (1): 142–177.

Staniland, Paul. 2012b. States, Insurgents, and Wartime Political Orders. *Perspectives on Politics* 10 (2): 243–264.

Stanton, Jessica. 2016. *Strategies of Violence and Restraint in Civil War: Civilian Targeting in the Shadow of International Law.* New York: Cambridge University Press.

Stead, William Thomas. 1898. The British Empire in Africa. In *Africa: Its Partition and Its Future,* edited by Harry Thurston Peck. New York: Dodd, Mead and Company, 49–82.

Stewart, Frances. 2002. Horizontal Inequalities: A Neglected Dimension of Development. QEH Working Paper No. 81. Oxford: Queen Elizabeth House.

Straus, Scott. 2012. Wars Do End! Changing Patterns of Political Violence in Sub-Saharan Africa. *African Affairs* 111 (443): 179–201.

Sullivan, Christopher. 2015. Undermining Resistance: Mobilization, Repression, and the Enforcement of Political Order. *Journal of Conflict Resolution* 60 (7): 1163–1190.

Tarrow, Sidney. 2010. The Strategy of Paired Comparison: Towards a Theory of Practice. *Comparative Political Studies* 43 (2): 230–259.

Thaler, Kai. 2018. From Insurgent to Incumbent: State Building and Service Provision after Rebel Victory in Civil Wars. Ph.D. Dissertation, Harvard University.

The Republic of Uganda, Ministry of Planning and Economic Development. 1987. Rehabilitation and Development Plan 1987/88 – 1990/91, Volume 1. Kampala: Government of Uganda.

Thomas, Jakana L., William Reed, and Scott Wolford. 2016. The Rebels' Credibility Dilemma. *International Organization* 70 (3): 477–511.

Thomas, Martin. 2008. *Empires of Intelligence: Security Services and Colonial Disorder after 1914.* Berkeley, CA: University of California Press.

Thompkins Jr., Paul J. 2013. Human Factors Considerations of Undergrounds in Insurgencies, Second Edition. Edited by Nathan Bos. United States Army Special Operations Command.

Thyne, Clayton L. 2006. ABCs, 123's and the Golden Rule: The Pacifying Effect of Education on Civil War, 1890–1999. *International Studies Quarterly* 50: 733–754.

Tilly, Charles. 2005. *Coercion, Capital, and European States AD 990–1992*. Cambridge, MA; Oxford, UK: Blackwell.

Tilly, Charles. 1985. War Making and State Making as Organized Crime. In *Bringing the State Back In*, edited by Dietrich Rueschemeyer, Peter B. Evans, and Theda Skocpol. Cambridge: Cambridge University Press, 169–187.

Toft, Monica Duffy. 2002. Indivisible Territory, Geographic Concentration, and Ethnic War. *Security Studies* 12 (2): 82–119.

Toft, Monica Duffy. 2010. *Securing the Peace: The Durable Settlement of Civil Wars*. Princeton, NJ: Princeton University Press.

Toft, Monica Duffy. 2003. *The Geography of Ethnic Violence: Identity, Interests, and the Indivisibility of Territory*. Princeton, NJ: Princeton University Press.

Tripp, Aili Mari. 2004. The Changing Face of Authoritarianism in Africa: The Case of Uganda. *Africa Today* 50 (3): 3–26.

Uchendu, V. C. and K. R. M. Anthony. 1975. *Agricultural Change in Teso District, Uganda*. Nairobi: East African Literature Bureau.

Uganda, Ministry of Finance, Planning and Economic Development. 1992. *Background to the Budget*.

UN Food and Agriculture Organization. 2005. *State of the World's Forests*. Rome.

Urdal, Hendrik. 2006. A Clash of Generations? Youth Bulges and Political Violence. *International Studies Quarterly* 50 (3): 607–629.

US Army and Marine Corps. 2007. *The U.S. Army/Marine Corps Counterinsurgency Field Manual*. University of Chicago Press.

Valentino, Benjamin A. 2004. *Final Solutions: Mass Killing and Genocide in the Twentieth Century*. Ithaca, NY: Cornell University Press.

Van der Windt, Peter and Macartan Humphreys. 2015. Crowdseeding Conflict Data. *Journal of Conflict Resolution* 60(4): 748–781.

Varshney, Ashutosh. 2003. *Ethnic Conflict and Civic Life: Hindus and Muslims in India*. 2nd ed. New Haven, CT: Yale University Press.

Vogt, Manuel, Nils-Christian Bormann, Seraina Rüegger, Lars-Erik Cederman, Philipp Hunziker, and Luc Girardin. 2015. Integrating Data on Ethnicity, Geography, and Conflict: The Ethnic Power Relations Data Set Family. *Journal of Conflict Resolution* 59 (7): 1327–1342.

Walter, Barbara F. 2004. Does Conflict Beget Conflict? Explaining Recurring Civil War. *Journal of Conflict Resolution* 41 (3): 371–388.

Walter, Barbara F. and Elaine K. Denny. 2014. Ethnicity and Civil War. *Journal of Peace Research* 51 (2): 199–212.

Webster, J. B., C. P. Emudong, D. H. Okalany, and N. Egimu-Okuda. 1973. *The Iteso During the Asonya*. Nairobi: East African Publishing House.

Webster, J. B., B. A. Ogot, and J. P. Chretien. 1992. The Great Lakes Region, 1500–1800. In *Africa from the Sixteenth to the Eighteenth Century*, edited by B. A. Ogot. Paris and California: UNESCO and University of California, Berkeley Press, 776–827.

Webster, Kaitlyn. 2019. Rethinking Civil War Onset and Escalation. Working Paper. https://kaitlynwebster.files.wordpress.com/2018/01/kwebsterrethinking civilwar.pdf

Weidmann, Nils. 2009. Geography as Motivation and Opportunity: Group Concentration and Ethnic Conflict. *Journal of Conflict Resolution* 53 (4): 526–543.

Weinstein, Jeremy M. 2005. Autonomous Recovery and International Intervention in Comparative Perspective – Working Paper 57. *Center for Global Development.*

Weinstein, Jeremy M. 2007. *Inside Rebellion.* Cambridge: Cambridge University Press.

Wickham-Crowley, Timothy. 1993. *Guerillas and Revolution in Latin America: A Comparative Study of Insurgents and Regimes since 1956.* Princeton, NJ: Princeton University Press.

Williams, Paul. 2011. *War & Conflict in Africa.* Cambridge: Polity Press.

Wilson, A. Jeyaratnam. 2000. *Sri Lankan Tamil Nationalism: Its Origins and Development in the Nineteenth and Twentieth Centuries.* Vancouver: UBC Press.

Wimmer, Andreas, Lars-Erik Cederman, and Brian Min. 2009. Ethnic Politics and Armed Conflict: A Configurational Analysis of a New Global Dataset. *American Sociological Review* 74: 316–337.

Woldemariam, Michael. 2018. *Insurgent Fragmentation in the Horn of Africa: Rebellion and its Discontents.* New York: Cambridge University Press.

Wood, Elisabeth. 2003. *Insurgent Collective Action and Civil War in El Salvador.* New York: Cambridge University Press.

Wood, Reed M. 2014a. From Loss to Looting? Battlefield Costs and Rebel Incentives for Violence. *International Organization* 68 (4): 979–999.

Wood, Reed M. 2014b. Opportunities to Kill or Incentives for Restraint? Rebel Capabilities, the Origins of Support, and Civilian Victimization in Civil War. *Conflict Management and Peace Science* 31 (5): 461–480.

Wood, Reed M. 2010. Rebel Capability and Strategic Violence against Civilians. *Journal of Peace Research* 47 (5): 601–614.

Zukerman-Daly, Sarah. 2012. Organizational Legacies of Violence: Conditions Favoring Insurgency Onset in Colombia, 1964–1984. *Journal of Peace Research* 49 (3): 473–491.

Index

Mchaka Mchaka, 184–188, 190–191,
   195–196
Mella subcounty, 149–151
Middleton, John, 52–53, 160
migration, 52, 129–130
   to Teso region, 143–144
   West Nile region and, 160
military capabilities, 43–44, 197–198
military effectiveness, 135–136, 196–197
military officials, 153
Min, Brian, 31, 104–106, 209–210
Ministry of Planning and Economic
   Development, 67–68
Minorities at Risk Project, 103–104
Mizo National Front, 80
Moi, Daniel arap, 73
Moro National Liberation Front, 80
motivation, 28–29, 33, 60, 217
Mount Elgon, 148–149
Mozambique, 8, 180, 198–199
Museveni, Yoweri, 55, 66–67, 68,
   69
   Bush War and, 76–77
   Dar es Salaam University and, 198–199
   era of, 84, 85
   governments before, 106
   Moi and, 73
   Okello and, 141
   swearing-in ceremony, 68–69, 182

NALU. *See* National Army for the
   Liberation of Uganda
nascent insurgency, 107
nascent rebels
   defeat and, 41–42
   deterring and ending, 189–196
   incubation period for, 196–197
   information and, 9
   information leaks and, 171–172
   initial material endowments of, 81
   intelligence institutions and, 178–179
   primary challenge for, 205
   violence and, 205–206
   vulnerability of, 9
   in weak states, 35–36
National Army for the Liberation of Uganda
   (NALU), 74
National Freedom Army (NFA), 90–92
national identity, 16
National Islamic Front, 72
National Leadership Institute, 185

National Resistance Army (NRA). *See*
   National Resistance Movement
National Resistance Movement (NRM), 36,
   63, 66–67, 111, 156
   Bush War and, 98–99, 101–102,
      138–139, 182–183
   counterinsurgency and, 79
   fledgling government of, 166–167,
      168–169
   focus on persuasion of, 192
   government of, 69–70
   government responses by, 165–166
   information-centric pathway to
      managing internal threats, 198
   LC system of, 180–184
   local officials installed by, 151
   power seized by, 92, 106, 139, 178
   reputation of, 68–69, 70
   state organizations disbanded by, 69
   state-building by, 181
   success of, 76–77
   weaknesses of, 192–193
nationalism, 103
natural resources, 94
Nazi Germany, 217
Nepal, 36
network density, 49–50
network distance, 49–51
networks of trust, 53
New Vision (newspaper), 117
NFA. *See* National Freedom Army
Nicaragua, 36
Nigeria, 57
Nile River, 65
Nilotic tribes, 64–65
non-government-aligned media, 220–221
nonviolent mobilization, 30
nonviolent opposition, 216
Northern Ireland, 5–7, 18–19
NRA. *See* National Resistance Army
NRM. *See* National Resistance Movement
Nyerere, Julius, 67, 198–199

Obote, Milton, 65–67, 108, 130–131, 169
   Bush War and, 141
   former members of military of, 150–151
   Omwero and, 150
   residents who served in military of, 148
   Special Forces and, 136–138, 141
oil, 94
Okello, Tito, 108, 141

Rory Truex, *Making Autocracy Work: Representation and Responsiveness in Modern China*

Lily Lee Tsai, *Accountability without Democracy: How Solidary Groups Provide Public Goods in Rural China*

Joshua Tucker, *Regional Economic Voting: Russia, Poland, Hungary, Slovakia and the Czech Republic, 1990–1999*

Ashutosh Varshney, *Democracy, Development, and the Countryside*

Yuhua Wang, *Tying the Autocrat's Hand: The Rise of The Rule of Law in China*

Jeremy M. Weinstein, *Inside Rebellion: The Politics of Insurgent Violence*

Stephen I. Wilkinson, *Votes and Violence: Electoral Competition and Ethnic Riots in India*

Andreas Wimmer, *Waves of War: Nationalism, State Formation, and Ethnic Exclusion in the Modern World*

Jason Wittenberg, *Crucibles of Political Loyalty: Church Institutions and Electoral Continuity in Hungary*

Elisabeth J. Wood, *Forging Democracy from Below: Insurgent Transitions in South Africa and El Salvador*

Elisabeth J. Wood, *Insurgent Collective Action and Civil War in El Salvador*

Deborah J. Yashar, *Homicidal Ecologies: Illicit Economies and Complicit States in Latin America*

Daniel Ziblatt, *Conservative Parties and the Birth of Democracy*